# Teaching
# U.S. History
# Through
# Children's Literature

## Post–World War II

Wanda J. Miller

1998
Teacher Ideas Press
A Division of
Libraries Unlimited, Inc.
Englewood, Colorado

To my late parents,
Marjorie Lookup Jansen and Arnold Jacob Jansen,
whom I miss very much.

TEACHER IDEAS PRESS
A Division of
Libraries Unlimited, Inc.
P.O. Box 6633
Englewood, CO 80155-6633
1-800-237-6124
www.lu.com/tip


*Production Editor:* Kevin W. Perizzolo
*Copy Editor:* Jan Krygier
*Proofreader:* Felicity Tucker
*Indexer:* Linda Running Bentley
*Typesetter:* Kay Minnis

**Library of Congress Cataloging-in-Publication Data**

Miller, Wanda J., 1959-
  Teaching U.S. history through children's literature : post-World War II / Wanda J. Miller.
    xiii, 229 p. 22x28 cm.
    Includes bibliographical references and index.
    ISBN 1-56308-581-X
    1. United States--History--1945- --Juvenile literature--Bibliography. 2. United States--History--1945- --Juvenile fiction--Bibliography. 3. United States--History--1945- --Study and teaching. I. Title.
Z1245.M54      1998
[E741]
016.97392--dc21                                        98-34575
                                                            CIP

# Contents

437909

# Acknowledgments

I'd like to thank my husband and children for their support throughout the writing of this book. It couldn't have been done without their patience and help.

Once again, Cheryl Gravelle from the Williamson Public Library was a whiz at locating materials.

Colleagues from Williamson Middle and Elementary Schools continued to be full of ideas, literature recommendations, and much encouragement!

Again, I'd like to thank my late parents, Arnold Jacob Jansen and Marjorie Lookup Jansen, for their encouragement to always do my best and keep trying.

The following permissions were obtained to reprint materials that appear in this book.

The Literature Response Guide (fig. 8-1), is reprinted with permission from Leslie Wood, Williamson Elementary School, Williamson, NY.

Excerpts from letters written by David W. Reilly, during the Vietnam War, dated July 14, 1968, August 16, 1968, August 17, 1968, September 16, 1968, November 18, 1968, and November 23, 1968, are reprinted with the permission of the letters' owner, Joan Reilly.

The speech given by Doris Wolf at the 149th anniversary celebrations of the first women's rights convention at Seneca Falls, New York, on July 19, 1997, is reprinted with the permission of Doris Wolf.

# Introduction

## Purpose

*Teaching U.S. History Through Children's Literature: Post–World War II* was written for use by teachers in grades four through eight. The purpose of this book is to provide teachers with information to begin or expand their use of quality children's literature in the teaching of United States history. Teachers who have already begun teaching history in this format have been forced to purchase their own materials and create their own questions, activities, vocabulary exercises, and lessons to supplement the trade books that they are using. With many demands on their time, including regular teaching duties, parent conferences, staff meetings, committee meetings, and paperwork, teachers do not have the time or energy to build a literature-based history program from the ground up. *Teaching U.S. History Through Children's Literature: Post–World War II* was written to help fill this need.

The core of any good literature-based curriculum is a collection of quality trade books. The trade books recommended for inclusion in this book were selected based on teacher recommendations, book reviews, and recommendations from librarians.

Teachers often have to purchase numerous trade book guides, as what is currently available, while often good, may only cover a certain historical time period, or a small sampling of books dealing with various time periods. In addition, many guides may have excellent activities, but do not include discussion questions or vocabulary, or vice versa.

## Advantages

The advantages of using children's literature to supplement your U.S. history lessons are numerous. The greatest advantage is having historical literature at your fingertips when teaching about a certain historical time period.

Nothing brings history alive better than reading quality literature about what life was like during that time. Although the facts learned in textbooks are very important, students more easily grasp a true understanding of the time period and hardships through an historical character's dilemmas, thoughts, and feelings.

Students forget facts and details learned strictly from textbooks more easily than those learned through immersion in literature based on the time period. Because a lasting impression and understanding of history is our ultimate goal for our students, use of historical literature in addition to textbook teaching is a must, whether it be in social studies class, English, or reading.

To immerse your students in quality historical literature, you should have available a classroom set of a novel to be read as a whole group (approximately thirty copies), several small group sets (four or five copies) of other titles to use in cooperative learning groups, and many individual titles for read-alouds, extra-credit opportunities, and research. In addition to recommending titles, this book includes ideas for the teacher in the development of the theme, including activities, writing ideas, and summaries of each large and small group title. Research topics are suggested in each chapter as well.

Although reading one historical novel or nonfiction trade book is beneficial, reading two or more is even better. This is the reason for having a class set of a novel to read, as well as several small group sets. This way, students can share information with one another. After sharing a variety of books about a certain time period, it becomes clearer that any single event in history is not a single story but several stories told from differing points of view. Reading a second or third story reinforces background information and fosters critical thinking through the comparison of different points of view. It is highly recommended that you read the trade books first to decide if they are appropriate for use in your classroom. Whole group titles may be interchanged with any of the small group titles. Decisions may be based on the availability of books, teacher preference, or students' needs. If class set quantities are not available, the book may be used as a read-aloud.

Finally, having these books available is a hassle-free way to incorporate quality literature with U.S. history. This book is an attempt to help teachers—be they history teachers, English teachers, reading teachers, or all of the above—build U.S. history libraries for use in their classrooms. As curriculum demands increase, interdisciplinary teaching becomes even more important.

## Author Information

It is my belief that it is important for student readers and writers to learn about the lives of authors. Therefore, where possible, author information has been included for whole group and small group titles.

## Vocabulary

Vocabulary words for each of the whole group and small group titles are listed and defined. Use them in whatever way you feel is most appropriate. These vocabulary words were not necessarily provided for use in testing students, but as a resource to help them better understand what they are reading. It has been my experience when working with small groups of students that teachers sometimes take for granted that all students know the more commonplace vocabulary in a novel. This is often not the case. Therefore, to provide a better understanding for all students, many of these more common words have been included.

Page numbers for the vocabulary words have been included for your reference. It is possible that these page numbers might be incorrect if you were to acquire different editions of any of the titles. If this occurs, I would suggest enlisting the help of a parent volunteer or teacher aide to locate the appropriate page numbers to correspond with your edition.

## Grade Levels of Trade Books

Although the focus of this book is on middle-grade students, it includes trade books encompassing a wide range of reading levels. As we all know, our students do not all read at the same level. Some students may need materials at a lower level for independent reading and small group reading, while others may need more challenging materials.

Also, regardless of independent reading level, the use of picture books as read-alouds with middle-grade students is an excellent way to introduce or expand on a theme. Picture books provide a visual stimulus for capturing students' interest in a subject.

# Building the Trade Book Collection

In a time of tighter budgets, we often need to find creative ways to fund projects such as this. If possible, ask your school's governing body to set aside at least 100 dollars in your school's reading, social studies, and English budgets for this purpose. It would be wise to start with one or two historical time periods in your proposal the first year, and add more in later years as funds become available. You could also purchase as many materials for an historical time period as your budget allows and add to it each year.

Often, school parent–teacher associations or parent–teacher organizations hold fund raisers to help with school programs. Try contacting the organization in your district to see if it would be willing to help fund your U.S. history library.

Book clubs, such as Scholastic, Trumpet, Troll, and Carnival, often offer selections that would be appropriate for your collection at a reduced cost. These savings, along with bonus points toward free books, can help stretch your budget.

Make use of the resources that are already available to you. Your school and public libraries most likely will have many of the titles you wish to use. Another possibility would be to inform parents and community members about your literature-based program. You could solicit donations by sending out a wish list of books for your library.

It may take a few years to have in place the books that you find most suitable for your use, but the payoff will make the initial investment in time, effort, and money worthwhile.

# How to Use This Book

Chapters 1 through 7 in this book contain the following sections: A suggested trade book for whole group reading, suggested trade books for use in small groups, a bibliography of individual titles, and theme resources. Chapter 8 provides a list of supplemental resources.

After reading a novel with your whole class, divide your class into cooperative learning groups of three to five students for small group reading. Books with summaries, author information, discussion questions, and activities are included for use by these groups. Choose from the activities listed in this book those that best fit the learning styles of your students and the time frame you have to complete the unit. Use these activities in reading, English, or social studies classes in the upper grades. In many classrooms today, there are times when remedial teachers, whether they are Title I teachers or special education teachers, work with classroom teachers and students in their classrooms, rather than in pull-out settings. An optimum time for these cooperative learning groups would be when other support personnel "push-in" to the room. The classroom teacher and resource person should rotate among the reading groups to provide guidance and direction when needed.

This book lists and summarizes many titles for independent reading and research by your students. These titles can be used in several different ways: For further research for a project; for extra credit toward their reading, social studies, or English grades; or as an independent reading assignment during your unit. In addition, chapter 8 of this book includes a literature response guide for journal writing for students to use.

A section on general theme resources in each chapter includes commercial resources, as well as some computer resources and videos.

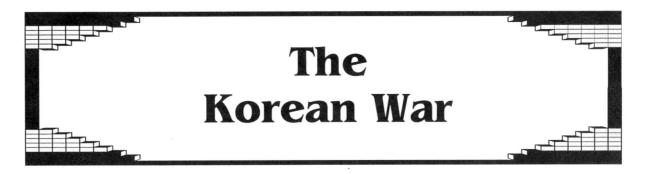

# Chapter 1

# The Korean War

## Introduction

The Korean War has been called "The Forgotten War." It was mostly ignored in the United States while it was being fought, and little has been written about it. Not surprisingly, as a result, few children's books focus on the Korean War.

Although it is called "The Forgotten War," undoubtedly the families of more than 54,000 Americans who died in Korea will never forget it.

On Sunday, June 25, 1950, the North Korean army invaded South Korea. For centuries, Korea had been a troubled country. Japan and China had fought for control of it. When Tsarist Russia's expansion extended to Korea's borders in the late 1800s, it, too, wanted control of Korea. In 1910, Imperial Japan formally annexed Korea as its colony. The Japanese were extremely harsh to the Koreans. Thus, many Koreans sought and welcomed leaders who promised to free the country from Japanese rule.

Near the end of World War II, the U.S.S.R. entered the war and quickly occupied the northern reaches of Korea. Fearful that the Soviets would take over the entire country, U.S. officers and diplomats held an emergency meeting in Washington, D.C., and drew up a plan to divide Korea at the 38th Parallel. Under the plan, to which the Soviets agreed, the U.S.S.R. would have an influence in North Korea, while the United States would have an influence in South Korea. This physical division of Korea also divided its people. South Korea was led by Syngman Rhee, who believed in democracy. North Korea was led by Kim Il Sung, a communist. Each man wanted to overthrow the other.

Following the invasion of North Korean troops in South Korea on June 25, 1950, President Harry S. Truman ordered the U.S. military to Korea to stop this aggression. What was intended as a police action soon became a war that would last until July 27, 1953, when the Korea armistice was signed at Panmunjon. A cease-fire resulted, and the war ended.

The Korean War, however, did not end in victory; it simply ended. The Korean political situation remained unchanged. The demilitarized zone just north of the old 38th Parallel now marked the border between North and South Korea. This new border gave South Korea approximately 1,500 square miles of land it did not have before the war.

American casualties totaled 54,246. In addition, more than two million Koreans, most of them civilians, died. Although the Chinese government did not release casualty figures, it is estimated that their forces lost about one million soldiers. Property damage was enormous. The Korean War was one of the most destructive wars in history.

As mentioned earlier, very little has been written for children about the Korean War. This is the reason for only two small group reading titles in this chapter. Following the whole group reading of *Year of Impossible Goodbyes*, two small groups of students could read *The Korean War Soldier at Heartbreak Ridge* and *Echoes of the White Giraffe*. The other students could select individual titles from the bibliography at the end of this chapter to read and respond to in their journals, using the Literature Response Guide (Figure 8.1) in chapter 8, "Supplemental U.S. History Resources."

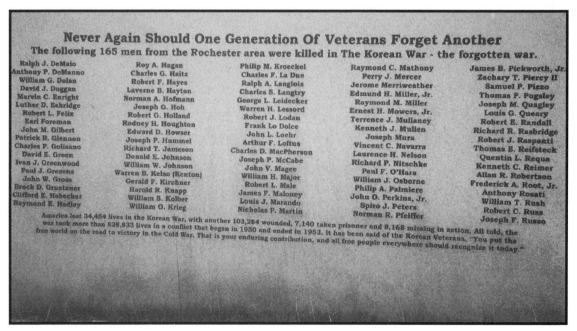

**Fig. 1.1.** Photograph of a tribute to Korean War veterans taken at the Greater Rochester Vietnam Veterans Memorial in Rochester, New York.

## Whole Group Reading

📖 Choi, Sook Nyul. *Year of Impossible Goodbyes.* Boston: Houghton Mifflin, 1991.

A young Korean girl survives the oppressive occupation of North Korea during the 1940s to later escape to freedom in South Korea. Grades 6 and up.

## Author Information

Sook Nyul Choi was born in Pyongyang, North Korea. She immigrated to the United States to attend college. She graduated from Manhattanville College and taught in New York City schools for close to twenty years. She spends most of her time writing.

*Year of Impossible Goodbyes* was prompted by Choi's love for both her native country and her adopted country. She wanted to share her experiences and foster greater understanding of the struggles that have taken place in Korea.

## Activities

1. On a world map, have students locate:

   Japan                                      Seoul, South Korea
   Manchuria, China                           Siberia
   North Korea

2. Have students illustrate the scene described in chapter 6 after the news of the end of the war had spread.

3. Discuss with the students what precious items they would hide if, like Sookan's family, they needed to hide possessions to keep them from being taken.

4. Have students create a time line of events that took place in Korea between the spring of 1945 and June, 1950. They may use additional sources of information if needed. Once finished, display the time line in your classroom.

## Discussion

Give the class the following instruction: As we read this book, we will be discussing the following.

1. What was Pyongyang, North Korea like in the spring of 1945?

2. Why is Sookan's mother afraid for her grandfather to meditate outside?

3. What do dragons symbolize in Korean culture?

4. Why can't Sookan learn to read and write in Korean or Chinese?

5. How are Sookan and her family treated by the Japanese?

6. Why must the Koreans eat millet and barley, when there is so much rice?

7. Where are Sookan's brothers? Where is her father?

8. Why aren't there any flowers around Sookan's home?

9. Why is Sookan's aunt called Aunt Tiger?

10. Why doesn't Sookan's mother polish her silver hairpin?

11. What made the surprise celebration for Haiwon such a special occasion?

12. What happened at the end of the celebration?

13. Why did Sookan suddenly wish that she were Japanese?

14. What stories did Sookan and Inchun's mother tell them about their family?

15. Why do you think that Sookan's grandfather insisted that Sookan and Inchun learn more about their family before he died?

16. What did Aunt Tiger mean when she said, "We are like mice trapped in a dungeon of wildcats"?

17. Why do Sookan and Inchun have to attend a Japanese school? How would you feel about it if you were them?

18. What did Narita Sensei make the children recite in school?

19. Describe Sookan's first day at the Japanese school.

20. Why do you think the Japanese tried to keep the Korean people hungry?

21. What did Kisa learn at the convent when he went to get medicine for Sookan's mother? How did everyone react to the news?

22. How were Unhi's brothers treated in the Japanese labor camp?

23. What did Sookan's grandfather mean when he said, "Korea was a little shrimp caught in a struggle between giants"?

24. How were the Russians a threat to Korea?

25. Where was Korea divided? Where were the Russians?

26. How did the Koreans feel about the Americans?

27. Why do you think Sookan's mother wants to flee to the south?

28. How do you feel about the way the Russians are treating the Koreans?

29. Why did Aunt Tiger call her family "Phony Reds" or "Pinks"?

30. Why do the Russians encourage the children to talk about their families?

31. How does Sookan's family plan to escape?

32. Why do Kisa and Aunt Tiger plan to stay in Kirimni?

33. What happened when Sookan, Inchun, and their mother tried to escape?

34. What advice did the old man at the train station give to Sookan and Inchun? What do you think they should do?

35. Discuss your feelings after reading chapter 10.

36. What happened in June of 1950?

## Vocabulary

**furrow** (p1)
a long, deep groove

**moat** (p1)
a ditch, usually full of water, around a castle, fortress, or other structure, that serves as a defense against attackers

**emanate** (p1)
to come or flow from a source

**harmony** (p1)
agreement; accord

**menacing** (p1)
threat of evil or harm

**glint** (p1)
a gleam; a flash

**respite** (p1)
a pause for rest

**oppressiveness** (p1)
a state of cruelty or harshness

**exhilaration** (p2)
high spirits

**benevolent** (p2)
desiring or showing the desire to do good; kind

**meditation** (p2)
the act of thinking quietly and deeply over a period of time; contemplation; reflection

**intensity** (p3)
extreme force or strength

**anticipation** (p3)
expectation

**permeate** (p3)
to spread itself or spread through

**dignified** (p3)
having dignity; proud; calm and stately

**prosperity** (p4)
a prosperous condition, including material wealth and success

**disdain** (p6)
scorn or haughty contempt, especially toward someone or something considered inferior

**vibrant** (p8)
full of energy; vigorous

**magpies** (p9)
large, noisy birds having long, tapering tails and black and white plumage

**frenetically** (p11)
   wildly

**quota** (p11)
   a number or amount that is required from or given to a person or group

**temperament** (p12)
   the nature or emotional makeup of a person; disposition

**azalea** (p14)
   a shrub having pointed leaves and showy red or orange flowers

**pestle** (p14)
   a tool with a blunt end used for pounding or crushing substances

**pensive** (p16)
   quietly and seriously thoughtful, often with a touch of sadness

**fable** (p16)
   a short story that teaches a lesson, often about animals who behave like people

**convent** (p20)
   the house or building where a group of nuns live together and follow set religious rules

**humble** (p23)
   modest; meek

**calligraphy** (p25)
   the art of handwriting

**savor** (p25)
   to taste or experience with pleasure; to relish

**monotone** (p27)
   a succession of syllables or words uttered in a single tone

**humiliated** (p28)
   stripped of pride or self-respect; embarrassed

**monk** (p29)
   a male member of a religious order who usually lives in a monastery under a rule and takes vows of poverty, chastity, and obedience

**nobility** (p30)
   in certain countries, a group of people who have hereditary titles and rank, such as kings, queens, duchesses, dukes, countesses, and earls

**bewildered** (p30)
   confused

**somber** (p33)
   gloomy and melancholy; sad

**catechism** (p39)
   a short book, written in the form of questions and answers, that teaches the principles of a religion

**massacre** (p39)
   a brutal killing of a large number of people or animals

**allay** (p40)
   to quiet, soothe, or reduce

**inconsolable** (p45)
   incapable of being comforted or cheered; brokenhearted

**subside** (p46)
   to become less violent or active

**prevail** (p46)
   to gain control; to be victorious; to win out

**vague** (p53)
   indefinite, unclear, imprecise, or indistinct

**revelation** (p56)
   something revealed to human beings by God

**apprehensive** (p57)
   fearful; worried

**stagnant** (p57)
   not flowing; motionless; still

**devout** (p61)
   heartfelt; sincere

**derisive** (p63)
   full of contempt; mocking

**defiance** (p63)
   bold opposition to power or authority; refusal to submit or obey

**kimono** (p69)
   a loose robe worn as an outer garment in Japan

**reverently** (p71)
   feeling or showing great respect

**dilapidated** (p74)
   half ruined by neglect; falling to pieces

**tedious** (p74)
   long, dull, and tiresome

**humid** (p84)
   containing water vapor; damp; moist

**delirium** (p84)
   a disturbance of the mind, marked by restlessness, excitement, and wild, confused thoughts and speech

**impetuous** (p88)
> acting on impulse and without thought; hasty; rash

**excursions** (p92)
> short trips

**liberators** (p98)
> people who set others free

**barbarian** (p98)
> a crude or brutal person

**ravenous** (p100)
> wildly hungry

**tungsten** (p104)
> a steel-gray, heavy metallic element, used in making electric light filaments and very hard steel alloys

**incredulous** (p104)
> feeling, having, or showing doubt or disbelief

**proletariat** (p106)
> the working class, especially those people who do manual labor or industrial work

**boisterous** (p107)
> noisy and wild

**refrain** (p108)
> a phrase in a poem or song repeated over and over, especially at the end of a stanza

**capitalists** (p108)
> people who believe in a system in which the factories, materials, and equipment for making and distributing goods are privately owned and operated for private profit rather than owned or controlled by a state or government

**imperialists** (p108)
> people who believe in the policy of increasing the power or dominion of a nation, such as by conquering other nations and exerting influence in political and economic areas

**Marxism** (p108)
> the political, economic, and social theories and policies of Karl Marx and Fredrick Engels that formed the basis for modern socialism and communism

**May Day** (p108)
> the first day of May, celebrated by such festivities as crowning a May queen and dancing around a Maypole; in some countries it is a holiday in honor of laboring people

**incessant** (p110)
> unceasing; continuing without letup

**candor** (p112)
> honesty; openness; frankness

**wary** (p114)
> watchful and suspicious; very careful; cautious

**Communist** (p114)
> a member of a political party that advocates a social system in which the means for producing economic goods belong to the entire community or the state, not to individuals

**tuberculosis** (p117)
> a disease caused by certain bacteria and marked by the formation of tubercles in various parts of the body; it chiefly affects the lungs and is accompanied by a slow wasting away of strength and vitality

**dysentery** (p117)
> a disease of the intestines, marked by the passing of blood and mucus in loose bowel movements

**timid** (p119)
> fearful or shy

**propaganda** (p119)
> a group of facts or ideas used to persuade people to adopt or support certain ideas, attitudes, or actions

**persimmon** (p139)
> the fruit of a North American tree, which puckers the mouth when green but is sweet to eat when ripe

**plight** (p142)
> a condition or situation, usually bad

**gesticulating** (p145)
> making emphatic or expressive gestures

**epaulets** (p147)
> ornaments worn on each shoulder of a naval or military officer's uniform

**ominous** (p149)
> threatening or foreboding, like a bad omen

**dissipate** (p161)
> to break up and scatter or dissolve

**turgid** (p163)
> unnaturally swollen

**diplomat** (p167)
> a person engaged in the handling of relations, friendly or unfriendly, short of war, between nations

**governess** (p168)
> a woman who cares for and teaches children in a private home

# Small Group Reading

📖 Choi, Sook Nyul. *Echoes of the White Giraffe*. Boston: Houghton Mifflin, 1993.

In this sequel to *Year of Impossible Goodbyes*, fifteen-year-old Sookan adjusts to life in the refugee village in Pusan but continues to hope that the Korean War will end so that she and her family can be reunited in Seoul. Grades 6 and up.

## Author Information

Sook Nyul Choi was born in Pyongyang, North Korea. She spent two and a half years as a refugee in Pusan, South Korea during the Korean War. She later graduated from Manhattanville College and taught in New York City schools for close to twenty years. She spends most of her time writing.

*Echoes of the White Giraffe* continues in fulfilling Choi's desire to share her experiences and foster greater understanding of the struggles that have taken place in Korea.

## Activities

1. On a world map, have students locate the following:
   France
   Pacific Ocean
   Pusan, South Korea
   Pyongyang, North Korea
   Seoul, South Korea

2. Have students illustrate Sookan's home and surrounding area in Pusan, which is described on page 10.

3. Have students write an epilogue for *Echoes of the White Giraffe*. It should take place ten years after the story ends and should tell what has happened to Sookan, Inchun, Sookan's mother, and Junho.

4. Have students in this group write a letter from Sookan to her brothers telling them what life has been like for her, Inchun, and their mother since they escaped from the bombing in Seoul.

5. Students who wish to read more about Sookan should be encouraged to read *Gathering of Pearls*, also by Sook Nyul Choi. *Gathering of Pearls* tells of Sookan's experiences during her first year in America.

## Discussion

Give the small group the following instruction: As your group reads this book, discuss the following.

1. Discuss Sookan's feelings upon looking at the completed school building.

2. How long had it been since Sookan attended school? Why?

3. Why did Sookan's mother go to the refugee information center every day?

4. What chore did Sookan and Inchun have to do when they got home?

5. Why did Sookan's mother scold Sookan for shouting from the mountain top?

6. Why does Sookan wish Inchun would join the choir?

7. How did Sookan escape from Seoul?

8. Why didn't Sookan want to talk to Haerin about the war?

9. What did Bokhi learn when her uncle was found?

10. What happened to the shouting poet?

11. What gift did Junho bring Sookan?

12. How did Sookan, her mother, and Inchun become separated from her father and brothers?

13. What does Sookan plan to do after finishing high school? Why?

14. What is expected of Junho after he finishes high school? Is this what he is really interested in?

15. Why did the letter Sookan received from Junho trouble Sookan?

16. Discuss the armistice agreement that was signed in July of 1953. What did this agreement mean to North and South Korea?

17. How did the refugees in Pusan react to the signing of the armistice?

18. Describe Sookan's feelings about leaving Pusan.

19. What did Sookan, Inchun, and their mother find when they reached their home in Seoul?

20. What did Father Lee find out about Sookan's father?

21. What did Sookan's mother do with the broken jewelry that she dug up in the yard?

22. Why do you think Junho came to visit Sookan in Seoul?

23. How did you feel when Sookan and her mother went to see Junho at the seminary?

## Vocabulary

**refugee** (p2)
    a person who flees from persecution or danger

**monsoon** (p2)
    the rainy season in India and adjacent countries, extending from June to September

**embossed** (p3)
    decorated with raised designs

**resignation** (p3)
    patient acceptance

**drawn** (p4)
    pulled tight

**tranquil** (p5)
    calm; serene

**determination** (p7)
    firmness of purpose; courage

**terrain** (p7)
    an area of land, especially as considered with respect to its use for military operations or some other purpose

**crevice** (p7)
    a narrow opening due to a crack or split, such as in a rock or wall

**ashen** (p7)
    of, like, or pale as ashes; gray

**stupefied** (p7)
    amazed; astounded

**frail** (p7)
    weak

**unbridled** (p8)
    not held in or controlled

**heartily** (p8)
    sincerely and enthusiastically

**taunted** (p8)
    scorned, mocked

**silhouette** (p8)
    the outline of a person or object seen against a light or a light background

**glistening** (p12)
    shining or sparkling

**anticipation** (p13)
    expectation

**resonant** (p13)
    deep, rich, and full in tone or sound

**reverberated** (p13)
    resounded or echoed back

**dissipating** (p13)
    breaking up and scattering or dissolving

**vast** (p13)
>of very large size; enormous; huge

**curiosity** (p14)
>eager desire to know or find out

**enchanting** (p14)
>charming; delightful

**disgrace** (p15)
>to bring shame or dishonor to

**abandon** (p16)
>to give in to a feeling or impulse

**reprimand** (p16)
>a severe or formal scolding

**admiration** (p17)
>a feeling of wonder, approval, and satisfaction for someone or something of quality

**composure** (p18)
>calmness; self-control

**altar boy** (p19)
>a boy who assists at the altar; an acolyte

**famished** (p21)
>extremely hungry

**persimmon** (p22)
>a tree that bears reddish, plum-like fruit

**ominous** (p22)
>threatening or foreboding, like a bad omen

**disdainful** (p23)
>scornful

**communion** (p27)
>a Christian ceremony in which bread and wine are blessed and consumed in memory of the death of Christ

**boisterous** (p28)
>noisy and wild

**arrogant** (p28)
>too proud and disdainful of others

**intriguing** (p28)
>arousing interest or curiosity; fascinating

**earnest** (p31)
>very serious, determined, or sincere

**enthralled** (p32)
>spellbound; fascinated

**somber** (p39)
>gloomy and melancholy; sad

**aloof** (p39)
>cool or distant in manner or action

**effusiveness** (p58)
>the condition of being overly emotional and enthusiastic

**acrid** (p60)
>burning; bitter; irritating, such as a taste or odor

**chaos** (p63)
>complete disorder and confusion

**convent** (p64)
>the house or buildings housing a group of nuns who live together, following set religious rules

**peninsula** (p65)
>a piece of land nearly surrounded by water and joined to a large land mass

**philosophy** (p66)
>a system that concerns itself with truth and wisdom and attempts to study and explain the meanings of life and death, of faith, and of religion, the differences between right and wrong, and the principles of art and beauty

**truce** (p67)
>a temporary stop in warfare or fighting by agreement of both sides

**pensive** (p67)
>quietly and seriously thoughtful, often with a touch of sadness

**destiny** (p68)
>the outcome or fate that is bound to come

**armistice** (p69)
>an agreement to stop fighting for a short time; truce

**perfunctorily** (p70)
>mechanically for the sake of getting through something

**reverie** (p71)
>distant and pleasant thoughts; daydreaming

**propriety** (p72)
>the quality of being proper; correctness

**docile** (p74)
>easy to teach, manage, or handle; obedient

**pristine** (p74)
>pure or fresh; untouched; unspoiled

**impetuous** (p75)
>acting on impulse and without thought; hasty; rash

**scruples** (p84)
>feelings of doubt that hold someone back from doing what seems to be wrong

**anguish** (p84)
   great suffering of mind or body; agony

**turbulent** (p86)
   being in violent agitation or commotion; disturbed

**sullied** (p88)
   soiled or tarnished

**Communist** (p90)
   a person who favors a political organization in which a single political party controls the state and manages the production and distribution of goods

**democratic** (p90)
   favoring a form of government in which the people rule, either by voting directly or by electing representatives to manage the government and make the laws

**meager** (p91)
   lacking in quality or quantity, not adequate, inferior

**exodus** (p91)
   a departure or going away

**queue** (p93)
   a line, such as one of persons or cars, waiting for something

**resilient** (p96)
   able to bounce back, such as from trouble or sorrow; buoyant

**archeologist** (p105)
   an expert in the study of past times and cultures, mainly carried on by digging up and examining remains, such as of the cities or tombs of ancient cultures

**vestment** (p108)
   a garment, especially any of various garments worn by the clergy in religious services

**vestibule** (p109)
   an entrance hall or lobby

**irony** (p113)
   a fact, result, or happening that seems the opposite of what one would naturally expect

**elation** (p116)
   a feeling of joy or triumph

**seminary** (p119)
   a school or college that trains ministers, priests, or rabbis

**proctor** (p125)
   an official in a school or college whose duties include keeping order and supervising examinations

**appalled** (p126)
   filled with dismay or horror

**austere** (p130)
   very plain and simple; without luxury or ornament

**stoic** (p136)
   unaffected by pleasure or pain

**remorse** (p136)
   great regret or anguish for something one has done; self-reproach

## Small Group Reading

📖 Green, Carl R., and William R. Sanford. *The Korean War Soldier at Heartbreak Ridge*. Mankato, MN: Capstone Press, 1991.
Through the career of Franklin "Ben" Moore, an African American soldier, the authors portray the politics, battles, and events of the Korean War, especially the Battle of Heartbreak Ridge. Grades 5–8.

## Activities

1.  On a world map, have students locate:

    Australia
    California
    China
    Columbia
    Fort Dix, NJ

    Fort Lewis, WA
    France
    Great Britain
    Greece
    Hungary

From *Teaching U.S. History Through Children's Literature.* © 1998 Wanda J. Miller. Teacher Ideas Press. (800) 237-6124.

North Korea
Poland
Seoul, South Korea
Commonwealth of Independent States
   (formerly the Soviet Union)

Sweden
Tokyo, Japan
Turkey
Washington, DC

2.  Have the students research the following people, focusing on their roles in the Korean War: General Douglas MacArthur, General Matthew Ridgeway, President Harry Truman, and General James Van Fleet.

3.  Have students write essays explaining why they believe that the Korean War should no longer be "The Forgotten War."

4.  Ask your local historian or a member of the Veterans of Foreign Wars (VFW) in your area to visit your class and talk about the soldiers in your area who fought in the Korean War.

## Discussion

Give the small group the following instruction: As your group reads this book, discuss the following questions.

1.  What is the purpose of the United Nations?

2.  How did President Truman attempt to stop the spread of communism in Eastern Europe and Asia?

3.  What was the Cold War?

4.  What caused the division between North and South Korea?

5.  Why did President Truman decide to send naval and air units to South Korea? Do you believe he made the right decision? Why or why not?

6.  Why did the Security Council of the United Nations ask its members to defend South Korea?

7.  Why do you think Ben decided to join the army?

8.  Why did Herbie tell Ben that the draft wouldn't get him if he was rich?

9.  Why was Ben's father concerned about Ben serving alongside white men?

10.  Why did Ben believe that the United States would not attempt to use atomic bombs to end the war?

11.  Where did Ben and Mark go for R & R?

12.  What did Ben mean when he said it "really is a United Nations army"?

13.  Why did the Republic of Korea depend on Americans?

14.  Why did President Truman fire General MacArthur and give command of the troops to General Ridgeway? What was President Truman afraid of?

15.  What did Captain Frasier mean when he said the soldiers had to "fight a limited war"?

16.  Captain Frasier said, "Korea is much like World War I." What did he mean?

17.  What bad news did Mark receive from home? How did Ben react to the news?

18.  Why did the communists refuse to sign a truce?

19.  Ben's regiment was ordered to take Hills 983, 940, and 773. Why did this seem impossible?

20.  How did Heartbreak Ridge get its name?

21.  When was a truce finally agreed upon? What was the final stumbling block?

22.  What did the United States learn from the Korean War?

23. What did the communists learn from the Korean War?

24. How many American soldiers died in the Korean War?

25. Why was General Van Fleet attacked in the newspapers?

26. How did Ben respond when he was asked if the war had been won or lost?

27. What did Ben do when his enlistment ended in 1953?

## Vocabulary

**economy** (p5)
: the management of the resources or finances of a country, business, home, or other entity

**communism** (p6)
: a social system in which the means for producing economic goods belong to the entire community or the state, not to individuals

**aggression** (p11)
: an attack, especially an unprovoked attack

**infantry** (p12)
: soldiers, or a branch of the army, trained and equipped to fight on foot

**draft** (p12)
: the forced selection of people for military service

**reserve units** (p12)
: troops who live as civilians and train at certain times to be ready to enter the regular armed services in an emergency

**deferment** (p13)
: a legal postponement given to someone who is scheduled to be drafted into the army

**barracks** (p13)
: a building (or buildings) used to house soldiers

**private** (p16)
: in the United States Army, the lowest ranking soldier

**corporal** (p16)
: in the United States Army, the lowest ranking noncommissioned officer, below a sergeant

**gooks** (p16)
: the American soldiers' slang term for North Korean soldiers

**bazooka** (p17)
: a long, tube-shaped portable weapon that fires an explosive rocket

**mortar** (p18)
: a short cannon, loaded through the muzzle and fired at a high angle

**hand grenades** (p18)
: small, hand-thrown bombs

**platoon** (p19)
: a basic fighting unit in the United States Army

**foxhole** (p19)
: a shallow hole dug by a soldier as a way of avoiding enemy fire

**kimchi** (p21)
: pickled cabbage, a national Korean dish

**C-rations** (p22)
: canned foods that can be prepared quickly for troops in the field

**atomic bomb** (p22)
: a powerful bomb using the energy suddenly released when the nuclei of atoms of uranium and plutonium are split

**R & R** (p25)
: army slang for Rest and Recuperation leave, which gives soldiers a chance to recover from the hardships of combat

**moat** (p25)
: a ditch, usually full of water, around a castle, fortress, or other structure, that serves as a defense against attackers

**kimono** (p26)
: a loose robe worn as an outer garment in Japan

**sukiyaki** (p27)
: a Japanese dish of thin-sliced meat and vegetables sautéed with seasonings

**shrine** (p27)
: a place or object, such as a tomb, chapel, or holy image, sacred to some holy person and often containing relics

**jade** (p28)
> a hard, usually green mineral used as a gem

**sergeant** (p30)
> in the United States Army, a noncommissioned officer ranking above a corporal

**casualties** (p31)
> soldiers who are killed or wounded in action

**bunker** (p32)
> a fortified earthwork, often reinforced with timbers and sandbags

**monsoon** (p32)
> the rainy season in India and adjacent countries, extending from June to September

**delegate** (p33)
> a person with authority to act for a group; a representative

**truce** (p33)
> an agreement to stop fighting while the two sides in a war try to work out a permanent peace treaty

**regiment** (p35)
> an army unit, larger than a battalion and smaller than a division, usually commanded by a colonel

**napalm** (p36)
> a jellied gasoline used in bombs and flamethrowers that burns everything it touches

**strafing** (p36)
> attacking group troops by firing on them from a low-flying plane

**camouflage** (p37)
> any material that hides soldiers by helping them blend into their surroundings

**artillery** (p37)
> large mounted guns; cannons

**barrage** (p37)
> a heavy, sustained volume of artillery fire

**outflank** (p38)
> to attack an enemy position by hitting it from the side where it is weakest

**grim** (p39)
> unyielding; fixed

**shrapnel** (p39)
> sharp fragments of metal produced by an exploding artillery shell

**ambush** (p43)
> a concealed place where troops lie hidden waiting to attack

# Bibliography

## Individual Titles

Bachrach, Deborah. *The Korean War.* San Diego, CA: Lucent Books, 1991.
Bachrach explains how the United States was involved in the Korean War. Grades 5 and up.

Choi, Sook Nyul. *Gathering of Pearls.* Boston: Houghton Mifflin, 1994.
In this sequel to *Year of Impossible Goodbyes* and *Echoes of the White Giraffe*, Sookan struggles to balance her life in the United States with expectations from her family in Korea. Grades 6 and up.

Darby, Jean. *Douglas MacArthur.* Minneapolis, MN: Lerner, 1989.
A biography of the general who butted heads with President Truman over whether to invade China during the Korean War. Grades 4–6.

Edwards, Richard. *The Korean War.* Vero Beach, FL: Rourke Enterprises, 1988.
A discussion of the origins, events, conclusion, and aftermath of the Korean War. Grades 7 and up.

Farley, Carol. *Korea: A Land Divided.* Minneapolis, MN: Dillon Press, 1983.
The author describes the history, geography, school life, sports and games, and folklore of Korea. She also discusses the problems created by the separation of the north and south into two nations, the Communist Democratic People's Republic of Korea, and the anticommunist Republic of Korea. Grades 4 and up.

Fincher, E. B. *The War in Korea.* New York: Franklin Watts, 1981.
Fincher describes major aspects of the Korean War, including events leading up to it, parts played by significant leaders, and the war's outcome. Grades 5–8.

McGowen, Tom. *The Korean War.* New York: Franklin Watts, 1992.
An overview of the three-year war that took more than two million lives and resolved none of the conflicts that split Korea into two irreconcilable nations. Grades 5–8.

Meltzer, Milton. *The American Promise: Voices of a Changing Nation.* New York: Bantam Books, 1990.

Meltzer provides an overview of the Korean War in this book that also examines the Cold War, the civil rights and women's movements, and the concerns of minority groups. Grades 7–8.

Rabinowitz, Richard. *What Is War? What Is Peace?* New York: Avon Books, 1991.

This book answers many of the questions that students have about war. It includes a glossary and an appendix that tells how students themselves can participate in the quest for world peace. Grades 4–7.

Smith, Carter. *The Korean War.* Englewood Cliffs, NJ: Silver Burdett, 1990.

This book focuses on the major battles and strategies used during the Korean War. Grades 5–8.

Smith, Nigel. *The United States Since 1945.* New York: Bookwright Press, 1989.

This series of two-page essays describes events since 1945, including the Korean battles, the Eisenhower presidency, McCarthyism, segregation, the Vietnam War, and the growing affluence of the middle class. Grades 4–7.

Stein, R. Conrad. *The Korean War: "The Forgotten War."* Hillside, NJ: Enslow, 1994.

Stein provides a history of the Korean War. Grades 6 and up.

Summers, Harry G., Jr. *Korean War Almanac.* New York: Facts on File, 1990.

Summers provides a detailed discussion of the Korean War, organized by topic from A to Z, with an overview and a chronology of events. An excellent research tool for students. Grades 7 and up.

## Theme Resources

### *Videos*

*Korea: The Forgotten War.* Easton, PA: Lou Reda Productions, 1987. (92 minutes)

Robert Stack narrates the events that shattered the peacetime atmosphere and plunged the United States into the Korean War.

*United States History Video Collection: Post–War U.S.A.* Bala Cynwyd, PA: Schlessinger Video Productions, 1996. (35 minutes)

This video covers the Korean War, along with post-war prosperity and the rise of the consumer society, roles of women, the Cold War, the early civil rights movement, and more.

## End-of-Unit Celebration

## The Korean War Research Project

In groups of three or four, have students research the following topics. When completed, hold a presentation day.

| | |
|---|---|
| The Battle of Heartbreak Ridge | General James VanFleet |
| Causes of the Korean War | General Matthew Ridgeway |
| The Division of North and South Korea | President Harry S. Truman |
| General Douglas MacArthur | The Role of the United States in the Korean War |

From *Teaching U.S. History Through Children's Literature.* © 1998 Wanda J. Miller. Teacher Ideas Press. (800) 237-6124.

# Chapter 2

# The Civil Rights Movement

## Introduction

The Constitution of the United States was written in 1787. The Fourteenth Amendment to the Constitution was added in 1868, a few years after the abolishment of slavery. This amendment mandated that all Americans, black or white, receive equal treatment under the law. The Fourteenth Amendment was first tested in the case of *Plessy v. Ferguson* in 1896. The lawyers for Homer Plessy argued that black people were being denied their civil rights. The Supreme Court disagreed, ruling that segregation was acceptable as long as both races had access to equal facilities. "colored only" and "white only" signs became commonplace, particularly in the South. These signs were found in restaurants, rest rooms, waiting rooms in train stations, and buses.

Since the early 1900s, the National Association for the Advancement of Colored People (NAACP) has fought to end segregation, discrimination, voting restrictions, and violence against blacks. A milestone in this fight occurred in 1954, when the case of *Brown v. Board of Education of Topeka, Kansas*, came before the Supreme Court. As a result of the decision in this case, the desegregation of all public schools became law.

The Montgomery bus boycott in 1955, led by E. D. Nixon, was a reaction to the arrest of Rosa Parks, who refused to give up her seat on the bus to a white person. This peaceful protest was organized to highlight segregation and demand equality. Following the Montgomery bus boycott, many other protests, rallies, and freedom rides were organized. Although these protests were nonviolent, in the spirit of the teachings of Dr. Martin Luther King, Jr., they were often met with violence and hatred.

By 1963, blacks were demanding total equality as their right as U.S. citizens. At an August 28th march on Washington, D.C., more than 310,000 people from all over the country listened to Dr. Martin Luther King, Jr.'s "I Have a Dream" speech.

Although significant progress has been made toward equality for all in the United States, racism continues to exist. Our best hope in reducing hatred and discrimination toward those who are considered "different" is education.

As teachers, we must promote the fair and equal treatment of all races by teaching our students that equality and acceptance of others is a goal worth striving for. The trade books in this chapter were selected to aid teachers in guiding their students toward a better understanding of the civil rights movement and the importance of equal opportunities for all.

# Whole Group Reading

📖 Davis, Ossie. *Just Like Martin*. New York: Simon & Schuster Books for Young Readers, 1992.

In the fall of 1963, after the deaths of two classmates in a bomb explosion at his Alabama church, fourteen-year-old Stone organizes a children's march for civil rights. Grades 5–8.

## Author Information

Ossie Davis was born December 18, 1917. He attended Howard University from 1935 to 1939 and Columbia University in 1948.

Davis has worked as an actor, playwright, screenwriter, director, and producer of stage productions and motion pictures. Motion pictures he has acted in include *Jungle Fever* (1991), *Grumpy Old Men* (1994), and *The Client* (1994). His television acting credits include "Roots: The Next Generation" (1979) and "Evening Shade" (1990–1994). He has also acted in many stage productions. Davis is a social activist and community leader.

In 1979, Davis's book *Escape to Freedom: A Play About Young Frederick Douglass* won the Coretta Scott King Book Award from the American Library Association and the Jane Addams Children's Book Award from the Jane Addams Peace Association.

Davis has been active in the civil rights movement. He was master of ceremonies for the 1963 March on Washington, and he spoke at the funerals of Malcolm X and Martin Luther King, Jr. *Just Like Martin*, his first novel, brings the civil rights struggle to life.

Davis, who grew up in a preaching and story-telling environment, always wanted to write. He is committed to bringing African American experiences to a wide audience.

## Activities

1. On a world map, have students locate:

   | | |
   |---|---|
   | Atlanta, GA | Montgomery, AL |
   | California | New Hampshire |
   | Chattanooga, TN | New York City |
   | Jackson, MS | Plaquemine, LA |
   | Korea | Washington, DC |
   | Little Rock, Arkansas | |

2. Have students illustrate the scene described on page 34 that takes place in Washington, D.C.

3. Ask a student volunteer to recite in front of the class the speech by Martin Luther King, Jr. that appears on page 35.

4. Have students research the following topics: Malcolm X, Ku Klux Klan, Rosa Parks, the Jim Crow laws, the assassination of President John F. Kennedy, and President Lyndon B. Johnson.

5. Ask your school music teacher to teach the song "Blowin' in the Wind" (found on page 44) to your class.

6. Have students write an epilogue that takes place fifteen years after *Just Like Martin* ended. Students should tell what has happened to Stone, his father, and Martin Luther King, Jr.

## Discussion

Give the class the following instruction: As we read this book, we will be discussing the following.

1. Why doesn't Stone's father want him to go to the March on Washington?

2. What is Stone's job at the church?

3. What did Stone's mother tell him about his father before she died?

4. How does Stone's father feel about white people?

5. Do you think Martin will ever be able to convince his father that marching, picketing, and demonstrating are right?

6. Why didn't Dorasthena go to the March on Washington?

7. How did Stone feel when listening to Dr. King speak on television?

8. What did Stone's father tell him that he is afraid of?

9. What did Reverend Cable give to Stone after the march? How did Stone feel about it?

10. Why might a march in Alabama be more dangerous than a march in Washington, D.C.?

11. Do you believe that children should be included in such marches?

12. What happened to Stone and his father on their way home after church?

13. What did Mr. Mac McIllister say about white people?

14. How do Stone and the other children feel about being included in the marches? Would you want to be included?

15. How would you feel about attending a workshop in creative nonviolence? Do you think it is something that would be useful for children and young adults today?

16. What caused the problem between Stone and Hookie Fenster?

17. What is more important than any textbook lessons at Stone's school?

18. What did Professor Duckett want to do for Stone?

19. What happened on the opening day of school?

20. What took place in Stone's church the Sunday after school started? How did it make you feel?

21. What did the children plan to do to show that they were not afraid?

22. What did Stone's father have to say about the children's march? Were you surprised by his reaction?

23. Why was Dorasthena worried about what Stone's father said about the children's march? What did Stone do about it?

24. Discuss what happened before the start of the children's march.

25. Where does Stone's father plan to go? Why?

26. When Stone's father came to school, what news did they hear on the radio? How did Stone's father react to the news?

27. What did Stone's father tell him at the lake?

28. Why do you think Stone's father changed his plans?

29. How do you think Stone felt when Martin Luther King, Jr. spoke at Holy Oak Baptist Church and a special visitor came?

From *Teaching U.S. History Through Children's Literature.* © 1998 Wanda J. Miller. Teacher Ideas Press. (800) 237-6124.

# Vocabulary

**deacon** (p3)
a church official who assists the clergy by performing duties not connected with actual worship

**civilize** (p4)
to bring from a primitive way of life into a state of civilization

**vouch** (p8)
to guarantee; to assure

**elders** (p16)
church officials

**provoke** (p16)
to make angry or resentful; to irritate

**blasphemy** (p17)
words or actions showing a lack of respect for God or sacred things

**conscience** (p18)
the inner understanding that tells a person when an action is right and when it is wrong

**infantry** (p18)
soldiers, or a branch of the army, trained and equipped to fight on foot

**decency** (p18)
the quality of being decent; proper character or behavior

**placard** (p21)
a poster that is publicly displayed

**sanctuary** (p22)
a holy or sacred place, especially the place in a church where the main altar is located

**foundry** (p28)
a place where molten metal is shaped in molds

**hypocrite** (p29)
a person who pretends to have but does not really have certain attitudes or qualities; an insincere person

**pulpit** (p35)
a raised platform or desk for a preacher in a church

**democracy** (p35)
a form of government in which the people rule, either by voting directly or by electing representatives to manage the government and make the laws

**desolate** (p35)
dreary; barren

**segregation** (p35)
the practice of separating a racial or religious group from the rest of society, such as in schools, housing, or parks

**creed** (p35)
a summary or formal statement of religious beliefs

**prodigious** (p36)
marvelous; amazing

**asthma** (p39)
a chronic illness that makes breathing difficult and causes wheezing and sometimes coughing

**trestle** (p41)
an open, braced framework used to support a road or railroad tracks

**congregation** (p45)
a group of people, especially those who gather to worship

**NAACP** (p45)
the National Association for the Advancement of Colored People

**AFL-CIO** (p46)
an organization of labor unions, formed when the American Federation of Labor and the Congress of Industrial Organizations merged in 1955

**Ku Klux Klan (KKK)** (p47)
a secret organization, founded in the southern United States after the Civil War, that advocates white supremacy

**telegram** (p47)
a message sent by a telegraph, which is a device for sending and receiving messages by means of a series of electrical or electromagnetic pulses

**vengeance** (p51)
punishment inflicted for a wrong done; revenge

**Pullman** (p61)
a railroad car having small, private compartments that can be converted into sleeping quarters

**porter** (p61)
an attendant on a train

**whipcord** (p61)
a strong braided or twisted cord

**jodhpurs** (p61)
riding breeches that fit tightly from ankle to knee and loosely from the knee upward

**timid** (p62)
fearful or shy

**skittish** (p63)
easily frightened

**dramatize** (p64)
to make something seem exciting or unusual

**verdict** (p68)
a judgment or decision

**dither** (p68)
a condition of nervous excitement or agitation

**quandary** (p68)
a dilemma or puzzle

**gentry** (p68)
people who are well born, but not of the nobility

**ardent** (p68)
very enthusiastic and eager

**indictment** (p69)
a formal written charge, delivered by a grand jury, accusing someone of a crime for which the person should be tried in court

**senile** (p69)
failing in body and mind because of old age

**eloquence** (p69)
a moving and skillful use of language, especially in speaking

**civil disobedience** (p70)
the refusal to obey laws that one considers unjust or wrong, especially as a means of publicly protesting these laws

**adjourn** (p70)
to stop with the intention of beginning again later

**rivals** (p71)
competitors

**lectern** (p77)
a stand having an inclined top on which a speaker may put books or papers from which to read

**gridiron** (p81)
a football field

**dignity** (p85)
the quality of character, worth, or nobility that commands respect

**composure** (p85)
calmness; self-control

**rosary** (p96)
a string of beads for keeping count of the prayers recited

**eulogy** (p97)
a speech or writing in praise of a person, especially when presented formally and in public

**despicable** (p111)
deserving to be despised; mean; contemptible

**adjutant** (p113)
an officer who helps a commanding officer by such duties as preparing orders, writing letters, and keeping records

**benediction** (p113)
an asking of God's blessing at the end of a religious service

**haberdashery** (p161)
a store that sells men's clothing

**jurisdiction** (p182)
the legal right to exercise official authority

**grits** (p199)
coarse meal made from grain, especially corn, with the husks removed

**righteousness** (p207)
the condition of being right according to morals or justice

## Small Group Reading

📖 Herlihy, Dirlie. *Ludie's Song*. New York: Dial Books, 1988.
In rural Georgia in the 1950s, a young white girl's secret friendship with an African American family exposes them all to unforeseen dangers. Grades 7 and up.

*A word of caution:* This book uses a derogatory word in referring to African Americans. Be sure to read the book yourself first to decide if it will be appropriate for your students to read. It might be better used with older students, but even so, discuss this term (and the reason for its use in the book) with them first. My feeling is that the story is excellent and worthwhile to use with older middle-school students.

## Author Information

Dirlie Ann Herlihy was born October 28, 1935, in Portsmouth, Virginia. She has worked as an advertising copywriter, secretary, department store clerk, dental assistant, and piano teacher, as well as a writer.

Herlihy attended Mercer University in Georgia, where she majored in theatre arts. Years later she studied creative writing at the University of North Florida.

*Ludie's Song* was named one of the ten best books of 1988 by United Press International and was recommended by *Parents'* magazine and the American Library Association in 1988.

## Activities

1.  On a map of the United States, have students locate:

    Augusta, GA                         Claxton, GA
    Baltimore, MD                       Macon, GA
    Caldwell, GA                        New York City
    Chicago, IL

2.  Have students write an epilogue for *Ludie's Song*. It should take place twenty years later and focus on Ludie and Martha and what they have been doing since Martha left Caldwell.

3.  Have students write a short skit to perform for the class. This skit should center on a discussion about the treatment of black people. It should include Ludie, Uncle Ray, Naomi, and Ludie's mother as characters.

4.  Have students research Booker T. Washington and George Washington Carver.

## Discussion

Give the small group the following instruction: As your group reads this book, discuss the following.

1.  Why did Martha's mother tell her that Sara couldn't sleep at their house?

2.  Why does Martha's Aunt Letty have Sister do the laundry for them, even though they have a washing machine?

3.  Who is Ludie? What does Martha think about Ludie and Sister?

4.  Why didn't Uncle Ray want Martha to see Jun?

5.  What did Martha overhear after church about Uncle Ray?

6.  Discuss your reactions to Thad's and Janelle's views about black people.

7.  Why were there separate drinking fountains for white people and black people at the Phelps store?

8.  Why wouldn't the dentist treat the Negro woman? After Martha overheard this encounter, what did she suddenly realize?

9.  What did Martha find out about Ludie and her animals?

10. Why did Martha decide to keep her visit with Sister and Ludie a secret?

11. Discuss the dream Martha had in chapter 8. What do you think it meant?

12. Why was Martha surprised that Ludie could write?

13. Discuss Uncle Ray's explanation to Martha about why black people and white people are separated.

14. How have Martha's feelings about Ludie changed? Why?

15. What is the special talent that Ludie has that Martha told Thad about?

16. What is Martha's hope for Ludie? Do you think her dream could come true?

17. What did Thad advise Martha regarding her relationship with Ludie?

18. When Uncle Ray accused Martha of doing something wrong in the mornings, what did Martha tell him she had been doing? Why?

19. What does Uncle Ray plan to do with the drawings?

20. Discuss Thad's warning to Martha. Do you think she has a reason to be afraid?

21. Why did Jewel want to frighten Martha?

22. What happened to Chili and Martha? Why? Who rescued them?

23. How did the truth about what happened to Chili and Martha finally come out?

24. Discuss your feelings about Thad's mother, Naomi. Why do you think she plans to take Thad to stay in Chicago?

25. How do Martha's parents feel about Ludie's questioning the separation of black people and white people?

26. What does Martha's Uncle Ray plan to do for Ludie?

27. Why do you think the author chose *Ludie's Song* as the title of this book?

## Vocabulary

**ravine** (p3)
a long, narrow, deep depression in the earth that has steep sides and is usually cut out by the flow of water; a gorge

**embankment** (p3)
a mound or bank, such as of stone, cement, or earth, built usually to hold back water or support a roadway

**silo** (p6)
a tower in which feed is stored for cattle

**pungency** (p7)
the condition of being sharp or piercing to taste or smell

**hickory** (p7)
any of several North American trees related to the walnut and having a hard wood and edible nuts

**haughty** (p8)
satisfied with oneself and scornful of others; arrogant

**disdainful** (p8)
scornful, especially toward someone or something considered inferior

**charity** (p10)
the giving of help, usually in the form of money, to the poor and unfortunate

**tolerable** (p11)
bearable

**phantom** (p14)
something that exists only in the imagination but seems to be real

**percolator** (p15)
a type of coffee pot in which boiling water keeps rising in a tube and then filters down through ground coffee to the bottom

**oxfords** (p17)
low shoes laced over the instep

**ignorant** (p17)
having little or no knowledge or learning

**pectin** (p23)
a carbohydrate substance found in various fruits and juices

**dispute** (p36)
to argue or challenge in debate

**pinafore** (p38)
a sleeveless, apronlike garment, worn as a dress or protective smock by girls and women

**commerce** (p49)
the buying and selling of goods, especially on a large scale between different places or nations; trade

From *Teaching U.S. History Through Children's Literature.* © 1998 Wanda J. Miller. Teacher Ideas Press. (800) 237-6124.

**patrician** (p50)
   a person having a high social position; an aristocrat

**aloofness** (p50)
   the condition of being cool or distant in manner or action

**parasol** (p51)
   a small, light umbrella carried to protect oneself from the sun

**vantage point** (p60)
   a position that offers a broad or commanding view

**discontent** (p67)
   an unhappy, dissatisfied feeling

**alibi** (p68)
   the fact or the defense that a person suspected of a crime was in another place when it was committed

**chintz** (p71)
   a cotton fabric, usually glazed and printed in bright colors

**sweatshop** (p73)
   a place where work is done under poor conditions, for very little pay, and for long hours

**Industrial Revolution** (p73)
   the great social and economic change, beginning in the eighteenth century in England and later spreading to the United States and Europe, that resulted from the replacement of hand tools with power-driven machinery

**metropolis** (p75)
   the largest or most important city of a country, state, or area

**Yankee** (p75)
   a person born or living in New England

**indignant** (p75)
   angry because of something that is not right, just, or fair

**War Between the States** (p75)
   the Civil War

**gingham** (p76)
   a cotton fabric woven in solid colors, stripes, checks, or plaids

**tonic** (p77)
   anything, such as certain medicines, that is supposed to make a person feel better or more energetic

**inferior** (p80)
   lower in rank, position, or importance

**utilitarian** (p86)
   possessing usefulness rather than beauty

**industrious** (p93)
   hardworking and diligent

**bolero** (p94)
   a short, vestlike jacket, open at the front

**stern** (p105)
   harsh in manner; strict

**bravado** (p106)
   a show of bravery without much courage or confidence underneath

**iota** (p109)
   a very small amount

**predominant** (p121)
   greater or superior in power, effect, or number

**dilapidated** (p128)
   half ruined by neglect; falling to pieces

**rancid** (p137)
   having the bad taste or smell of spoiled fat or oil

**dignity** (p147)
   the quality of character, worth, or nobility that commands respect

**exasperation** (p152)
   the feeling of being annoyed or irritated almost to the point of anger

**turmoil** (p182)
   a condition of great confusion or agitation

**putrid** (p182)
   decaying; rotten

**misconstrued** (p195)
   interpreted wrongly; misunderstood

**inquisitive** (p205)
   full of questions; eager for knowledge; curious

**retaliation** (p207) something done to get even, such as for an injury or wrong

# Small Group Reading

📖 Nelson, Vaunda Micheaux. *Mayfield Crossing*. New York: G. P. Putnam's Sons, 1993.

When the school in Mayfield Crossing closes, the students are sent to a larger school, where the black children encounter racial prejudice for the first time. Baseball seems the only means of bringing people together. Grades 3–5.

## Author Information

Vaunda Micheaux Nelson grew up in a small Pennsylvania town, the youngest of five children. She lives in Pittsburgh, Pennsylvania, where she is a children's librarian. Nelson says her parents inspired her to become a writer. *Mayfield Crossing* was based on some of her own experiences as one of only a few black children in her school. These experiences, along with the strong family values with which she was raised, became the backbone for Meg's story.

## Activities

1. Have students write an epilogue for *Mayfield Crossing*. It should take place one year later, and tell how things have changed at Parkview School.

2. Have students write a journal entry from Ivy's point of view, telling how she feels about the new students from Mayfield Crossing.

3. Have students write a short skit based on *Mayfield Crossing* and perform it for the class. It should include the black students' first encounter with racial prejudice in their new school.

4. Following the reading of *Mayfield Crossing*, have students write essays explaining their feelings about racial prejudice.

## Discussion

Give the small group the following instruction: As your group reads this book, discuss the following questions.

1. What did Papa say about being different?

2. How do you think the children feel about going to a new school?

3. What did Fitch's mother say about them going to Parkview School?

4. What happened to Meg and Mo at lunchtime their first day at Parkview School?

5. How were the new students treated at recess?

6. Why are Meg and the other children afraid of Old Hairy?

7. What happened when Meg offered Ivy half of her sandwich? How would you have felt if you were Meg?

8. How did Old Hairy end up helping Meg and her friends at school?

9. What did Old Hairy leave at the Crossing for Billie and Meg?

10. What helped Meg remember all fifty states?

11. Why did Clayton go after Meg at recess?

12. How did the principal handle Clayton, Meg, and Billie after recess?

13. How did Mrs. Carmichael treat Billie and the other kids from Mayfield Crossing?

14. What did Billie plan to try to make the Parkview kids treat the kids from Mayfield Crossing with respect?

15. Why do you think Ivy agreed to play baseball on the Mayfield Crossing team?

16. Do you think baseball will really bring the kids together?

## Vocabulary

**riled** (p11)
annoyed or irritated

**commotion** (p13)
great confusion; excitement; disturbance

**cowlick** (p19)
a tuft of hair that sticks up and will not easily lie flat

**pneumonia** (p32)
a disease caused by a bacterial or viral infection and marked by inflammation in one or both lungs

**glider** (p33)
a swing made of a seat hung in a metal frame so it can glide back and forth

**redeem** (p36)
to make amends for

**hobo** (p38)
a person who lives by doing odd jobs and begging

**knapsack** (p42)
a large bag for supplies, worn strapped to the back; a backpack

**air raid** (p47)
an attack or raid by aircraft

**curfew** (p47)
a rule or law requiring certain persons to keep off the streets at certain times, usually evening

**doe** (p51)
the female of the deer, antelope, rabbit, kangaroo, and certain other animals

**accusation** (p53)
a charge of having done something wrong or illegal or of being something bad

**smug** (p70)
full of or showing much self-satisfaction

**varnish** (p76)
a solution of certain gums or resins, such as those in alcohol or linseed oil, used to give a shiny coat to a surface

**forfeit** (p82)
to lose or give up as a penalty for an offense or mistake

**traitor** (p86)
a person who betrays friends, a cause, or an obligation; especially a person who betrays a country

## Small Group Reading

Rochelle, Belinda. *Witnesses to Freedom: Young People Who Fought for Civil Rights*. New York: Lodestar, 1993.

Rochelle describes the experiences of young African Americans who were involved in such significant events in the civil rights movement as *Brown vs. Board of Education of Topeka, Kansas*, the Montgomery bus boycott, and the sit-in movement. Grades 4–8.

## Author Information

Belinda Rochelle lives in Washington, D.C. Her poetry and articles have appeared in many magazines. *Witnesses to Freedom: Young People Who Fought for Civil Rights* is Rochelle's first book. She wrote this book because "most of the books about the civil rights movement focus on the contributions of one person, yet the movement was successful because of many people. I wanted to write this book for children because it shows how children themselves can affect history."

Rochelle has also served as a lobbyist and community organizer, providing public health policy to more than 800 community-based organizations in Africa and the United States.

## Activities

1. On a map of the United States, have students locate:

| | |
|---|---|
| Albany, GA | Memphis, TN |
| Anniston, AL | Mississippi |
| Atlanta, GA | Mobile, AL |
| Birmingham, AL | Montgomery, AL |
| Charleston, SC | Nashville, TN |
| Chicago, IL | Raleigh, NC |
| Farmville, VA | Selma, AL |
| Florida | Texas |
| Greensboro, AL | Topeka, KS |
| India | Tuskegee, AL |
| Little Rock, AR | Virginia |
| Louisiana | Washington, DC |

2. Have students research the following people and organizations to find out more about the roles they played in the civil rights movement:

| | |
|---|---|
| Congress of Racial Equality (CORE) | E. D. Nixon |
| President Dwight Eisenhower | Rosa Parks |
| President John F. Kennedy | Asa Philip Randolph |
| Martin Luther King, Jr. | President Franklin D. Roosevelt |
| Thurgood Marshall | |

   Students should incorporate the information they obtain onto small posters to be hung in the classroom.

3. Have students in this group first write essays explaining their feelings about the Jim Crow laws, then read their essays to the rest of the class.

4. Have students write personal reactions in their journals to the "I Have a Dream" speech given by Martin Luther King, Jr. at the March on Washington on August 28, 1963.

## Discussion

Give the small group the following instruction: As your group reads this book, discuss the following.

1. Describe what school was like for Barbara Johns.

2. What were the Jim Crow laws?

3. Compare black high schools with white high schools in the 1950s.

4. What did Barbara Johns and other students from R. R. Morton High School do to improve the conditions in their school?

5. What advice does Barbara Johns give to young people today?

6. Why did Barbara go to Montgomery, Alabama, to stay with her uncle?

7. Why couldn't Spottswood and Wannamaker Bolling attend Sousa Junior High School?

8. What did Linda Brown's father, Oliver Brown, do to force school officials to let Linda attend Sumner Elementary School?

9. What ruling did the Supreme Court make in *Plessy v. Ferguson*?

From *Teaching U.S. History Through Children's Literature.* © 1998 Wanda J. Miller. Teacher Ideas Press. (800) 237-6124.

10. What other cases were combined under *Brown v. Board of Education of Topeka, Kansas*?

11. What ruling did the Supreme Court make on May 17, 1954?

12. Why was it necessary for the Supreme Court to issue another ruling on May 31, 1955?

13. How long did it take for some schools to obey the Supreme Court's decision and desegregate?

14. Who were the "Little Rock Nine"? What did they do that was so brave?

15. What did Orval Faubus, the governor of Arkansas, do to prevent integration?

16. What did President Dwight Eisenhower do to protect the "Little Rock Nine"?

17. How were the "Little Rock Nine" treated by the white students and parents?

18. Why did Governor Faubus close Central High School?

19. Are all schools integrated today?

20. What happened to Claudette Colvin on March 2, 1955?

21. What did the law in Montgomery, Alabama say about public buses and black ridership?

22. What was the lawsuit that Rosa Parks filed in Montgomery, Alabama? Why did she file this lawsuit?

23. What did Martin Luther King, Jr. learn about Mahatma Gandhi? What tactics of Gandhi's did he use as the leader of the Montgomery bus boycott?

24. What was the three-point plan that was presented to Montgomery city officials?

25. Discuss the outcome of the Montgomery bus boycott.

26. What did Joseph McNeil, Ezell Blair, Jr., Franklin McCain, and David Richmond do to protest discrimination?

27. What role did the Freedom Singers play in the civil rights movement?

28. What did Freedom Riders do in 1961? Why did the first Freedom Ride end?

29. Why does Diane Nash believe that voting is not enough?

30. Discuss the Children's Crusade in Birmingham, Alabama in May of 1963.

31. What was Asa Phillip Randolph's role in the fight for civil rights for all?

32. What was the goal of the March on Washington?

33. What happened at Youth Day at the Sixteenth Street Baptist Church in Birmingham, Alabama on September 15, 1963?

34. What does the Civil Rights Act of 1964 guarantee?

35. Discuss the things that were done to black people to keep them from registering to vote.

36. What was the reason for the fifty-mile march from Selma, Alabama to Montgomery, Alabama on March 7, 1965?

37. Why was passage of the Voting Rights Act considered to be the most important battle won for the civil rights movement?

38. Why do we have a national holiday honoring Dr. Martin Luther King, Jr.?

39. In the afterword to her book, Belinda Rochelle tells readers that you don't have to be an adult to work to end discrimination and injustice. What can you do in your community to fight inequality?

# Vocabulary

**segregation** (p1)
    the practice of separating a racial or religious group from the rest of society, such as in schools, housing, or parks

**custom** (p2)
    something that has become an accepted practice by many people

**boycott** (p4)
    to unite in refusing to buy from, sell to, use, deal, or associate with a certain business, organization, or group of people

**truant** (p4)
    a person who is absent without permission from a duty or task, especially from school

**idol** (p4)
    a person or thing that is greatly loved or admired

**Ku Klux Klan (KKK)** (p5)
    a secret organization, founded in the southern United States after the Civil War that advocates white supremacy

**NAACP** (p9)
    the National Association for the Advancement of Colored People

**desegregation** (p9)
    the act of abolishing the separation of races

**integrate** (p9)
    to make the use or occupancy of schools, parks, neighborhoods, or other facilities available to persons of all races

**prohibit** (p11)
    to forbid, especially by authority or law

**comply** (p11)
    to act in agreement

**deteriorating** (p12)
    becoming worse

**moral** (p18)
    good or virtuous in behavior or character

**mortal** (p18)
    very great

**jeering** (p19)
    ridiculing; mocking

**reprimanded** (p20)
    formally blamed

**provoke** (p20)
    to cause; to bring on

**confrontation** (p20)
    the act of standing face to face with; the act of facing boldly

**expelled** (p20)
    dismissed permanently from school

**torment** (p20)
    great bodily pain or mental agony

**transition** (p22)
    the act or condition of changing from one form, place, or type of existence to another

**taunted** (p24)
    insulted, provoked, or made fun of with scornful, mocking, or sarcastic remarks

**glee club** (p25)
    a group organized to sing songs

**humanity** (p28)
    kindness

**noble** (p28)
    having or showing outstandingly good or moral qualities

**discrimination** (p32)
    prejudice in one's attitudes or actions

**atmosphere** (p32)
    surrounding influence; background

**prejudice** (p32)
    hatred of or dislike for a particular race

**tactics** (p34)
    the art, technique, or means used to achieve one's goals

**traumatic** (p37)
    caused by a severe emotional shock that has long-lasting psychological effects

**pursuit** (p40)
    the act of trying to get or obtain

**dignity** (p40)
    the quality of character, worth, or nobility that commands respect

**mentor** (p44)
    a wise, devoted advisor

**admiration** (p45)
    a feeling of wonder, approval, and satisfaction for someone or something of quality

**dismantle** (p47)
    to take apart

**agenda** (p47)
    a list of things to be done or discussed

**veteran** (p48)
  a person who has had much experience in doing something

**harassment** (p51)
  the act of annoying with small, repeated attacks

**critical** (p52)
  extremely important; crucial

**liberation** (p53)
  the act of setting free

**barricade** (p55)
  an obstruction hastily built to prevent passage or for defense

**billy club** (p55)
  a short club, such as that carried by some police officers

**slogan** (p57)
  an often-repeated phrase or motto used to draw attention

**injustice** (p59)
  lack of justice, fairness, or equal treatment

**gospel** (p60)
  the teaching of Christ and his apostles

**podium** (p69)
  a small platform on which a speaker stands

**prodigious** (p71)
  marvelous; amazing

**disperse** (p72)
  to scatter or spread in many directions

**literacy** (p75)
  the ability to read and write

**inspiration** (p78)
  a person who fills others with a certain thought, feeling, or desire to do something

**resolution** (p82)
  a formal expression of the feelings or will of an assembly

**commemorating** (p84)
  honoring or keeping fresh the memory of

## Small Group Reading

📖 Siegel, Beatrice. *The Year They Walked: Rosa Parks and the Montgomery Bus Boycott*. New York: Four Winds Press, 1992.

Siegel examines the life of Rosa Parks, an African American woman who refused to give up her seat on a segregated bus in Montgomery, Alabama, and was arrested as a result. Her act of nonviolent resistance sparked the Montgomery bus boycott in which thousands of African Americans made their economic influence felt by choosing not to ride the bus and instead walking for freedom through the streets of Montgomery. Grades 7 and up.

## Author Information

Beatrice Siegel was born in New York City. She received her bachelor of arts degree from Brooklyn College (now the City University of New York) in 1933. She received her master's degree from Cornell University in New York in 1936.

Siegel worked for the Retail Drug Employees Union, Local 1199 from 1950 to 1955. She worked for a Neighborhood Youth Corps from 1966 to 1968, and began her writing career in 1971.

Siegel has written several books for children, including *Indians of the Woodland: Before and After the Pilgrims*, *A New Look at the Pilgrims: Why They Came to America*, and *Lillian Wald of Henry Street*. *Fur Trappers and Traders: The Indians, the Pilgrims, and the Beaver* was selected as an ALA Notable Children's Trade Book in the field of Social Studies.

# Activities

1. On a map of the United States, have students locate:

   | | |
   |---|---|
   | Alabama River, AL | Mobile, AL |
   | Atlanta, GA | Monteagle, TN |
   | Birmingham, AL | Montgomery, AL |
   | Chicago, IL | Nashville, TN |
   | Cleveland, OH | Richmond, VA |
   | Columbia, SC | Scottsboro, AL |
   | Detroit, MI | Tallahatchie River |
   | Gulf of Mexico | Tuscaloosa, AL |
   | Mississippi | Tuskegee, AL |

2. Have students research the following civil rights-related topics:

   | | |
   |---|---|
   | *Brown v. Board of Education of Topeka, Kansas* | E. D. Nixon |
   | | Rosa Parks |
   | Coretta Scott King | Scottsboro Case |
   | Martin Luther King, Jr. | Booker T. Washington |

3. Ask your school music teacher to teach the song "Onward, Christian Soldiers" to your class.

4. Have students act out the speech appearing on page 46.

5. Civil rights for United States citizens are guaranteed under the Thirteenth, Fourteenth, Fifteenth, and Nineteenth Amendments to the Constitution. Have students read these amendments and summarize them for the class.

# Discussion

Give the small group the following instruction: As your group reads this book, discuss the following.

1. Discuss the bus laws in Montgomery, Alabama.

2. Why was Rosa Parks arrested?

3. As a child, how did Rosa first realize that there was a black world and a white world?

4. Describe the school that Rosa attended.

5. How was Rosa's church important to her and to other black people?

6. Describe Rosa's life as a child.

7. How do you think Rosa felt the first time she voted?

8. Why was Alabama called the "heart of Dixie"?

9. Why was racism a large part of life in the South following the Civil War?

10. What was the ruling of the U.S. Supreme Court regarding *Brown v. the Board of Education of Topeka, Kansas*?

11. What was the White Citizens Council?

12. What did Rosa Parks learn at Highlander Folk School in Monteagle, Tennessee?

13. Why did many black people hesitate to speak out against segregation?

14. Why was riding city buses a daily humiliation for black people?

15. Discuss the Montgomery bus boycott.

16. How was Dr. Martin Luther King, Jr.'s approach to the civil rights movement different from others?

17. What resolutions did the Montgomery Improvement Association demand of the bus company?

18. Discuss the jobs that volunteers performed to make the Montgomery bus boycott a success.

19. What was the first concession that the Montgomery Improvement Association won? Why were city officials afraid to agree to more of the demands?

20. How did the White Citizens Council try to put a stop to the boycott?

21. How were Rosa Parks and her family treated as a result of the boycott?

22. How did Robert S. Graetz help the Montgomery Improvement Association?

23. What treatment did Juliette Morgan receive because of her belief that segregation was evil?

24. As news of the Montgomery bus boycott traveled around the world, how did people react?

25. Discuss the outcome of the Montgomery bus boycott, how long it lasted, its effects on blacks and whites, and your feelings regarding the issue of segregation.

26. Why did Martin Luther King, Jr. call the boycott a "social revolution"?

27. Describe Rosa Parks's life after the boycott.

28. Why do you think it is important for students to learn about Rosa Parks?

# Vocabulary

**bursitis** (p 12)
inflammation of the bursa (a pouch or saclike cavity in the body), especially one between the parts of a joint

**tailor** (p12)
a person who makes or repairs outer clothing

**rebuke** (p13)
a strong statement of disapproval; a sharp scolding

**segregation** (p15)
the practice of separating a racial or religious group from the rest of society, such as in schools, housing, or parks

**rural** (p15)
in the country; outside of city areas

**barren** (p16)
empty

**spiritual** (p16)
a religious folk song originating among the blacks of the southern United States

**solidarity** (p16)
the condition of being strongly united or in unison

**Ku Klux Klan (KKK)** (p16)
a secret organization, founded in the southern United States after the Civil War, that advocates white supremacy

**integration** (p17)
the act of making the use or occupancy of a school, park, neighborhood, or other facility available to persons of all races

**persecution** (p17)
mistreatment or oppression because of religion, race, or beliefs

**overseer** (p17)
a person who supervises laborers at their work

**endure** (p17)
to bear up under; to stand firm against

**vocation** (p18)
a profession, career, or trade, especially the one a person chooses or for which a person is best suited

**genial** (p18)
friendly and kind; cheerful

**civil rights** (p18)
the rights and privileges of a citizen; especially in the United States, the rights guaranteed by the Thirteenth, Fourteenth, Fifteenth, and Nineteenth Amendments to the Constitution

**activist** (p18)
a person who participates in public action in support of a cause

**crusade** (p18)
a vigorous struggle in favor of a cause

**racist** (p19)
a person who shows prejudice in favor of a particular race

**domestic** (p19)
having to do with the home or family

**militant** (p19)
taking or ready to take aggressive action, as on behalf of beliefs or rights

**intimidate** (p22)
to frighten into doing or not doing something

**desegregation** (p25)
the act of abolishing the separation of races

**textile** (p27)
having to do with weaving or woven fabrics

**Confederacy** (p27)
The Confederate States of America; southern states in the United States that joined together during the Civil War

**secede** (p27)
to withdraw from a union or association, especially a political or religious one

**inaugurated** (p27)
installed in an office with a formal ceremony

**meager** (p27)
lacking in quality or quantity; inadequate; inferior

**democracy** (p28)
a form of government in which the people rule, either by voting directly or by electing representatives to manage the government and make the laws

**extremist** (p28)
a person who holds extreme opinions, favors extreme measures, or goes to extremes in actions or behavior

**prominent** (p28)
well-known

**abolish** (p29)
to do away with; to put an end to

**humiliation** (p30)
the act or an instance of being stripped of pride or self-respect; embarrassment

**Reconstruction** (p30)
the bringing back into the Union the seceded Southern states after the Civil War; the time period during which this process took place (1865–1877)

**malady** (p32)
a disease, sickness, or illness

**faction** (p32)
a party or group exhibiting angry disagreement or strife

**passive** (p32)
not showing resistance; yielding; submissive

**genteel** (p32)
polite or well-bred; refined

**NAACP** (p36)
the National Association for the Advancement of Colored People

**boycott** (p36)
to unite in refusing to buy from, sell to, use, deal, or associate with a certain business, organization, or group of people

**indignity** (p38)
something that humiliates someone or injures someone's self-respect

**dormant** (p42)
inactive

**quiescent** (p42)
in a state of rest; inactive; quiet

**philosophy** (p44)
a system of thought that concerns itself with truth and wisdom in an attempt to study and explain the meanings of life and death, of faith, and of religion; the differences between right and wrong; and the purposes and principles of art and beauty

**enclave** (p44)
a distinctly separate community or area lying within another

**eloquence** (p46)
a moving and skillful use of language, especially in speaking

**abyss** (p47)
the lowest depth, too deep to measure

**aspiration** (p47)
a great hope or desire; ambition

**resolution** (p56)
something determined or decided on, such as a course of action

**exhorting** (p62)
advising or urging strongly

**provocation** (p62)
something that provokes, angers, or stirs up

**coercive** (p62)
tending to force someone into doing something, such as by threats or violence

**radicals** (p63)
people who favor rapid and widespread changes or reforms, especially in politics or government

**anguish** (p67)
great suffering of mind or body; agony

**besiege** (p67)
to bother; to harass

**patriarch** (p68)
a father who is the founder, ruler, or head, such as of a family or tribe

**staunch** (p69)
firm and dependable; loyal

**aristocratic** (p70)
superior; exclusive; snobbish

**liberal** (p70)
not narrow-minded or prejudiced; tolerant

**parsonage** (p71)
the house that a church provides for its minister

**recluse** (p72)
a person who lives alone, shut away from the world

**elegiac** (p75)
sad; mournful

**morale** (p77)
state of mind, especially in terms of confidence, courage, or hope

**turmoil** (p87)
a condition of great confusion or agitation; disturbance

**upheaval** (p88)
a violent disturbance or change

**apartheid** (p92)
the government policy of racial segregation and social, economic, and educational discrimination in the Republic of South Africa

# Small Group Reading

Taylor, Mildred D. *The Gold Cadillac.* New York: Dial Books for Young Readers, 1987.

Two black girls are proud of their family's new, all gold 1950 Cadillac until they visit the South and encounter racial prejudice for the first time. Grades 4–6.

## Author Information

Mildred D. Taylor was born September 13, 1943, in Jackson, Mississippi. Taylor received her bachelor's degree in Education from the University of Toledo in 1965. In 1969, she received her master's degree from the University of Colorado.

Taylor has worked as an English and history teacher, study skills coordinator, proofreader, editor, and writer.

Taylor has won many awards for her books, including a *New York Times* notable book citation in 1977, and the Christopher Award in 1988, both for *The Gold Cadillac. Roll of Thunder, Hear My Cry* was the 1977 Newbery Medal winner.

Through her writing, Taylor shares her pride in her racial heritage by providing historical fiction about black American life. She believed that school history texts diminish the contributions and struggles of blacks, and vowed to write stories that offer a truer version of black families and racial struggles. Taylor draws on her own family's experiences in writing her books.

## Activities

1. Have students write essays describing their feelings about racial prejudice and the treatment of blacks in the 1950s. They can then present these essays to the class.

2. On a map of the United States, have students locate:

   Bowling Green, OH        Maumee River
   Chicago, IL              Memphis, TN
   Cincinnati, OH           Mississippi
   Cleveland, OH            Ohio River
   Dayton, OH               Peoria, IL
   Detroit, MI              Toledo, OH
   Kentucky

3. Have students design posters promoting an end to racial prejudice. Then display them in your classroom or in the main hallway of your school.

4. Have students in this group write and perform a short skit based on *The Gold Cadillac*. It could include the arrival of the gold Cadillac, the incident with police in Mississippi, and the girls' reaction to racial prejudice.

## Discussion

Give the small group the following instruction: As your group reads this book, discuss the following.

1. How did Wilma and 'lois react to the brand-new Cadillac?

2. How did Wilma and 'lois's mother feel about the Cadillac?

3. What did 'lois and her family do on Sundays in the summer?

4. Why did 'lois's aunts and uncles worry about them driving the Cadillac to Mississippi?

5. How does Wilbert feel about what white people think?

6. Why did their mother tell Wilma and 'lois that she didn't want them to talk in front of white people?

7. What signs did 'lois and her family see when they reached Tennessee? Where were the signs located?

8. How did 'lois feel about the signs?

9. Why had 'lois's mother packed a picnic lunch for them?

10. What happened when the family crossed into Mississippi with the Cadillac?

11 Why did 'lois and her family leave Mississippi and go back to Tennessee before returning to visit with their family in Mississippi?

12. How did 'lois's father explain to her the way they were treated in the South?

13. Discuss your feelings about the treatment of black people during this time period.

14. What dream does 'lois's father have for the future?

15. Why do you think 'lois's father didn't drive the Cadillac after they returned home?

16. What did 'lois's father do with the gold Cadillac? Why?

17. Discuss how their trip to Mississippi affected the whole family.

## Vocabulary

**parlor** (p11)
a room for receiving visitors or entertaining guests

**duplex apartment** (p11)
an apartment that has rooms on two floors

**proclaimed** (p11)
announced publicly

**caravan** (p19)
a group of cars traveling together

**evident** (p22)
easily seen or understood; apparent

**rural** (p24)
in the country; outside of city areas

**uppity** (p24)
snobbish or arrogant

**lynch** (p24)
to kill a person by mob action, such as by hanging

**heedful** (p26)
paying careful attention to

**dusk** (p33)
the darkest part of twilight, just before night falls

**lurk** (p33)
to lie hidden; to stay out of sight

**dawn** (p35)
the first appearance of light in the morning

**splendor** (p36)
brilliance or magnificence

**ignorance** (p37)
the condition of having little or no learning or knowledge

**migrate** (p45)
to move from one country or region to settle in another

## Small Group Reading

Walter, Mildred Pitts. *The Girl on the Outside*. New York: Scholastic, 1982.

The small Southern town of Mossville is turned upside down in 1957 when the Supreme Court orders the desegregation of all public schools. Nine black students enroll at the all-white Chatman High School. Two girls (one white and one black) are caught up in the town's anger and are bound together by their courage and strength. Grades 6 and up.

## Author Information

Mildred Pitts Walter was a teacher in Los Angeles in the 1960s. Her husband, Earl Walter, was the city chairperson of the Congress of Racial Equality (CORE).

As members of CORE, Walter and her husband worked to have the case of *Crawford v. Los Angeles Board of Education* heard in 1968. They hoped a decision in this case would end segregation in the Los Angeles school system.

*The Girl on the Outside* was inspired by the desegregation crisis in Little Rock, Arkansas; it is a fictional re-creation of that incident.

## Activities

1. On a map of the United States, have students locate:
   Little Rock, AR          Mississippi
   Louisiana                Tennessee

2. Have students illustrate the scene on the first day of school at Chatman High, when Eva and the other eight black students arrive to enroll at the school.

3. Have students write a letter from Eva to Sophia after Sophia helps her escape from the angry mob at Chatman High School. Then have the students share their letters with the rest of the class.

4. Have students write three diary entries from Sophia's point of view. The first entry should take place when Sophia learns that her school will be integrated by nine black students. The second entry should take place when Sophia begins to have mixed feelings about integration. The final entry should take place after Sophia helps Eva escape the angry mob at Chatman; this entry should include her feelings about integration.

## Discussion

Give the small group the following instruction: As your group reads this book, discuss the following.

1. How does Sophia feel about Arnold coming to visit her?

2. Discuss Sophia's reaction to Negroes attending Chatman High School.

3. How does Burt feel about school desegregation?

4. Describe Eva's reaction to the possibility of her attending Chatman High School.

5. Eva's father said many times, "Dying ain't the worst thing in the world. When y' can't choose what y' wanta do, and where y' wanta go, that, havin' no choice, is worse 'n death." Discuss your feelings about this statement.

6. Why do Eva's parents want her to go to her Aunt Shirley's?

7. When did Sophia first learn that her family felt that black people were different?

8. Where did Arnold take Sophia? How did she react?

9. How does Arnold feel about integration?

10. How does Cecil feel about Eva leaving Carver High School to go to Chatman? Why?

11. What do you think Aunt Shirley meant when she told Eva, "Oh, but y' gonna do some teachin', too. They can learn as much from you as y' can learn from them. Otherwise, what's the point o' this integration?"?

12. Why do you think Sophia had never realized before that Rod is black? Did this realization change her feelings toward Rod?

13. What did Sophia and her friends plan at the skating rink?

14. Why did the governor bring in the National Guard to Mossville?

15. What news did Mrs. Floyd bring to Eva and her family the night before school was to start?

16. Why did Sophia change her mind about what to wear the first day of school?

17. Why do you think Sophia is beginning to have mixed feelings about integration?

18. Why didn't Sophia want Arnold to know about the pact that she and her friends had made?

19. Contrast Sophia's and Eva's reactions to the news of Judge Pomeroy's decision.

20. What happened when Sophia and Eva met at school?

21. How did Sophia's family react to what she did?

22. Discuss your feelings about *The Girl on the Outside*.

## Vocabulary

**cultivated** (p4)
planted and cared for

**humid** (p4)
containing water vapor; damp; moist

**distinction** (p5)
a difference that can be seen

**legislature** (p5)
a group of persons who make the laws of a nation or state

**integration** (p5)
the act of making the use or occupancy of a school, park, neighborhood, or other facility available to persons of all races

**somber** (p5)
gloomy and melancholy; sad

**denounce** (p6)
to speak against openly and strongly; to condemn

**Communist** (p6)
a person who supports or is in favor of a social system in which the means for producing economic goods belongs to the entire community or state, not to individuals

**monotonous** (p6)
boring because of lack of variety or change

**NAACP** (p11)
the National Association for the Advancement of Colored People

**humiliation** (p18)
the act or an instance of being stripped of pride or self-respect; embarrassment

**solemnly** (p20)
seriously

**anxiety** (p22)
an uneasy, worried feeling about what may happen; concern

**organdy** (p22)
a thin, crisp, cotton cloth, used mainly for clothing, such as dresses, collars, and cuffs

**heirloom** (p22)
an object that has been passed down through several generations of a family

**silhouette** (p29)
the outline of a person or object seen against a light or a light background

**tedious** (p40)
long, dull, and tiresome

**desegregation** (p42)
the act of abolishing the separation of races

**dowry** (p43)
the money or property a wife brings to her husband when they marry

**ebony** (p43)
a hard, heavy wood, usually black

**tranquil** (p44)
calm; serene

**parasol** (p45)
a small, light umbrella carried to protect oneself from the sun

**kosher** (p47)
clean or proper, according to Jewish religious laws

**bodice** (p55)
the upper portion of a dress

**mirage** (p57)
an optical illusion, such as of a lake and palm trees in a desert or an upside-down ship at sea, appearing quite close, which is actually an image of a distant object reflected by the atmosphere

**bedlam** (p69)
noisy confusion

**animosity** (p89)
strong dislike or hatred; enmity

**pall** (p95)
something that covers, especially something that is dark and gloomy

**sanction** (p96)
final and official approval or confirmation of something

**hue** (p102)
a color, or shade of a color

**exotic** (p106)
strangely different and fascinating

**alliance** (p111)
a formal agreement or union made between nations, states, or individuals

**chastisement** (p111)
the condition of being punished, especially by beating

**accord** (p112)
a state of agreement; harmony

**deftly** (p122)
quickly and skillfully

**saunter** (p123)
　　to walk along in a slow, casual way; to stroll

**vengeance** (p137)
　　punishment inflicted in return for a wrong done; revenge

**destiny** (p139)
　　the outcome or fate that is bound to come

**aspiration** (p146)
　　great hope or desire; ambition

**thwart** (p146)
　　to keep from doing or succeeding

# Small Group Reading

Wilkinson, Brenda. *Not Separate, Not Equal*. New York: Harper & Row, 1987.

Malene is one of six black students to integrate a Georgia public high school in the mid-sixties. Malene experiences hatred and racism, as well as the beginnings of the civil rights movement. Grades 5–8.

## Author Information

Barbara Wilkinson grew up in Waycross, Georgia. She attended Hunter College in New York City, where she currently lives.

Wilkinson's other novels include *Ludell*, which was chosen as a Best Children's Book in 1975 by *School Library Journal*; *Ludell and Willie*, which was chosen by the American Library Association as a Best Books for Young Adults in 1977; and *Ludell's New York Time*.

## Activities

1.　On a map of the United States, have students locate:

| | |
|---|---|
| Alabama | Pineridge, GA |
| Atlanta, GA | Savannah, GA |
| Milledgeville, GA | South Carolina |
| Mississippi | |

2.　Have students write an epilogue for *Not Separate, Not Equal* that takes place twenty years after the novel ends. It should include what has happened to Malene and each of the other five students who were the first black students to attend Pineridge High School.

3.　Have students write a letter from Malene to her sister Moochie, telling her what it is like to attend a white high school for the first time. The letter should include specific incidents, as well as Malene's feelings. Students should then share their letters with the rest of the class.

4.　Have students research school integration, then make an oral presentation to the rest of the class summarizing what they have learned.

## Discussion

Give the small group the following instruction: As your group reads this book, discuss the following.

1.　What happened to Malene on her way to school? Who rescued her?

2.　How are Malene and the five other black students treated at Pineridge High School?

3. Why did Malene's new adoptive parents decide she should go to Pineridge?

4. Describe Pineridge, Georgia in the 1960s. Is it a place where you would want to live? Why or why not?

5. What was Malene's life like before being adopted by the Freemans?

6. What happened to Malene's family?

7. Why were some white students, who had nothing against black people, afraid to be nice to them?

8. Describe Malene's first day at Pineridge High School. How would you have reacted if you were Malene?

9. Why is Malene afraid to answer questions in school? Have you ever felt that way?

10. Share your opinions about Ronnie's speech to Eva and Malene about judging people.

11. Why does Stanley think so highly of his first-grade teacher, Miss Baker?

12. What did Malene mean when she said they have to "believe that a sacrifice can't be in vain"?

13. What did Stanley learn at the emergency meeting at the Baptist church?

14. Why did the principal ask the six black students to leave the school? What happened after they left?

15. What do you think will happen to Malene and the other students?

16. After what happened at Wiley's house, what plans do the parents of the six black students have for them?

17. Discuss your feelings about integration in schools.

## Vocabulary

**feeble** (p4)
   inadequate or ineffective

**integration** (p4)
   the act of making the use or occupancy of a school, park, neighborhood, or other facility available to persons of all races

**pity** (p5)
   a feeling of sorrow for the misfortunes or sufferings of others

**intruder** (p6)
   someone who forces himself or herself in where not invited or wanted

**ignorance** (p6)
   the condition of having little or no learning or knowledge

**adversity** (p11)
   great hardship, misfortune, or trouble

**stamina** (p11)
   vitality; vigor; strength; endurance

**justification** (p11)
   the act of showing something to be just, right, or reasonable

**discourtesies** (p12)
   acts of rudeness

**complexion** (p12)
   the color and appearance of the skin, especially of the face

**dissuaded** (p13)
   persuaded not to do something

**undaunted** (p13)
   not discouraged or fearful

**corridors** (p13)
   hallways

**ultimately** (p14)
   in the end; at last; finally

**elite** (p14)
   the social or professional group considered to be the best

**authentic** (p14)
   genuine

**contradictory** (p14)
   expressing the opposite

**prima donna** (p16)
   a vain, temperamental person

**taunted** (p16)
   scorned; mocked; made fun of with sarcastic remarks

**debutante** (p16)
   a young woman making a formal entrance into society

**inception** (p19)
a beginning; a start; an origin

**tuberculosis** (p19)
a disease caused by certain bacteria that affects the lungs, and is accompanied by a slow wasting away of strength and vitality

**proprietors** (p19)
the legal owners of something, such as a store or business

**shanty** (p20)
a crude, hastily built shack or cabin

**sharecropped** (p20)
land that is farmed by someone who does not own it in return for a portion of the crop as rent

**disdain** (p22)
scorn or contempt, especially toward someone or something considered inferior

**prestige** (p24)
fame, importance, or respect based on a person's reputation, power, or past achievements

**ordeal** (p26)
a very difficult or trying experience

**derogatory** (p27)
meant to lessen the value or merit of someone or something; belittling

**flabbergasted** (p28)
greatly amazed; astounded

**rabble-rouser** (p33)
a person who tries to arouse the passions or prejudices of the public

**activists** (p33)
people who participate in public action in support of a cause

**credentials** (p34)
something, such as a letter or certificate, that identifies the owner and shows the person's position, authority, or right to be trusted

**prejudice** (p41)
hatred of or dislike for a particular group, race, or religion

**distraught** (p43)
extremely upset

**inquisition** (p47)
an official investigation

**Pharaoh** (p59)
any one of the kings of ancient Egypt

**deter** (p67)
to prevent from doing something through fear or doubt; to discourage

**Jim Crow laws** (p75)
the policy of segregating and discriminating against black people

**exasperated** (p77)
annoyed or irritated almost to the point of anger

**vain** (p77)
taking or showing too much pride in oneself, one's looks, or one's abilities

**implemented** (p79)
put into effect; carried out

**unperturbed** (p79)
not disturbed or agitated

**divisive** (p79)
causing people to disagree sharply

**rhetoric** (p79)
extravagant or insincere language

**jurisdiction** (p79)
the legal right to exercise official authority

**skepticism** (p88)
the tendency to question or doubt beliefs that others accept

**transgression** (p95)
the act of breaking a law or an oath

**tribulations** (p97)
things that cause great misery or suffering

**adamantly** (p110)
stubbornly

**Ku Klux Klan (KKK)** (p124)
a secret organization, founded in the southern United States after the Civil War that advocates white supremacy

**vicinity** (p138)
a nearby region; a neighborhood

**chaos** (p146)
complete disorder and confusion

**uprising** (p149)
a revolt; a rebellion

**vice versa** (p149)
the same action or idea reversed; the other way around

**boycott** (p150)
to unite in refusing to buy from, sell to, use, deal, or associate with a certain business, organization, or group of people

From *Teaching U.S. History Through Children's Literature.* © 1998 Wanda J. Miller. Teacher Ideas Press. (800) 237-6124.

# Bibliography

## Individual Titles

Adler, David A. *Martin Luther King, Jr.: Free at Last.* New York: Holiday House, 1986.
This is a biography of the Baptist minister who worked unceasingly for his dream of a world without hate, prejudice, or violence, and was assassinated in the attempt. Grades 4–7.

——. *A Picture Book of Martin Luther King, Jr.* New York: Holiday House, 1989.
A brief, illustrated biography of Martin Luther King, Jr. Grades 2–6.

——. *A Picture Book of Rosa Parks.* New York: Holiday House, 1993.
This is a biography of the black woman whose refusal to give up her seat on a bus helped launch the civil rights movement. Grades 2–6.

Adoff, Arnold. *Malcolm X.* New York: HarperCollins, 1970.
This biography of Malcolm X, the civil rights activist, is for younger students. Grades 3–6.

Altman, Susan. *Extraordinary Black Americans: From Colonial to Contemporary Times.* Chicago: Childrens Press, 1989.
Altman presents short biographies of African Americans from colonial times to the present, highlighting their achievements and contributions to the growth of American society. Grades 5–9.

Archer, Jules. *They Had a Dream: The Civil Rights Struggle from Frederick Douglass to Marcus Garvey to Martin Luther King and Malcolm X.* New York: Viking, 1993.
Archer traces the history of the civil rights movement and its effect on history through biographical sketches of four influential African Americans. Grades 7 and up.

Bray, Rosemary L. *Martin Luther King.* New York: Greenwillow Books, 1995.
Folk art paintings by Malcah Zeldis illustrate this biography of Martin Luther King, Jr. Grades 3–6.

Bullard, Sara, ed. *Free at Last: A History of the Civil Rights Movement and Those Who Died in the Struggle.* Montgomery, AL: The Civil Rights Education Project, 1989.
Through text and photographs, this book gives a history of the civil rights movement from early America to the present. The book includes profiles of forty people who died in the struggle for civil rights. Grades 5 and up.

Cavan, Seamus. *Thurgood Marshall and Equal Rights.* Brookfield, CT: Millbrook Press, 1993.
Cavan examines the life and accomplishments of the first African American judge to be appointed to the Supreme Court. Grades 4–7.

Celsi, Teresa. *Rosa Parks and the Montgomery Bus Boycott.* Brookfield, CT: Millbrook Press, 1991.
This is a biography of Rosa Parks, whose refusal to give up her bus seat to a white person in 1955 launched the Montgomery bus boycott and led to important civil rights gains for blacks. Grades 4–7.

Clifton, Lucille. *The Lucky Stone.* New York: Delacorte Press, 1979.
In this fictional story, a lucky stone passed from one generation to the next in Tee's family has brought good fortune to its owners since the days of slavery. The stone originally saved the life of a runaway slave who used the stone to let others know where she was hiding by throwing it at them from a hidden cave. They in turn found ways to bring food to her. Grades 3–5.

Cwiklik, Robert. *A. Philip Randolph and the Labor Movement.* Brookfield, CT: Millbrook Press, 1993.
This book tells the story of the civil rights activist who organized the Brotherhood of Sleeping Car Porters and crusaded for equal rights for blacks in the armed forces, military industries, and labor unions. Grades 4–8.

——. *Stokely Carmichael and Black Power.* Brookfield, CT: Millbrook Press, 1993.
Cwiklik describes the life and accomplishments of the civil rights worker who took a controversial, aggressive stance in the struggle for civil rights in the 1960s. Grades 4–8.

Davis, Thulani. *1959: A Novel.* New York: Grove Weidenfeld, 1992.
Willie Tarrant becomes aware of the prejudice surrounding her and how easily it can turn into violence when an African American is shot in her Virginia community. Grades 7–9.

Duncan, Alice Faye. *The National Civil Rights Museum Celebrates Everyday People.* Mahwah, NJ: BridgeWater Books, 1995.
This book explores the civil rights movement in the United States from 1954 to 1968, using select museum exhibits as a framework. Grades 4 and up.

Durham, Michael S. *Powerful Days: The Civil Rights Photography of Charles Moore.* New York: Stewart, Tabori & Chang, 1991.

Charles Moore became famous for his photographs of the civil rights movement. His pictures became instant symbols of the black struggle for equality. This book brings together the most significant pictures of the civil rights movement in the South from 1958 to 1965. The text is written by journalist Michael Durham, who worked with Moore on some of his most important stories. Grades 5 and up.

Elish, Dan. *James Meredith and School Desegregation.* Brookfield, CT: Millbrook Press, 1994.

This is a biography of James Meredith and the events surrounding his efforts to attend the University of Mississippi in 1962. Grades 4–7.

Feelings, Tom, ed. *Souls Look Back in Wonder.* New York: Dial Books, 1993.

Artwork and poems by such writers as Maya Angelou, Langston Hughes, and Asia M. Touré reflect the creativity, strength, and beauty of their African American heritage. Grades 4–8.

Fireside, Harvey, and Sarah Betsy Fuller. *Brown v. Board of Education: Equal Schooling for All.* Hillside, NJ: Enslow, 1994.

Both sides of the *Brown v. Board of Education of Topeka, Kansas* landmark case are presented. Grades 6–9.

Fleischner, Jennifer. *The Dred Scott Case: Testing the Right to Live Free.* Brookfield, CT: Millbrook Press, 1997.

This book gives a thorough account of the Dred Scott case and decision. Grades 5 and up.

Freedman, Suzanne. *Ida B. Wells-Barnett and the Antilynching Crusade.* Brookfield, CT: Millbrook Press, 1994.

Freedman traces the life of the journalist Ida B. Wells-Barnett, focusing on her lifelong fight to stop lynching and to direct the nation's attention to the injustices suffered by blacks. Grades 4–7.

Golenbock, Peter. *Teammates.* San Diego, CA: Harcourt Brace Jovanovich, 1990.

Golenbock describes the racial prejudice experienced by Jackie Robinson when he joined the Brooklyn Dodgers and became the first black player in Major League baseball, along with the acceptance and support he received from his white teammate Pee Wee Reese. Grades 2–4.

Greene, Carol. *Martin Luther King, Jr.: A Man Who Changed Things.* Chicago: Childrens Press, 1989.

This is an easy-to-read biography of Martin Luther King, Jr., the Baptist minister and civil rights leader who helped African Americans win many battles for equal rights. Grades 2–5.

Griffin, John Howard. *Black Like Me.* Boston: Houghton Mifflin, 1977.

The author tells of his experiences after he darkened his skin to travel to the South and find out how it feels to be black. Grades 8 and up.

Hakin, Rita. *Martin Luther King, Jr. and the March Toward Freedom.* Brookfield, CT: Millbrook Press, 1991.

This biography of civil rights leader Martin Luther King, Jr. describes his role in blacks' struggle for equality in the 1950s and 1960s. Grades 4–8.

Harris, Janet. *The Long Freedom Road: The Civil Rights Story.* New York: McGraw-Hill, 1967.

Harris gives a history of the civil rights movement, including the Montgomery bus boycott, sit-ins, and freedom rides. Grades 7 and up.

Haskins, James. *Freedom Rides: Journey for Justice.* New York: Hyperion Books for Children, 1995.

Haskins details the struggle to overturn the laws of segregation that dealt with transportation from *Morgan v. Commonwealth of Virginia* to the Freedom Riders, whose purpose was to see that bus and train companies were upholding the courts' declaration that segregated transportation was illegal. Grades 5–12.

———. *I Am Somebody! A Biography of Jesse Jackson.* Hillside, NJ: Enslow, 1992.

Haskins presents the life, accomplishments, and goals of civil rights activist and politician Jesse Jackson, from his childhood in North Carolina through his years in Chicago and Washington, D. C. Grades 5 and up.

———. *The Life and Death of Martin Luther King, Jr.* New York: Lothrop, Lee & Shepard, 1977.

This biography of the man who dedicated his life to the cause of civil rights reexamines unanswered questions about his assassination. Grades 7 and up.

———. *The March on Washington.* New York: HarperCollins, 1993.

Haskins discusses the people and events connected with the 1963 March on Washington, as well as the consequences of this well-known civil rights demonstration. Grades 5 and up.

———. *Thurgood Marshall: A Life for Justice.* New York: Henry Holt, 1992.

This is a biography of Thurgood Marshall, the first African American judge to be appointed to the Supreme Court. Grades 5–9.

Haskins, Jim. *The Day Martin Luther King, Jr. Was Shot: A Photo History of the Civil Rights Movement.* New York: Scholastic, 1992.

Through text and photographs, Haskins gives a thorough history of the civil rights movement. Grades 5 and up.

———. *I Have a Dream: The Life and Words of Martin Luther King, Jr.* Brookfield, CT: Millbrook Press, 1992.

Haskins profiles Martin Luther King, Jr. and the civil rights movement in America. Photographs, historical illustrations, and newspaper headlines are included. Grades 6 and up.

———. *One More River to Cross: The Stories of Twelve Black Americans.* New York: Scholastic, 1992.

This book includes twelve brief biographies of African Americans who courageously fought against racism to become leaders in their fields, including Marian Anderson, Ralph Bunche, Fannie Lou Hamer, Shirley Chisholm, Madam C. J. Walker, and Malcolm X. Grades 6 and up.

Herda, D. J. *Thurgood Marshall: Civil Rights Champion.* Springfield, NJ: Enslow, 1995.

This biography of Thurgood Marshall describes both his personal and professional accomplishments. Grades 5–9.

Jakoubek, Robert. *Martin Luther King, Jr.* New York: Chelsea House, 1989.

Jakoubek examines the life of the Baptist minister and civil rights leader who helped African Americans win many battles for equal rights. Grades 7 and up.

Jakoubek, Robert E. *James Farmer and the Freedom Rides.* Brookfield, CT: Millbrook Press, 1994.

Jakoubek presents the life and times of the black civil rights activist who formed the Congress of Racial Equality (CORE) and organized the freedom rides. Grades 4–8.

———. *Walter White and the Power of Organized Protest.* Brookfield, CT: Millbrook Press, 1994.

The author describes the details of the life and career of the black reporter and civil rights activist who became secretary of the National Association for the Advancement of Colored People (NAACP). Grades 4–8.

Kallen, Stuart A. *Thurgood Marshall: A Dream of Justice for All.* Edina, MN: Abdo & Daughters, 1993.

This is a biography of the first African American Supreme Court justice, who fought to preserve civil rights for all Americans. Grades 5–8.

King, Coretta Scott. *My Life with Martin Luther King, Jr.* New York: Henry Holt, 1993.

This is a revised edition of the 1969 title. It offers an inside look at the life and work of the noted civil rights leader from the viewpoint of his wife, Coretta Scott King. Grades 8 and up.

Kosof, Anna. *The Civil Rights Movement and Its Legacy.* New York: Franklin Watts, 1989.

Kosof describes the civil rights movement in the United States. Grades 7 and up.

Krug, Elisabeth. *Great Lives: Thurgood Marshall, Champion of Civil Rights.* New York: Fawcett Columbine, 1993.

This is a biography of the first African American appointed to the Supreme Court. Thurgood Marshall successfully argued the landmark *Brown v. Board of Education of Topeka, Kansas* case before the Supreme Court which in 1954 put an end to legal segregation in public schools. Grades 4–8.

Levine, Ellen. *Freedom's Children: Young Civil Rights Activists Tell Their Own Stories.* New York: G. P. Putnam's Sons, 1993.

Levine gives first-person accounts of individuals who were children or young adults during the civil rights movement. They relate their experiences with segregation in schools and communities, and their participation in sit-ins, freedom rides, and other forms of protest. Grades 7–9.

Livingston, Myra Cohn. *Let Freedom Ring: A Ballad of Martin Luther King, Jr.* New York: Holiday House, 1992.

Well-known poet Myra Cohn Livingston tells the story of Martin Luther King, Jr.'s life in a ballad, using quotes from King's speeches and sermons. Grades 3–8.

Lowery, Linda. *Martin Luther King Day.* Minneapolis, MN: Carolrhoda, 1987.

Lowery gives a brief account of the life of the black minister who devoted his life to civil rights and discusses the national holiday honoring him. Grades 2–4.

Marzollo, Jean. *Happy Birthday, Martin Luther King.* New York: Scholastic, 1993.

J. Brian Pinkney illustrates this celebration of the life of Martin Luther King, Jr. Grades K–3.

McKissack, Patricia. *Martin Luther King: A Man to Remember.* Chicago: Childrens Press, 1984.

This is a biography of the Baptist minister from Georgia who led a nonviolent crusade against racial segregation and, in the process, raised awareness among all Americans of the principles on which our nation was founded. Grades 5–8.

McKissack, Patricia C. *Jesse Jackson: A Biography*. New York: Scholastic, 1989.

This is a biography of the African American minister and civil rights worker who ran for the Democratic presidential nomination in 1984 and 1988. Grades 5–8.

——. *Mary McLeod Bethune: A Great American Educator*. Chicago: Childrens Press, 1985.

This is a biography of the life of black educator Mary McLeod Bethune, from her childhood in the cotton fields of South Carolina to her success as a teacher, crusader, and presidential advisor. Grades 6 and up.

McKissack, Patricia, and Fredrick McKissack. *A Long Hard Journey: The Story of the Pullman Porter*. New York: Walker, 1989.

This book describes the first black-controlled union, made up of Pullman porters. Grades 5 and up.

——. *Mary Church Terrel: Leader for Equality*. Hillside, NJ: Enslow, 1991.

Through text and illustrations, the authors describe the life and accomplishments of this civil rights activist. Grades 2–4.

——. *Taking a Stand Against Racism and Racial Discrimination*. New York: Franklin Watts, 1990.

The authors examine racism and racial discrimination in the United States, and the individuals and organizations who have fought against it. Grades 7 and up.

Medearis, Angela Shelf. *Dare to Dream: Coretta Scott King and the Civil Rights Movement*. New York: Lodestar, 1994.

This is a biography of Coretta Scott King, the wife of Martin Luther King, Jr. Grades 4–7.

Meltzer, Milton, ed. *The American Promise: Voices of a Changing Nation 1945–Present*. New York: Bantam Books, 1990.

Meltzer provides an overview of the civil rights movement, along with information on the Cold War, the Korean War, the women's movement, and the concerns of minority groups. Grades 7 and up.

——. *Mary McLeod Bethune: Voice of Black Hope*. New York: Viking Kestrel, 1987.

Meltzer details the courage of the woman who rose from poverty to become a famous educator, civil rights leader, and champion of women's rights. Grades 3–6.

Meriwether, Louise. *Don't Ride the Bus on Monday: The Rosa Parks Story*. Englewood Cliffs, NJ: Prentice-Hall, 1973.

This is a brief biography of the Alabama woman whose refusal to give up her seat on the bus marked the beginning of the civil rights movement. Grades 4–8.

Miller, Marilyn. *The Bridge at Selma*. Morristown, NJ: Silver Burdett, 1985.

Miller discusses the far-reaching repercussions of the events of March 7, 1965, when 535 men, women, and children in Alabama attempted to march from Selma to the state capitol in Montgomery to register to vote. Grades 4–8.

Milton, Joyce. *Marching to Freedom: The Story of Martin Luther King, Jr.* New York: Dell, 1987.

This biography of Martin Luther King, Jr. describes his triumphs, his struggles, and his dream of freedom and a better life for all people. Grades 4–8.

Moore, Yvette. *Freedom Songs*. New York: Orchard, 1991.

In the 1960s, when Sheryl's Uncle Pete joins the Freedom Riders in the South, she organizes a gospel concert in Brooklyn to help him by raising money for the freedom workers. Grades 5–8.

Myers, Walter Dean. *The Glory Field*. New York: Scholastic, 1994.

This novel follows a family's 250-year history, from the capture of an African boy in the 1750s through the lives of his descendants, as their dreams and circumstances lead them away from and back to the small plot of land in South Carolina that is known as the Glory Field. Grades 6 and up.

——. *Malcolm X: By Any Means Necessary*. New York: Scholastic, 1993.

This is a biography of Malcolm X, a controversial African American who believed that violence was justified in the fight for civil rights. Grades 7 and up.

——. *Now Is Your Time! The African-American Struggle for Freedom*. New York: HarperCollins, 1991.

This well-documented history of the African American struggle for freedom and equality begins with the capture of Africans in 1619, then continues through the American Revolution, the Civil War, the civil rights movement of the 1960s, and into contemporary times. Grades 5 and up.

——. *Young Martin's Promise*. Austin, TX: Raintree Steck-Vaughn, 1993.

Myers relates events in Martin Luther King, Jr.'s childhood that sowed the seeds for his quest for equal rights for all people, regardless of their color. Grades 2–4.

O'Neill, Laurie A. *Little Rock: The Desegregation of Central High*. Brookfield, CT: Millbrook Press, 1994.

In September 1957, a high school in Little Rock, Arkansas became a civil rights battleground when nine black students attempted to enroll. This book tells their story and explains its importance to the civil rights movement. Grades 5 and up.

Parks, Rosa, with Jim Haskins. *Rosa Parks: My Story*. New York: Dial Books, 1992.

In her autobiography, Rosa Parks describes in detail her refusal on December 1, 1955 to give up her bus seat to a white man on a segregated bus. This act sparked the Montgomery, Alabama bus boycott. Grades 5 and up.

Parks, Rosa, with Gregory J. Reed. *Dear Mrs. Parks: A Dialogue with Today's Youth*. New York: Lee & Low Books, 1996.

In this book, Parks and Reed present letters written to Parks by children throughout her life. She answers their questions and encourages them to reach their highest potential. Grades 5 and up.

Patrick, Diane. *Martin Luther King, Jr*. New York: Franklin Watts, 1990.

Patrick traces the life of the Baptist minister, from his early days and education to his leadership in the civil rights movement. Grades 5–8.

Patterson, Lillie. *Martin Luther King, Jr., and the Freedom Movement*. New York: Facts on File, 1989.

This biography of a Baptist minister focuses on his leadership role in the civil rights movement. Grades 7 and up.

Plowden, Martha Ward. *Famous Firsts of Black Women*. Gretna, LA: Pelican, 1993.

Readers are introduced to twenty African American women who have changed history. The book includes chapters on Rosa Parks, Wilma Rudolph, Harriet Tubman, and Maggie L. Walker. Grades 4 and up.

Powledge, Fred. *We Shall Overcome: Heroes of the Civil Rights Movement*. New York: Charles Scribner's Sons, 1993.

Powledge is a journalist who covered the civil rights movement in the 1960s for the *Atlanta Journal* and the *New York Times*. He interweaves the stories of Martin Luther King, Jr., Rosa Parks, and Medgar Evers with personal accounts of lesser-known heroes. Grades 7–12.

Quayle, Louise. *Martin Luther King: Dreams for a Nation*. New York: Fawcett Columbine, 1989.

This is a biography of civil rights leader Martin Luther King, Jr. Grades 6-9.

Ringgold, Faith. *My Dream of Martin Luther King*. New York: Crown, 1995.

Ringgold recounts the life of Martin Luther King, Jr. in the form of her own dream. Grades 2–4.

Schlank, Carol Hilgartner, and Barbara Metzger. *Martin Luther King, Jr.: A Biography for Young Children*. Rochester, NY: The Rochester Association for the Education of Young Children, 1989.

This is an easy-to-read biography of Martin Luther King, Jr. Grades 1–3.

Schloredt, Valerie. *Martin Luther King, Jr.: America's Great Nonviolent Leader in the Struggle for Human Rights*. Milwaukee, WI: Gareth Stevens, 1988.

Through text and photographs, the author presents a biography of Martin Luther King, Jr. and a history of the civil rights movement. Grades 5 and up.

Schulke, Flip, and Penelope Ortner McPhee. *King Remembered*. New York: W. W. Norton, 1986.

This biography of Martin Luther King, Jr. includes a foreword by Jesse Jackson. Grades 7 and up.

Smith, Nigel. *The United States Since 1945*. New York: Bookwright Press, 1990.

This book includes a series of two-page essays that describe events since 1945. Descriptions include the Korean battles, the Eisenhower presidency, McCarthyism, segregation, and the growing affluence of the middle class. Grades 4–6.

Smothers, Ethel Footman. *Down in the Piney Woods*. New York: Alfred A. Knopf, 1992.

An African American family of sharecroppers in rural Georgia suffers violence and prejudice when white people move onto the family's land. Grades 4–6.

———. *Moriah's Pond*. New York: Alfred A. Knopf, 1995.

While she and her sisters are staying with their great-grandmother, ten-year-old Annie Rye learns about prejudice firsthand when a local white girl causes Annie's sister to be unjustly punished. Grades 5–8.

Sterling, Dorothy. *Tear Down the Walls: A History of the American Civil Rights Movement*. New York: Doubleday, 1968.

This is an excellent book for older students to use to research the civil rights movement. Grades 7 and up.

Tate, Eleanora E. *Thank You, Dr. Martin Luther King, Jr.!* New York: Franklin Watts, 1990.

The children of Gumbo Grove Elementary School discover the contributions of many famous African Americans during Black History Month. Grades 4–8.

Taylor, Mildred D. *The Friendship*. New York: Dial Books for Young Readers, 1987.

Four children witness a confrontation between an elderly black man and a white storekeeper in rural Mississippi in the 1930s. Grades 3–6.

———. *Let the Circle Be Unbroken*. New York: Dial Books, 1981.

The Logan family struggles against poverty and prejudice. From their parents, the four Logan children learn the pride and self-respect they need to survive. Grades 5 and up.

———. *The Road to Memphis*. New York: Dial Books, 1990.

Horribly teased by three white boys in 1940s rural Mississippi, a black youth severely injures one of the boys with a tire iron and enlists the help of Cassie Logan in trying to flee the state. Grades 5 and up.

———. *The Well: David's Story*. New York: Dial Books for Young Readers, 1995.

In Mississippi in the early 1900s, ten-year-old Danny Logan's family generously shares their well water with both white and black neighbors in an atmosphere charged with the potential for racial violence. Grades 4–8.

Turner, Glennette Tilley. *Take a Walk in Their Shoes*. New York: Cobblehill Books, 1989.

Turner presents fourteen biographical sketches of notable African Americans, including Martin Luther King, Jr., Rosa Parks, and LeRoy "Satchel" Paige, accompanied by brief skits that readers can use to act out imagined scenes from their lives. Grades 4 and up.

Walker, Alice. *Langston Hughes, American Poet*. New York: Thomas Y. Crowell, 1974.

This is a biography of Langston Hughes, an American poet whose work articulated the despair of African Americans over social and economic conditions. Grades 3–5.

Walter, Mildred Pitts. *Mississippi Challenge*. New York: Bradbury Press, 1992.

Walter describes the struggle for civil rights for blacks in Mississippi, from slavery to the signing of the Voting Rights Act in 1965. Grades 8 and up.

Williams, Juan. *Eyes on the Prize: America's Civil Rights Years, 1954–1965*. New York: Viking, 1987.

This book brings to life the struggle for civil rights through text and photographs. An excellent research tool for older students. Grades 7 and up.

# Theme Resources

## *Commercial Resources*

Atherton, Herbert M., and J. Jackson Barlow, eds. *1791–1991 The Bill of Rights and Beyond*. Washington, DC: Commission on the Bicentennial of the United States Constitution, 1991.

This resource describes in detail the first twenty-six amendments to the Constitution. Suggested activities for teachers and librarians are included. For use with students in grades 5 and up.

*Cobblestone: The History Magazine for Young People*. Peterborough, NH: Cobblestone.

The focus of the February 1983 issue for students in grades 5 and up is African American history. Articles include "Black Codes and Jim Crow," "Five Leaders for Freedom," and "W. E. B. DuBois and the Niagara Movement."

The focus of the February 1994 issue for students in grades 4 and up is Martin Luther King, Jr. and the civil rights movement. Articles include "From Jim Crow to Justice" and "To the Promised Land: The Civil Rights Years."

The subject of the January 1995 issue for students in grades 4 and up is "Famous Dates." It includes an article titled "1929–1968: Timely Leader." The article tells of the work of Dr. Martin Luther King, Jr. during the civil rights movement.

The focus of the February 1996 issue for students in grades 4 and up is Mary McLeod Bethune. Articles include "Changing America" and "A Force for Constructive Action."

*Educational Oasis: The Magazine for Middle Grades 5–9*. Carthage, IL: Good Apple.

The January/February 1991 issue for students in grades 5 through 9 includes the following articles: "Black Leaders," "28 Ways to Commemorate Black History Month," and "Black History Quiz."

The January/February 1994 issue for use with students in grades 5 through 9 includes a short biography of Martin Luther King, Jr. and activities for students to complete to learn more about King and the civil rights movement.

Scriabine, Christine, historian. *Jackdaw: Black Voting Rights*. Amawalk, NY: Jackdaw Publications, 1992.

This is a portfolio of primary source material including nineteen reproduction historical documents. Among them are the "Hands Off Democracy" handbill from the NAACP in 1949 and "The Fifteenth Amendment" poster, printed in full color. Comprehensive notes on the documents and a reading list and critical thinking questions are also included. This resource can be used with students in grades 5 and up.

Snodgrass, Mary Ellen, ed. *Black History Month Resource Book*. Detroit, MI: Gale Research, 1993.

This resource contains ideas to generate interest in and understanding of black history among all races. For use with students in grades 4 and up.

## Videos

*An Amazing Grace*. Solar Home Video, 1991. (60 minutes)

This documentary chronicles the life of Dr. Martin Luther King, Jr. and his role in the civil rights movement.

*And the Children Shall Lead: WonderWorks*. Chicago: Public Media Video, 1984. (58 minutes)

This WonderWorks PBS video depicts events in the summer of 1964 in the segregated town of Catesville, Mississippi. There, people measure integration by whether a young black girl can use a "whites only" bathroom. Freedom riders arrive, hoping to organize a rally to promote voting rights. The town's sheriff and his longtime friend, a black carpenter, soon find themselves on opposite sides of the civil rights issue, causing conflict for their children.

*The Assassination of Martin Luther King, Jr.* Orland Park, IL: MPI Home Video, 1993. (85 minutes)

This program examines the government's involvement in the harassment of Martin Luther King, Jr. and uses a variety of recently declassified pieces of information to reexamine the counterintelligence programs that preceded the assassination. It also investigates the conviction of James Earl Ray.

*Eyes on the Prize: America's Civil Rights Years 1954 to 1965: Awakenings (1954–1956)*. Boston: Blackside, 1987. (60 minutes)

This video presents the brave struggle of African Americans for freedom in their own country. From "separate but equal," to *Brown v. Board of Education of Topeka, Kansas*, to the murder of Emmett Till, a fourteen-year-old boy whose murder in Mississippi shocked the nation, this video reveals the courage of people who stood up against what was wrong and inspired others to join them.

*Ghosts of Mississippi*. Columbia Tristar Home Video, 1996. (131 minutes)

This video recounts the decades-long fight by Myrlie Evers to see the white supremacist who murdered her husband, civil rights leader Medgar Evers, convicted of the crime. The film features special appearances by three children of Medgar Evers, along with Yolanda King, the daughter of Reverend Martin Luther King, Jr.

*Martin Luther King: "I Have a Dream."* Orland Park, IL: MPI Home Video, 1988. (25 minutes)

This is a video of the famous "I Have a Dream" speech that Martin Luther King, Jr. made at the steps of the Lincoln Memorial in Washington, D.C. on August 28, 1963.

*Martin Luther King Jr. and the Civil Rights Movement*. Chatsworth, CA: Aims Multimedia. (20 minutes)

This program reviews the career of Martin Luther King, Jr. through the events of the civil rights movement.

*The Martin Luther King, Jr., Center for Nonviolent Social Change*.

This organization is dedicated to eliminating worldwide poverty, racism, ignorance, violence, and war. For information about available materials, call the center at (404) 524-1956, or write: 449 Auburn Avenue, N.E., Atlanta, GA 30312.

*Mary McLeod Bethune*. Bala Cynwyd, PA: Schlessinger Video Productions, 1994. (30 minutes)

This video examines Bethune's importance in society today and the inspirational forces that helped shape her life.

*Separate but Equal*. Los Angeles: Republic Pictures Home Video, 1991. (193 minutes)

The dramatic events leading from a small rural classroom to the Supreme Court decision that outlawed segregation are reenacted in this video. The cast includes Sidney Poitier as Thurgood Marshall, Burt Lancaster as John W. Davis, and Richard Kiley as Chief Justice Earl Warren.

*United States History Video Collection: Post–War U.S.A.* Bala Cynwyd, PA: Schlessinger Video Productions, 1996. (35 minutes)

Included in this video covering post-war prosperity and the rise of the consumer society, roles of women, the Cold War, and the Korean War, is a segment focusing on the early civil rights movement.

# End-of-Unit Celebration

## Civil Rights Movement Research Project

Individually or in groups of two, have your students research the following topics pertaining to the civil rights movement. When completed, hold a presentation day.

Asa Philip Randolph

*Brown v. Board of Education of Topeka, Kansas*

Congress of Racial Equality (CORE)

Coretta Scott King

Dr. Martin Luther King, Jr.

*The Dred Scott Case*

E. D. Nixon

The Freedom Riders

Ida B. Wells-Barnett

Jesse Jackson

The Jim Crow Laws

The 'Little Rock Nine'

Malcolm X

The March on Washington, D.C., August 28, 1963

Mary Church Terrel

Mary McLeod Bethune

The Montgomery Bus Boycott

National Association for the Advancement of Colored People (NAACP)

*Plessy v. Ferguson* (1896)

Rosa Parks

Thurgood Marshall

## Civil Rights Movement Vocabulary Activity

In addition to the research project, you might wish to celebrate the end of the unit by having students work in teams to complete the vocabulary activity presented in figure 2.1 (p. 48). This could be competitive or noncompetitive, with appropriate prizes awarded to all.

**Directions:** Place the letter of the correct definition in the blank next to the vocabulary word.

1.   segregation _____

2.   solidarity _____

3.   derogatory _____

4.   Ku Klux Klan (KKK) _____

5.   adversity _____

6.   civil rights _____

7.   desegregation _____

8.   racist _____

9.   activist _____

10.  discrimination _____

11.  integration _____

12.  prejudice _____

**a.**   hatred of or dislike for a particular race

**b.**   a person who shows prejudice in favor of a particular race

**c.**   prejudice in one's attitudes or actions

**d.**   the condition of being strongly united or in unison

**e.**   the practice of separating a racial or religious group from the rest of society, such as in schools, housing, or parks

**f.**   a secret organization, founded in the United States after the Civil War, that advocates white supremacy

**g.**   the act of abolishing the separation of races

**h.**   great hardship, misfortune, or trouble

**i.**   meant to lessen the value or merit of someone or something; belittling

**j.**   a person who participates in public action in support of a cause

**k.**   the act of making the use or occupancy of a school, park, neighborhood, or other facility available to persons of all races

**l.**   the rights and privileges of a citizen, especially in the United States, the rights guaranteed by the Thirteenth, Fourteenth, Fifteenth, and Nineteenth Amendments to the Constitution

**Fig. 2.1.** Civil rights movement vocabulary activity.

# Chapter 3

# The Women's Rights Movement

## Introduction

On July 19, 1997, I attended the 149th anniversary celebration of the first Women's Rights Convention, which was held in Seneca Falls, New York, on July 19, 1848.

Doris Wolf, a reporter for the Rochester *Democrat and Chronicle*, gave a wonderful speech following a reenactment of the first convention. With her permission, I have included this speech here for you to read to your students to begin your study of women's rights. Depending on the age of your students, you may wish to exclude selected parts.

**Fig. 3.1.** The Woman's Rights National Historical Park in Seneca Falls, New York.

As we gather here, some women driving their own cars, wearing shorts or slacks, our purses carrying our checkbooks and credit cards, our cellular phones and college reunion invitations, it's hard to imagine the life of women and girls a century and a half ago.

It was a difficult time, and for those who dared to challenge the established order, it was even more difficult—and dangerous.

Women were beaten, jailed, and shunned for daring to suggest they were entitled to rights we take for granted today—organizing a committee, signing a petition, voting.

But the fires of change had been ignited across the country in the mid-1800s and nowhere did they burn brighter than here, in upstate New York.

At seances, revival meetings, lectures, and conventions, passions were so inflamed the area became known as the "burned over district."

In Hydesville, near Newark, the Fox sisters, those high priestesses of Spiritualism, were hearing rappings and conducting seances.

In Geneva, Elizabeth Blackwell received her degree from Geneva Medical College, the forerunner of Hobart and William Smith Colleges, as the first woman doctor in the United States. In the small white clapboard Congregational Church in South Butler, her sister-in-law, Antoinette Brown Blackwell, was ordained the first woman minister of a recognized denomination.

Marcus Whitman and his bride, Narcissa Prentice, had left Gorham for Oregon Territory with Henry and Eliza Spalding, a 2,250-mile journey during which Narcissa and Eliza became the first white women to cross the Rockies. Their massacre sparked a rush of settlers that determined the area would belong to the United States and not Great Britain.

In Auburn, Harriet Tubman, the Moses of her people, rested between trips to guide runaway slaves north, following the drinking gourd, traveling on the Underground Railroad.

Many found the way to Pultneyville, where sympathetic ship captains smuggled them across Lake Ontario to Canada. Others traveled east to the Utica area, where Gerrit Smith of Peterboro and a network of loyal Quakers were Underground Railroad stationmasters and conductors.

In Rochester, the man who was born the slave Fred Bailey in Maryland had become the great orator Frederick Douglass and was publishing the anti-slavery paper *The North Star* between speaking engagements.

His neighbor, Susan B. Anthony, had moved to Rochester from the Berkshires in Massachusetts and was also on the lecture circuit, speaking for women's issues.

In Seneca Falls, the Irish immigrants who had come to build the Erie Canal stayed on to work in the mills. Their families were large; their paychecks small. Alcoholism and domestic abuse were common; malaria and other illnesses plagued the area. Food and medical care were scarce.

Because women weren't allowed to own property, bank accounts or other assets—even the money they earned—many of these families found themselves homeless and destitute when their husbands died or simply left.

Some of those families lived next to the Stantons—the abolitionist Henry B. and his wife, Elizabeth Cady—in the flats section, on Washington Street.

Elizabeth was touched and saddened by the plight of these women and children and did her best to help them. The daughter of a prominent judge, Daniel Cady, Elizabeth had free access to her father's fine library and had learned Greek and Latin at an early age. When it came time for her to attend college, she thought she'd go to Union College to study law. But she was soon to discover that the college doors were closed to her—because she was a woman. She was educated instead at Emma Willard's Troy Female Seminary.

Later, Elizabeth met and married Henry Stanton and they attended the World Anti-Slavery Convention in London on their honeymoon. There she met the prominent Quaker Lucretia Mott. As a Quaker, Mott was accustomed to having an equal voice in meetings, and so the two women were shocked and outraged to learn that they would not be allowed to sit on the convention floor, but were relegated to the balcony—just because they were women.

Returning to Seneca Falls and her family of four active and unruly boys, Elizabeth chafed at the restrictions of women, which confined them to the tedium of household tasks while men were free to roam about, exercising their minds and pursuing their varied interests.

And then, one day, Elizabeth received an invitation to a tea. Her friend, Lucretia Mott, had come to Auburn to visit Mott's sister, Martha Wright, and to lend encouragement to Waterloo Quakers who supported the abolitionist movement.

Jane Hunt, whose Quaker husband, Richard, operated a nonslave woolen mill in Waterloo, was hosting the tea that afternoon on July 9, 1848. She had invited Quaker Mary Ann M'Clintock. M'Clintock's husband, Thomas, operated a store on Main Street that sold cookies baked without sugar, because it was a product of the slave trade.

During the tea, Stanton reminded Mott of their pledge, made at the World Anti-Slavery Convention, to call a meeting to discuss the oppressed condition of women. It was decided that the women would meet the following Sunday at M'Clintock's home to draw up a list of grievances to be presented at a meeting in the Wesleyan Methodist Chapel in Seneca Falls two weeks hence.

And so it was that Martha Wright, Jane Hunt, Mary Ann M'Clintock, Lucretia Mott, and Elizabeth Cady Stanton gathered around the tiny mahogany tea table in M'Clintock's parlor to pen the words that would change the lives of women forever: "The history of mankind is a history of repeated injuries and usurpations on the part of man toward woman. . . . To prove this, let facts be submitted to a candid world. . . ."

Their document called on women to right those wrongs, demanding the right to an education, a career, to own property, and control her own money. To custody of her children in divorce, to leadership positions in government and the church, and, most significantly, the right to vote.

The day of that first women's rights convention dawned bright and clear. The people began arriving in the early morning light. Working women from the mills came, piled together in a democrat wagon. The Quakers came from Waterloo and beyond. And so did the Free Soil party members, some of whom were mill owners and professional men, looking for a platform for their cause. A few of them even brought their wives.

Frederick Douglass arrived from Rochester, joining the cause of abolition to that of women's rights.

Forty men came that first day, in spite of the call which had declared that day exclusively for women, and it was agreed that they could stay.

As they arrived at the chapel, they discovered the door was locked, but the women hoisted Cady Stanton's nephew through a window so that he could let them in.

And, since not one of the women had experience leading a convention, they appointed James Mott as chairman. Mary Ann M'Clintock had been secretary of conventions so many times, it was only right that she would be again. For keynote speaker Elizabeth Cady Stanton, the day would be the start of a whole new life.

For it was on that day, 149 years ago, that Stanton first read the immortal words "that all men AND WOMEN are created equal." The Declaration of Sentiments, modeled after the Declaration of Independence, was presented here, in the Wesleyan Methodist Chapel, at the first Women's Rights Convention, in Seneca Falls, July 19, 1848.

Today, women's history is no longer sad and dark. Women have made great strides in the past century and a half. But although the struggle to achieve an independent women's movement may seem distant from us today, the struggle for equality continues. Indeed, the perceptions of women's roles in society may have altered dramatically from that fateful day at Seneca Falls when women wrote a "womanifesto," but much remains to be done.

The women of Seneca Falls were not content just to call conventions. They petitioned Congress, they organized local campaigns, they buttonholed state legislators, and many hundreds and thousands of women tirelessly sought to improve women's status. And so we must today.

Prior to the nineteenth-century feminist campaign, wives were treated as the property of their husbands; the majority of American women were leading lives of social and economic dependency. Today, women continue to earn less than a man is paid for similar jobs. Statistics continue to demonstrate the "feminization of poverty." We must have equal pay for equal work.

And, although women are no longer considered unfit for business, the glass ceiling that prevents women from taking an equal place at the top of major corporations still exists. We must break through!

In the 1850s, many children were confined to a life of poverty, darkness, and danger, working in mills, suffering from lack of food and medical care. Many of today's children still live in poverty, darkness, and danger. We are all too familiar with the issues: Child abuse and neglect, homelessness, inadequate health care, the struggle of single-parent families, lack of child care crowd our newspapers and television screens. Schools serve breakfasts and hold counseling sessions to try to make children "fertile for learning" while battling drugs, weapons, and teen pregnancies. The future belongs to the children of the world. We must help them survive in a world of equality, security, and hope.

The suffrage campaign was one of but many issues of the first Women's Rights Convention, and it was a long-fought and hard-won battle. Of all the women who attended that 1848 convention, only one, Charlotte Woodward, lived to vote in the 1920 presidential election.

Today women not only vote, we serve in Congress, as mayors of major cities, in the president's cabinet and on the highest court in the land. We are astronauts, newspaper editors, heads of colleges, ministers, and county supervisors.

Women serve as judges, prosecuting attorneys and district attorneys throughout the land. We also see signs of improvement in women's legal status. However, in 1848, domestic violence was an issue. In 1997, domestic violence continues to be an issue. We need more shelters for victims, and better treatment for victims before the law.

We have made great strides in science and medicine, but we need more research on women's health issues, especially those associated with menopause and breast cancer.

Women are not only admitted to colleges and universities, but women's studies is a recognized course. We celebrate not only Convention Days, but also Equality Day and Women's History Week. We have a national park dedicated to women's rights and a national hall of fame which recognizes the outstanding accomplishments of American women—both here, in Seneca Falls. Soon, in Washington, D.C., that bastion of male superiority, we will have a National Women's Museum. And finally, this year, a statue of our suffrage leaders has been moved to the rotunda of the U.S. Capitol, the first women to be honored there.

We still look for equality in leadership, in religion, and the arts. We have yet to elect a woman president, or to accord women the respect of an equal partner of the president. Women are still not equal in numbers in the state legislature or the U.S. Congress. We need more women as state education commissioners and social service commissioners. Where are our women police chiefs and sheriffs? Our women priests? Our women motion picture directors, theater directors?

The road continues to be rocky: Sexual harassment threatens American women who move toward equality in business and the military. In many African countries, female castration is a rite of passage for young women. In Eastern nations, contraception and family planning advice is scarce—or forbidden.

The pebble dropped in the ocean here must continue to send in ripples to distant shores.

Through the effort of concerned individuals, through the raising of issues and the articulation of women's demands, we can continue to change the world around us.

We must EACH seek our OWN causes, those which we hope will create free and equal opportunities for women in our society.

It is crucial that we look to women's history for inspiration, support, and comfort. It was their sense of justice and commitment which sustained women through their long and hard campaigns.

We can best honor our foremothers, whose struggles have so improved our lives, by each of us becoming a loving memorial to their efforts. In devoting our time and energies to the cause of improving women's status, we will create a better future not just for ourselves but for all the world.

**Fig. 3.2.** The Women's Rights Hall of Fame.

"Women must try to do the things men have tried," Amelia Earhart said in 1937. "When they fail, their failure must be but a challenge to others." The trade books selected in this chapter were chosen to attempt to help students understand how these women struggled and sacrificed to make the United States truly a land of freedom.

**Fig. 3.3.** Reenactment of the first woman's rights convention. Portrayed were Frederick Douglass, Susan B. Anthony, Elizabeth Cady Stanton, and James Mott.

## Whole Group Reading

Sullivan, George. *The Day the Women Got the Vote: A Photo History of the Women's Rights Movement.* New York: Scholastic, 1994.

Through text and photographs, Sullivan reveals the hard work and achievements of the women's movement in business, government, sports, and the arts. Grades 5 and up.

## Author Information

George Sullivan was born August 11, 1927, in Lowell, Massachusetts. Sullivan has worked in public relations, as an adjunct professor of nonfiction writing from 1969 to 1972 at Fordham University in Bronx, New York, and as a freelance writer since 1972.

Sullivan has written well over 100 nonfiction books, including *Mathew Brady, His Life and Photographs*; *Slave Ship: The Story of Henrietta Marie*; and *Black Artists As Photographers, 1840–1940*. In addition to his writing, Sullivan takes many of the photographs that appear in his books. He has written many books about sports, particularly baseball and football. Sullivan has written books for adults, but prefers to write for young people.

Getting ideas for his books has never been a problem for Sullivan. He says, "The ideas spring from my curiosity about people, places, and events."

## Activities

1. On a map of the United States, have students locate:

| | | |
|---|---|---|
| Adams, MA | Delaware | Philadelphia, PA |
| Albany, NY | Dover, NH | Poughkeepsie, NY |
| Atlanta, GA | Fall River, MA | Rochester, NY |
| Atlantic City, NJ | Hartford, CT | Seneca Falls, NY |
| Berlin, CT | Idaho | South Hadley, MA |
| Birmingham, AL | Indiana | Tennessee |
| Boston, MA | Kentucky | Topeka, KS |
| California | Lowell, MA | Troy, NY |
| Cape Cod, MA | Lynn, MA | Utah |
| Caterbury, CT | Milwaukee, WI | Waltham, MA |
| Charleston, SC | Missouri | Waterloo, NY |
| Cleveland, OH | Montgomery, AL | West Virginia |
| Colorado | Nantucket, MA | Wyoming |
| Columbia, SC | Oswego, NY | |

2. Have students find out how Title IX of the Higher Education Act of 1972 changed things for girls at your school by interviewing the principal and teachers who have taught at your school for many years.

3. Have students research the following women and their roles in the fight for equal rights for women:

| | | |
|---|---|---|
| Susan B. Anthony | Ella Grasso | Jeanette Rankin |
| Catherine Beecher | Angelina Grimke | Janet Reno |
| Joan Benoit | Sarah Grimke | Sally Ride |
| Mary McLeod Bethune | Dr. Mae Jemison | Eleanor Roosevelt |
| Dr. Elizabeth Blackwell | Barbara Jordan | Elizabeth Cady Stanton |
| Carrie Chapman Catt | Belva Lockwood | Gloria Steinem |
| Hillary Rodham Clinton | Mary Lyon | Lucy Stone |
| Anna Dickinson | Lucretia Mott | Sojourner Truth |
| Joycelyn Elders | Antonia Novella | Emma Willard |
| Geraldine Ferraro | Sandra Day O'Connor | Frances Willard |
| Betty Friedan | Rosa Parks | Mary Wollstonecraft |
| Ruth Ginsburg | Alice Paul | Victoria Woodhull |

4. Have students write a short essay describing the inequalities that still exist today for women.

5. Have students think of a woman they admire, then list her accomplishments on a poster. Display these posters in your classroom for all to see.

6. Have students interview their mothers and grandmothers or community members to find out how things have changed for women in their lifetime.

## Discussion

Give the class the following instruction: As we read this book, we will be discussing the following.

1. In what way was November 2, 1920 important to women in the United States?

2. Discuss the reasons women were denied the right to vote. What are your feelings about this?

3. What does it take for a Constitutional amendment to be ratified?

4. When did the Nineteenth Amendment to the Constitution become law?

5. Being able to vote affected women's status only slightly. What barriers did women still face?

6. Angelina and Sarah Grimke called women "the white slaves of the North." What did they mean?

7. Why was being a woman a hardship for Emma Willard? What did Willard accomplish in 1821?

8. What is Catherine Beecher known for?

9. What were Mary Lyon's accomplishments?

10. What new choice for work did single women have by the 1820s?

11. Describe the working conditions in the textile mills.

12. What is Lucretia Mott known for?

13. What happened at the World Anti-Slavery Convention in London in 1840 that shocked Lucretia Mott?

14. What did Lucretia Mott and Elizabeth Cady Stanton do to further the cause of women's rights in the United States?

15. What was the Declaration of Sentiments?

16. What is Seneca Falls, New York known for?

17. What role did Lucy Stone play in the women's movement?

18. Following Lucy Stone's marriage, why did other women become known as "Lucy Stoners"?

19. Describe the relationship between Elizabeth Cady Stanton and Susan B. Anthony.

20. Why do you think "bloomers" attracted so much attention in the 1850s?

21. How has women's clothing changed since the 1850s?

22. What role did Dr. Elizabeth Blackwell play during the Civil War?

23. During the Civil War, what new jobs were women able to perform?

24. Why were Elizabeth Cady Stanton and Susan B. Anthony wary of President Abraham Lincoln?

25. What was the purpose of the Emancipation Proclamation?

26. What was the goal of the National Women's Loyal League?

27. Why did the rights of women have to wait following the Civil War?

28. Why was the Fourteenth Amendment to the Constitution frustrating for women?

29. What did the Fifteenth Amendment to the Constitution guarantee?

30. Who was the first woman to receive votes in a presidential election?

31. What territory was the first to give women the right to vote? Why?

32. Why did many women become involved in the temperance movement? How did this involvement harm the women's suffrage movement?

33. How did World War I expand the job opportunities available to women? Did these opportunities remain once the war ended?

34. Discuss the significance of Spellman College in Atlanta, Georgia.

35. What did the Nineteenth Amendment to the Constitution guarantee?

36. In what ways did Eleanor Roosevelt support equal rights for women?

37. During World War II, more new job opportunities became available to women. What were they? What changed after the war ended?

38. What was the finding of *Brown v. Board of Education of Topeka, Kansas* in 1954?

39. What did Rosa Parks do to further the cause of civil rights?

From *Teaching U.S. History Through Children's Literature.* © 1998 Wanda J. Miller. Teacher Ideas Press. (800) 237-6124.

40. What were the findings of the Commission on the Status of Women in 1963? What resulted from these findings?

41. Through her book *The Feminine Mystique*, what did Betty Friedan urge women to do? What faults did *The Feminine Mystique* have?

42. How did the passage of the Civil Rights Act in 1964 help women?

43. In what ways were the goals set by the National Organization for Women (NOW) similar to the goals set in Seneca Falls, New York more than a century earlier?

44. Discuss the laws passed by Congress in the 1970s that were intended to improve the status of women.

45. How does Title IX of the Higher Education Act of 1972 help women and girls?

46. What protection does the Equal Opportunity Act provide for women?

47. What criticisms have been made about the Equal Rights Amendment? What prevented the Equal Rights Amendment from being ratified?

48. Following the 1992 presidential election, what gains did women make in politics?

49. How have the goals of women's organizations changed today?

50. In what ways does inequality for women still exist?

51. Why was Take Your Daughter to Work Day started?

## Vocabulary

**triumph** (p5)
   a victory or success

**liberty** (p6)
   freedom to think or act as one wishes, regarded as a very important human right

**amendment** (p7)
   a change, such as to a law or bill

**abridge** (p7)
   to deprive of or lessen

**women's suffrage** (p8)
   women's right to vote

**militant** (p8)
   taking or ready to take aggressive action, such as on behalf of beliefs or rights; fighting or ready to fight

**electoral** (p8)
   having to do with an election or electors

**stenographer** (p9)
   a person whose work is taking dictation, usually in shorthand, and typewriting

**rebellious** (p10)
   full of the disobedient spirit of a rebel

**inferiority** (p10)
   the quality or condition of being lower in rank, position, or importance

**vindication** (p10)
   the act of defending successfully against challenge or attack; justification

**abolitionist** (p10)
   one of the people who wanted to end slavery in the United States

**feminism** (p12)
   the belief that women should have social, economic, legal, and political equality

**domestic** (p12)
   of or having to do with the home or family affairs

**balked** (p14)
   caused to stop; thwarted; hindered

**seminary** (p14)
   a high school or school of higher education, especially a boarding school

**textile** (p17)
   of or having to do with weaving or woven fabrics

**abide** (p17)
   to put up with; to endure

**curfew** (p17)
   a rule or law requiring certain persons to keep off the streets after a certain hour in the evening

**advocate** (p19)
   to speak or write in favor of; to defend; to support

**Quaker** (p19)
   a member of the Society of Friends, whose name came from their founder's statement to tremble at the word of the Lord

**tactics** (p20)
   the art, technique, or means to achieve one's goals; methods

**delegation** (p20)
   a group of people sent with authority to act for a larger group; a representative

**liberal** (p21)
   favoring progress, reform, and the use of governmental power to achieve social or political goals

**reform** (p21)
   a change for the better, such as by the correction of wrongs or abuses

**memoirs** (p21)
   the story of a person's life or experiences

**inalienable rights** (p23)
   rights that cannot be taken away or transferred

**pursuit** (p23)
   the act of seeking to gain something

**resolution** (p23)
   a formal expression of the feelings or will of an assembly

**vital** (p24)
   having great or essential importance

**virtually** (p24)
   the condition of being in effect, though not in name or in fact

**temperance** (p25)
   the rule or practice of consuming no alcoholic drinks

**exploited** (p25)
   used selfishly or unfairly

**virtue** (p25)
   because of or by means of

**corset** (p26)
   a close-fitting undergarment worn to give support and shape to the hips and waist

**innovation** (p26)
   something newly introduced

**ridicule** (p26)
   words or actions intended to make another person or thing seem foolish; mockery

**pantaloon** (p26)
   trousers, especially tight-fitting ones with straps that fit under the instep, worn in former times

**hostility** (p27)
   opposition

**delicacy** (p27)
   refinement, such as of feeling or manner; sensitivity

**jeer** (p27)
   to make fun of with insulting words; to ridicule; to mock

**frenzy** (p27)
   a wild, excited fit or condition suggesting madness

**toiled** (p28)
   worked hard

**arsenal** (p29)
   a public building for making or keeping such supplies as guns and ammunition

**compromise** (p29)
   an adjustment or settlement in which each side gives up part of its demands

**eloquent** (p29)
   showing much feeling; expressive

**servitude** (p33)
   slavery

**brash** (p33)
   acting too hastily; rash

**platform** (p34)
   a set or statement of principles, ideas, or aims put forth by a political party or other group

**defraud** (p34)
   to take (such as money or rights) by tricking or deceiving

**repealing** (p37)
   revoking; canceling

**enfranchised** (p37)
   allowed to vote

**crusade** (p39)
   a vigorous struggle against an evil or in favor of a cause

**racism** (p47)
   prejudice in favor of a particular race

From *Teaching U.S. History Through Children's Literature.* © 1998 Wanda J. Miller. Teacher Ideas Press. (800) 237-6124.

**plantation** (p49)
> a farm or estate of many acres on which is grown cotton, tobacco, rice, or other products planted and tended by laborers who live there

**vigil** (p53)
> the act of staying awake to observe or protect; watch

**bleak** (p55)
> gloomy; dismal

**zealous** (p63)
> filled with great interest and devotion, such as when working for a cause; enthusiastic

**defiant** (p71)
> full of bold opposition to power or authority; resisting

**formative** (p72)
> of or related to formation or development

**essential** (p81)
> extremely important or necessary; vital

# Small Group Reading

Duffy, James. *Radical Red*. New York: Charles Scribner's Sons, 1993.
The life of a twelve-year-old Irish girl named Connor O'Shea undergoes many changes when she and her mother become involved with Susan B. Anthony and her suffragists. Grades 5–8.

## Author Information

James Duffy lives in Arlington, Massachusetts. He is the author of several books, including *The Christmas Gang*, *The Man in the River*, *Cleaver & Company*, and *Uncle Shamus*. Duffy has received fellowships from the Bollingen Foundation, the Guggenheim Foundation, and the Rockefeller Foundation.

## Activities

1. On a map of the United States, have students locate:

   Albany, NY          Massachusetts
   Baltimore, MD       Philadelphia, PA
   Chicago, IL         Rochester, NY
   Hudson River, NY    Washington

2. If possible, bring in an oil lamp, an early iron, and a small icebox for the class to see.

3. Have students research Susan B. Anthony and the National-American Woman Suffrage Association (which had come into existence following a merger of the National Woman Suffrage Association and the American Woman Suffrage Association), then share what they have learned with the rest of the class.

4. Ask a student or a parent volunteer to make soda bread and bring it in for the students to try. If possible, this could be made in school with the assistance of staff or parent volunteers.

5. Have students illustrate the scene at the capitol building described on page 132 or the scene described on page 150.

6. Ask your school music teacher to teach the song "Mine Eyes Have Seen the Glory" to your class. The women sang it on the way to the train station when Susan B. Anthony was leaving for California.

# Discussion

Give the small group the following instruction: As your group reads this book, discuss the following questions.

1. Why does Connor envy boys?

2. What did Sister Mary Francis tell Connor about reading?

3. Why did Connor and her family have to move to Canal Street?

4. What does Connor's father do for a living? What does her mother do to earn money?

5. What was the pamphlet about that a woman tried to give Connor and her mother at the capitol square? Why did they refuse it?

6. How did Connor's father react to seeing Connor talk to the woman at the capitol square?

7. What did Connor's father tell her about why women can't vote? Discuss your feelings about this.

8. How do the O'Sheas keep their food cold?

9. How does Mrs. O'Shea iron clothes?

10. What is Connor teaching her mother? Why?

11. How did Doreen react when Connor told her that women can't vote?

12. Why are Susan B. Anthony and her friends in Albany?

13. Why can't Mr. O'Shea vote?

14. How does Mrs. O'Shea feel about women being able to vote?

15. Why was Connor surprised to find a note from her mother after school?

16. What did the pamphlet mean about women being prisoners?

17. What do the O'Sheas use to heat their home?

18. Why doesn't Connor's father want her mother to speak Irish?

19. How did Mr. and Mrs. O'Shea happen to marry?

20. Why do you think Mrs. O'Shea had been so anxious to come to America?

21. Why does Mrs. O'Shea miss Martinville?

22. What was Senator Phelan's plan for Susan B. Anthony and the other women?

23. Why did Connor's father hurt her mother?

24. How did Connor and her mother meet Susan B. Anthony?

25. What did Mrs. O'Shea tell Susan B. Anthony about her feelings regarding women voting?

26. What are Doreen and Connor going to do to help the suffragists? How is Mrs. O'Shea going to help?

27. How long has Susan B. Anthony been working for women's suffrage?

28. Why do the suffragists wear red ribbons in their bonnets?

29. What did Mr. O'Shea do when his wife told him that she and Connor had been working with the suffragists? What did Connor and her mother do afterward?

30. What did the men do to try to keep the suffragists from entering the capitol building?

31. What punishment did Sister Mary Francis receive for taking the children to the capitol?

32. What did Bertha ask Mrs. O'Shea and Connor?

# Vocabulary

**reverie** (p3)
distant and pleasant thoughts; a daydream

**livery** (p4)
the uniform worn by servants

**linger** (p4)
to stay on as if unwilling to go

**shanties** (p4)
crude, hastily built shacks or cabins

**derby** (p4)
a stiff felt hat having a curved, narrow brim and a round crown

**condemned** (p4)
declared unfit or unsafe for use

**menace** (p4)
a threat

**tenement** (p5)
an apartment house that is poorly built or maintained, usually overcrowded, and often located in a slum

**rubbish** (p5)
trash, garbage, or refuse

**assembly** (p7)
a group of persons gathered together for a common purpose; a meeting

**scowled** (p10)
frowned

**tannery** (p10)
a place where hides are tanned to make leather

**timidly** (p11)
fearfully or shyly

**parlor** (p16)
a room for receiving visitors or entertaining guests

**cape** (p21)
a sleeveless outer garment that fastens at the neck and hangs loosely from the shoulders

**vocation** (p24)
a profession, career, or trade, especially one a person chooses or is best suited for; a calling

**convention** (p26)
a meeting or assembly for some purpose

**democracy** (p26)
a form of government in which the people rule, either by voting directly or electing representatives to manage the government and make the laws

**delegate** (p27)
a person with authority to act for a group; a representative

**charity** (p32)
the giving of help, usually money, to the poor and unfortunate

**suffrage** (p33)
the right to vote

**lass** (p35)
a young woman or girl

**uppity** (p35)
snobbish or arrogant

**destiny** (p38)
the outcome or fate that is bound to come

**scuttle** (p39)
a bucketlike container in which coal may be kept or carried

**Yankee** (p40)
a person born or living in the northern United States

**parish** (p41)
in certain religious groups, a district, usually part of a diocese, having its own church and clergy

**taunted** (p45)
insulted, provoked, or made fun of

**slum** (p45)
a shabby, dirty, run-down section of a city where the poor live in crowded conditions

**boisterous** (p47)
noisy and wild

**spectacles** (p49)
a pair of eyeglasses

**disgrace** (p50)
a condition of shame or dishonor

**hooligan** (p50)
a person who goes about committing violent or destructive acts for little or no purpose; a ruffian

**shroud** (p53)
anything that wraps up or conceals

**wardrobe** (p54)
a cabinet or other storage place for clothing or costumes

**parasol** (p57)
a small, light umbrella carried to protect oneself from the sun

From *Teaching U.S. History Through Children's Literature*. © 1998 Wanda J. Miller. Teacher Ideas Press. (800) 237-6124.

**stern** (p59)
> harsh in nature or manner; strict; severe

**countenance** (p59)
> the expression of the face

**ignorant** (p62)
> having little or no learning or knowledge

**convert** (p63)
> a person who has been won over to a new religion or belief

**endorse** (p64)
> to give support or approval to

**petition** (p64)
> a formal, written request, often with many signatures, sent to a person or group in authority

**sorrow** (p65)
> sadness or distress of mind because of some loss or misfortune

**prevail** (p65)
> to gain control; to be victorious; to win out

**drone** (p67)
> to speak in a dull, monotonous manner

**elegant** (p74)
> tasteful, luxurious, and beautiful

**turret** (p81)
> a small tower, often at the corner of a large building or castle

**grim** (p82)
> stern or forbidding

**fortnight** (p84)
> a period of two weeks

**seminary** (p87)
> a high school or school of higher education, especially a boarding school

**Quaker** (p99)
> a member of the Society of Friends, whose name came from their founder's statement to tremble at the word of the Lord

**universal** (p113)
> involving all

**liberty** (p113)
> freedom to think or act as one wishes, regarded as a very important human right

**noble** (p117)
> having or showing outstandingly good or moral qualities

**daft** (p120)
> crazy or foolish

**carpetbag** (p122)
> an old-fashioned suitcase or bag made of carpeting

**camphor** (p127)
> a white, crystalline substance with a strong odor, obtained from an Asian tree or made synthetically, that is used in medicine, lacquers, and mothballs

**pungent** (p127)
> sharp or piercing to the taste or smell

**salve** (p127)
> a soothing or healing ointment, such as for wounds, burns, or sores

**chamber** (p131)
> one house of a legislature or congress

**desist** (p134)
> to stop what one is doing; to cease

**minion** (p136)
> a servant or follower

**magistrate** (p137)
> a minor judge, such as a justice of the peace

**abide** (p145)
> to put up with; to endure

**optimism** (p146)
> the belief that everything in life works out to a good end

**tardy** (p148)
> late; delayed

**lapel** (p150)
> either part of the front of a coat that is folded back below the collar

# Small Group Reading

Fritz, Jean. *You Want Women to Vote, Lizzie Stanton?* G. P. Putnam's Sons, 1995.

This is a biography of Elizabeth Cady Stanton, a woman who wanted the same rights as men, which included the right to vote. She spoke out at a convention in Seneca Falls, New York in July 1848, and traveled around the country to advocate equality for everyone, men and women, black and white. Grades 4–8.

## Author Information

The daughter of missionary parents, Jean Fritz spent the first twelve years of her life in China. As a child, she often wondered about America and what it meant to be an American.

Fritz began writing after she married and had two children, with articles appearing in such magazines as *The New Yorker* and *Redbook*.

Each of Fritz's historical novels grew from her personal interest in the subject. Her enthusiasm for her subjects brings the past to life in an entertaining, informative, and detailed fashion.

Jean Fritz was the 1986 recipient of the Laura Ingalls Wilder Award of the American Library Association, which is given once every three years to an author whose work has made a "substantial and lasting contribution to literature for children."

## Activities

1.  On a world map, have students locate:

    | | |
    |---|---|
    | Albany, NY | New York City |
    | Atlantic Ocean | Ohio |
    | Boston, MA | Oregon |
    | California | Peterboro, NY |
    | Colorado | Philadelphia, PA |
    | Gardner, MA | Rochester, NY |
    | Harpers Ferry, VA | Seneca Falls, NY |
    | Indiana | South Carolina |
    | Iowa | Tenafly, NJ |
    | Johnstown, NY | Troy, NY |
    | Kansas | Waterloo, NY |
    | London, England | Worcester, MA |
    | Maine | Wyoming |

2.  Have students research the following people and their contributions to the women's suffrage movement:

    | | |
    |---|---|
    | Susan B. Anthony | Abraham Lincoln |
    | President Cleveland | Lucretia Mott |
    | Frederick Douglass | Gerrit Smith |
    | William Lloyd Garrison | Lucy Stone |
    | President Grant | |

3.  Have students write a speech that Elizabeth might have given had she lived to see women receive the right to vote, then present the speech to the rest of the class.

4.  At the end of chapter 2, on page 15, we are told that women had to be silent during the convention. Have students write a speech that might have been made if the women had been allowed to speak.

## Discussion

Give the small group the following instruction: As your group reads this book, discuss the following.

1.  Why couldn't Elizabeth's father help Flora Campbell?

2.  How do you think Elizabeth felt when her father told her, "I wish you were a boy!"? Why do you think he felt that way?

3. What did Elizabeth do to make up to her father for not being a boy?

4. Discuss the difference in treatment of men and women during this time period.

5. Why did Elizabeth enjoy visiting her cousin Libby Smith in Peterboro, New York?

6. How did Elizabeth's father feel about her marrying Henry Stanton?

7. How were women treated at the World Anti-Slavery Convention in London, England?

8. How did Henry Stanton feel about women's rights and the anti-slavery movement?

9. What did Elizabeth mean when she said that she suffered from "mental hunger"?

10. How did taxation without representation apply to women of this time period?

11. Discuss the grievances that women demanded in the Declaration of Sentiments at the Women's Rights Convention in Seneca Falls, New York.

12. Which demand was at first opposed at the convention? Who persuaded women and men to vote in favor of it?

13. After the convention, why did some women ask that their names be removed from the Declaration of Sentiments?

14. What style of clothing did Elizabeth's cousin Libby introduce her to? Why were people upset with this new style?

15. In what ways did Elizabeth Cady Stanton and Susan B. Anthony support each other?

16. How do you think Elizabeth felt when she spoke about the rights of women to the New York State Legislature at Albany?

17. Why do you think Elizabeth's family opposed her public speaking?

18. What did Abraham Lincoln mean when he said, "A house divided against itself cannot stand"?

19. Why didn't abolitionists believe that the Emancipation Proclamation was enough?

20. Why did the Fourteenth and Fifteenth Amendments to the Constitution upset Elizabeth?

21. What was the difference between the National Woman Suffrage Association and the American Woman Suffrage Association?

22. In what way did Susan B. Anthony, along with fourteen other women in Rochester, New York, put the Fourteenth Amendment to the test? What were the consequences?

23. How was the International Council of Women, held in 1888, different from the original Women's Rights Convention that was held forty years earlier?

24. How had rights for women changed by 1890?

25. When did women gain the right to vote?

## Vocabulary

**outlandish** (p1)
  strange or unfamiliar

**obscene** (p1)
  offensive to accepted standards of morality or decency

**legislators** (p5)
  members of a lawmaking body, such as members of Congress

**forlorn** (p6)
  sad due to being alone or neglected

**seminary** (p7)
  a high school or school of higher learning, especially a boarding school

**reformer** (p8)
  a person who tries to make things better, such as by correcting wrongs or abuses

**abolition** (p8)
the ending of slavery in the United States

**broadcloth** (p9)
a closely woven, fine cloth of cotton, silk, or other fabric, used for clothing

**inferiority** (p9)
the condition of being not as good, such as in quality, worth, or usefulness

**vivacious** (p9)
full of life and spirit; lively by nature

**hasty** (p10)
quick

**delegate** (p10)
a person with authority to act for a group; a representative

**elope** (p10)
to run away in secret to get married

**masthead** (p12)
the part of a newspaper or magazine that lists the names of the editors, staff, and owners, and tells where it is published

**Quaker** (p12)
a member of the Society of Friends, whose name came from their founder's statement to tremble at the word of the Lord

**provoked** (p12)
made angry or resentful; irritated

**staunchly** (p12)
loyally

**demure** (p12)
quiet, modest, and shy

**revelation** (p16)
making or becoming known

**gale** (p17)
a strong wind

**devotions** (p19)
prayers; worship

**drudgery** (p20)
dull, hard, unpleasant work

**inalienable rights** (p23)
the rights of a citizen that cannot be taken away or transferred

**injustice** (p23)
lack of justice, fairness, or equal treatment

**dignity** (p23)
the quality of character, worth, or nobility that commands respect

**tyranny** (p23)
absolute power unfairly or cruelly used

**sordid** (p24)
mean, selfish, or spiteful

**heretics** (p27)
people who believe or teach a belief different from an accepted belief of a church, profession, or science

**petticoat** (p29)
a skirt, usually hanging from the waist and worn as an undergarment

**corset** (p29)
a close-fitting undergarment, worn to give support and shape to the hips and waist

**scandalized** (p30)
shocked or offended, such as by something that is wrong or improper

**charismatic** (p33)
having a personal quality that attracts many devoted followers

**exploits** (p35)
brave or daring acts

**eloquent** (p38)
showing much feeling; expressive

**orator** (p41)
a person who delivers a serious public speech, usually at a formal occasion

**hindrances** (p42)
persons or things that interfere with something

**arsenal** (p43)
a public building for making or keeping such supplies as guns and ammunition

**secede** (p45)
to withdraw from a union or association, especially a political or religious one

**emancipate** (p46)
to set free, such as from slavery or oppression

**pacifist** (p47)
a person who refuses, for moral or religious reasons, to bear arms during a war

**Emancipation Proclamation** (p47)
an order issued by President Lincoln on January 1, 1863, abolishing slavery in those areas still at war with the Union

**illiterate** (p49)
lacking the ability to read and write

**suffrage** (p49)
> the right to vote

**egotistical** (p54)
> inclined to think too highly of oneself; conceited

**conservative** (p56)
> wishing to keep things as they have been; opposed to change

**platform** (p58)
> a set or statement of principles, ideals, or aims put forth by a political party or other group

**pardoned** (p61)
> freed from further punishment

**veranda** (p63)
> a long outdoor porch, usually roofed, along the outside of a building

**eulogy** (p65)
> a speech or writing in praise of a person or thing, especially when presented formally and in public

**agape** (p67)
> in a condition of wonder, surprise, or excitement

**pneumonia** (p67)
> a disease caused by a bacterial or virus infection and marked by inflammation of one or both lungs

**merger** (p72)
> the act of combining two groups into one

**lavish** (p74)
> profuse; exceedingly generous

**tableau** (p74)
> a picture or scene

**steadfast** (p75)
> not moving or changing; constant

**perpetual** (p75)
> continuing indefinitely; eternal

# Small Group Reading

Jacobs, William Jay. *Mother, Aunt Susan and Me: The First Fight for Women's Rights*. New York: Coward, McCann & Geoghegan, 1979.

Jacobs uses the voice of sixteen-year-old Harriot Stanton to tell the story of her mother, Elizabeth Cady Stanton; her mother's friend Susan B. Anthony; and their effort to win equal rights for women. Grades 4–7.

## Author Information

William Jay Jacobs was born August 23, 1933, in Cincinnati, Ohio. He received a bachelor of arts degree in history from the University of Cincinnati in 1955. In 1956 he received a master of arts degree from Columbia University. He also received an educational doctorate degree from Columbia University in 1963.

Jacob's teaching experiences have been numerous. He has taught history in public schools as well as at several universities. In 1974, Jacobs formed William Jay Jacobs Associates, Inc. (educational consultants), of which he is president. He has also worked as a consultant to several publishers, including McGraw's Junior Book Division and Scholastic.

Among Jacobs's awards are a Notable Children's Books in Social Studies selection from the National Council for Social Studies and the Childrens Book Council, and a Best Children's Books selection by the Child Study Association; both of these were awarded in 1979 for *Mother, Aunt Susan and Me: The First Fight for Women's Rights*.

## Activities

1. On a map of the United States, have students locate:

   Adirondack Mountains, NY  
   Albany, NY  
   Baltimore, MD  
   Catskill Mountains, NY  
   Englewood, NJ  
   Hudson River, NY  
   Johnstown, NY  

   Kansas  
   New York City  
   Rochester, NY  
   Seneca Falls, NY  
   Seneca River, NY  
   Tenafly, NJ  
   Washington, DC  

2. Have students research the following people and their roles in the women's rights movement:

   Susan B. Anthony  
   Frederick Douglass  
   President Andrew Johnson  
   Abraham Lincoln  
   John Stuart Mill  

   Lucretia Mott  
   Wendell Phillips  
   Elizabeth Cady Stanton  
   Sojourner Truth  
   Mary Wollstonecraft  

3. At Susan B. Anthony's trial following her arrest for illegal voting, she was asked if she had anything to say. She responded with a speech that became a summary of the feminist position. This speech begins on page 44 and ends on page 47. Have students in this group divide this speech into equal parts and recite it for the rest of the class.

4. Susan B. Anthony delivered her final speech in 1906, at age 86, a month before she died. In it, she said there was only one certainty in the future of the women's movement: "FAILURE IS IMPOSSIBLE!" Have students write a short essay reflecting this title.

## Discussion

Give the small group the following instruction: As your group reads this book, discuss the following.

1. Why did Harriot change the spelling of her name?

2. Why do Harriot's friends think it is strange that she attends private schools?

3. What is Harriot's mother known for throughout the United States?

4. What is Harriot's father known for?

5. What was the Declaration of Sentiments that Elizabeth Cady Stanton wrote for the women's rights meeting in Seneca Falls, New York in 1848?

6. How is the Declaration of Sentiments different from the Declaration of Independence?

7. Discuss the difference in women's rights today and in 1848.

8. Why did people object to Amelia Bloomer's pantaloons (or "bloomers" as they became known)?

9. Who is Elizabeth Cady Stanton's closest friend?

10. What did the Thirteenth Amendment to the Constitution change?

11. Why did the Fourteenth and Fifteenth Amendments to the Constitution make Susan B. Anthony and Elizabeth Cady Stanton angry?

12. Why did Elizabeth and Susan go to Kansas to speak?

13. Why did many men oppose women being granted the right to vote?

14. How did George Francis Train help Susan and Elizabeth's cause?

15. Why did someone call Susan B. Anthony "the invincible Susan"?

16. Why did many merchants refuse to advertise in *The Revolution*?

17. Why did some women want Elizabeth and Susan to stop printing *The Revolution*?

18. Why was Susan arrested in 1872?

19. How did Elizabeth compare Susan's trial with the Battle of Bunker Hill during the American Revolution?

20. Discuss life in Elizabeth's home.

21. What became of Harriot Stanton as an adult?

22. What right did women gain upon passage of the Nineteenth Amendment to the Constitution?

# Vocabulary

**foliage** (p10)
  the leaves on a tree or other plant

**mahogany** (p12)
  a reddish brown hardwood used for furniture

**smokehouse** (p15)
  a building or closed room where foods and other things, such as hides, are hung and treated with smoke to preserve them

**delegate** (p17)
  a person with authority to act for a group; a representative

**distinguished** (p18)
  having the look of a notable person; dignified

**corset** (p19)
  a close-fitting undergarment, worn to give support and shape to the hips and waist

**pantaloons** (p19)
  trousers, especially tight-fitting ones with straps that fit under the instep, worn in former times

**efficient** (p28)
  producing results with the least effort or waste; capable

**merchant** (p29)
  a storekeeper

**masthead** (p30)
  the part of a newspaper or magazine that lists the names of the editors, staff, and owners, and tells where it is published

**defiance** (p30)
  bold opposition to power or authority; refusal to submit or obey

**impeach** (p36)
  to formally charge with wrongdoing in office

**eloquently** (p44)
  said in an effective or skillful way

**leniency** (p46)
  the quality of being mild; gentleness

**prosecution** (p46)
  the starting and carrying out of a legal action to obtain a right or punish a wrong

**tyranny** (p47)
  absolute power unfairly or cruelly used

**debate** (p49)
  the act of arguing for or against, especially in a formal way between persons taking opposite sides of a question

**illustrious** (p53)
  very famous; distinguished

**suffragettes** (p55)
  women who fought for women's right to vote

**suffrage** (p55)
  the right to vote

**agitation** (p57)
  the arousing of public interest to change something

**dignity** (p58)
  the quality of character, worth, or nobility that commands respect

**indomitable** (p60)
  not easily defeated or overcome; persevering

# Small Group Reading

📖 McPherson, Stephanie Sammartino. *I Speak for the Women: A Story About Lucy Stone*. Minneapolis, MN: Carolrhoda, 1992.

McPherson tells the story of Lucy Stone, an outspoken nineteenth-century supporter of women's rights. Grades 4–7.

## Author Information

Stephanie Sammartino McPherson is a high school English teacher-turned-writer. *I Speak for the Women: A Story About Lucy Stone* is her third book in Carolrhoda's Creative Minds biography series. Her first book, *Rooftop Astronomer: A Story About Maria Mitchell*, was named a Best Children's Book of 1990 by *Science Books & Films* magazine.

## Activities

1.  On a map of the United States, have students locate:

    Boston, MA            Orange, NJ
    Chicago, IL           Paxton, MA
    Cincinnati, OH        Salem, OH
    Cleveland, OH         Seneca Falls, NY
    Lake Erie             Syracuse, NY
    Niagara Falls, NY     Viroqua, WI

2.  Have students research the following people and their roles in the struggle for women's rights:

    Susan B. Anthony       William Lloyd Garrison
    Elizabeth Blackwell    Elizabeth Cady Stanton
    Antoinette Brown       Sojourner Truth
    Frederick Douglass

3.  A dove with an olive branch was used to illustrate any victory for women's suffrage. Have students draw this symbol to hang in your classroom.

4.  Have students write an essay telling how women's lives have changed since the nineteenth century. It could take the form of a letter to Lucy Stone, telling her what women are able to do today. Students can then share these letters with the rest of the class.

## Discussion

Give the small group the following instruction: As your group reads this book, discuss the following questions.

1.  Why did Lucy's mother wish that Lucy had been a boy?

2.  What was life like for Lucy's mother, Hannah Stone?

3.  Do you think that if you were Lucy, you would have also questioned women's roles? Why or why not?

4.  Why did Lucy have to earn the money for her schoolbooks?

5.  In the nineteenth century, what was considered important for a woman to learn?

6.  Why did Lucy think so highly of her sister Rhoda?

7.  As a child, what were Lucy's responsibilities?

8. Why did Mary Lyon's speech excite Lucy?

9. What was Lucy's first job? In what way was she treated differently from a man in this job?

10. What was Lucy saving her money for?

11. Why did Lucy want to attend Oberlin College in Ohio?

12. Oberlin College was a stop on the Underground Railroad. What did this mean? How did Lucy feel about it?

13. Why were the former slaves insulted to have Lucy as their teacher? How did their feelings change?

14. What did her students learn that Lucy herself was not allowed to study?

15. Why wasn't Lucy allowed to read a graduation essay that she was asked to write? How did she react?

16. Who was William Lloyd Garrison?

17. What did Lucy want for all women?

18. Why did Hannah Stone worry about Lucy?

19. How did Lucy's father feel about women speaking out for women's rights?

20. How did Lucy help to change her father's feelings about the women's movement?

21. Why were some people afraid of women being granted equal rights?

22. How did Lucy compare women's rights to the argument of taxation without representation used by American colonists during the Revolutionary War?

23. Why did Lucy feel the need to ignore her dreams of being married and having children?

24. Why did Lucy finally agree to marry Henry Blackwell?

25. How do you feel about the speech Henry made just before he and Lucy were married?

26. What did the Thirteenth Amendment to the Constitution accomplish?

27. In what ways did women make advances toward equality during the Civil War?

28. What caused problems between Lucy and Elizabeth Cady Stanton and Susan B. Anthony so that they could no longer work together?

29. What symbol was used whenever there was a victory for women's suffrage?

30. What was the result of the Fifteenth Amendment to the Constitution?

31. Which amendment to the Constitution guaranteed women the right to vote? When did it become law?

# Vocabulary

**obedient** (p10)
willing or tending to obey; complying, such as with rules, regulations, or laws

**blacksmith** (p11)
a person who works with iron by heating it in a forge and then hammering it into shape

**fatigue** (p12)
a tired condition resulting from hard work, effort, or strain; weariness

**injustice** (p13)
lack of justice, fairness, or equal treatment

**turban** (p13)
an oriental headdress consisting of a sash or shawl, twisted around the head

**seminary** (p13)
a high school or school of higher education, especially a boarding school

**ambitious** (p13)
eager to succeed

**abolitionist** (p14)
one of the people who wanted to end slavery in the United States

**hostility** (p14)
  resentful opposition

**deacon** (p14)
  a church official who assists the clergy by performing duties not connected with actual worship

**indignation** (p16)
  anger caused by something that is not right, just, or fair

**skeptical** (p16)
  not believing readily; inclined to question or doubt

**board** (p16)
  food or meals, especially meals furnished for pay

**tuition** (p17)
  the charge or payment for instruction in a school

**controversial** (p18)
  tending to stir up an argument

**curriculum** (p18)
  all of the subjects or courses taught in a school or in any particular grade

**carpetbag** (p19)
  an old-fashioned suitcase or bag made of carpeting

**schooner** (p20)
  a ship having two or more masts rigged with fore-and-aft sails

**tension** (p22)
  mental strain; nervous anxiety

**dismay** (p22)
  a feeling of alarm, uneasiness, and confusion

**sympathized** (p23)
  shared the feelings or ideas of another

**debate** (p24)
  to discuss or argue for or against, especially in a formal way between persons taking sides

**rebel** (p24)
  a person who refuses to submit to authority and fights against it instead

**uproar** (p25)
  a condition of violent agitation, disturbance, or noisy confusion

**endure** (p26)
  to last for a long time

**pulpit** (p27)
  a raised platform or desk for a preacher in a church

**convictions** (p29)
  strong, firm beliefs

**inspiration** (p29)
  a good idea or impulse that comes to someone, usually suddenly

**scandalized** (p32)
  shocked or offended, such as by conduct that is wrong or improper

**typhoid fever** (p35)
  an infectious disease caused by a bacterium found in infected food or water

**dingy** (p35)
  looking dirty; dull; shabby

**fugitive** (p36)
  fleeing, such as from danger or arrest

**elaborate** (p36)
  fancy and usually costly or luxurious in its details or parts

**petticoats** (p36) skirts, usually hanging from the waist and worn as undergarments

**liberate** (p38)
  to set free; to release

**earnest** (p41)
  very serious, determined, or sincere

**matronly** (p50)
  like a married woman or widow, especially one no longer young

**suffrage** (p52)
  the right to vote

**jubilant** (p57)
  expressing great joy; joyful; exultant

**scorn** (p61)
  to treat with contempt; to despise

**ridicule** (p61)
  words or actions intended to make another person or thing seem foolish; mockery

**eloquence** (p61)
  a moving and skillful use of language, especially in speaking

# Small Group Reading

📖 Oneal, Zibby. *A Long Way to Go: A Story About Women's Right to Vote.* New York: Viking, 1990.

Eight-year-old Lila deals with the women's suffrage movement during World War I. Grades 4–7.

## Author Information

Elizabeth (Zibby) Oneal was born March 17, 1934, in Omaha, Nebraska. She attended Stanford University from 1952 to 1955, and received a bachelor's degree from the University of Michigan in 1970.

Oneal was a lecturer in English at the University of Michigan from 1976 to 1985. She has written several books for children, including *War Work, The Language of Goldfish, In Summer Light*, and *Grandma Moses: Painter of Rural America*.

Oneal came from a family who loved books. Her parents encouraged her early attempts at writing. Because of this background in literature, Oneal can't remember a time when she didn't want to be a writer.

## Activities

1. On a map of the United States, have students locate New York City and Washington, D.C.

2. Ask your school music teacher to teach the songs "Over There" and "Tipperary" to your class.

3. Have students research the following:
   - Susan B. Anthony
   - the Fourteenth Amendment to the Constitution
   - Lucretia Mott
   - Elizabeth Cady Stanton
   - President Woodrow Wilson

4. Have students illustrate the parade scene on page 47 in which hundreds of women of all races and ages are carrying flags and banners, some in nurses' uniforms, some in Red Cross uniforms, and some with yellow chrysanthemums in their hats.

5. Have students in this group recite the speech about women's rights in this book to the rest of the class.

## Discussion

Give the small group the following instruction: As your group reads this book, discuss the following.

1. Why was Lila's grandmother arrested?

2. What did Lila's mother do to help in the war effort?

3. How did Lila's father feel about women voting?

4. How was Lila treated differently from girls today?

5. When Lila thought of her brother George being able to vote someday, how did she feel?

6. Why did Lila feel like an animal in the zoo?

7. What new things did Lila see when she went home with Katie Rose?

8. What did Annie do to Mike? Why?

9. What did Lila read about the suffragists in the newspaper?

10. What did Lila prove to Mike?

11. Discuss Lila and her grandmother's talk about women working and voting. How have things changed for women since then?

12. Why do you think Lila's father decided to let her go to the parade?

13. How do you think Lila felt at the parade? Why?

14. What made Lila's grandmother believe that someday women would be able to vote?

15. When were women in New York given the right to vote? How was this a turning point in the suffragist movement?

16. Discuss the Nineteenth Amendment to the Constitution. In what ways did it change women's lives?

## Vocabulary

**parlor** (p3)
a room for receiving visitors or entertaining guests

**telegram** (p4)
a message sent by telegraph, which sends and receives messages by means of a series of electrical or electromagnetic pulses

**suffrage** (p4)
the right to vote

**suffragist** (p4)
a person who advocates extension of the right to vote, especially to women

**spectacle** (p6)
an unusual or painful sight

**amendment** (p6)
a change, such as to a law or bill

**Constitution** (p6)
the fundamental law of the United States

**democracy** (p8)
a form of government in which the people rule, either by voting directly, or by electing representatives to manage the government and make the laws

**convict** (p11)
a person found guilty of a crime and serving a prison sentence

**riot** (p11)
a violent disturbance made by a large group of people behaving in a wild, disorderly way

**Victrola** (p17)
an early record player

**prim** (p19)
very precise and formal; stiffly proper and neat

**shirtwaist** (p19)
a woman's tailored blouse that looks something like a man's shirt

**tenement** (p20)
an apartment house that is poorly built or maintained, usually overcrowded, and often located in a slum

**trolley** (p26)
a vehicle for public transportation that runs on rails and is powered by electricity obtained from overhead wires running through it

**torpedo** (p29)
a large, underwater projectile that moves under its own power, is shaped like a cigar, and is filled with high explosives that blow up when it strikes a ship

**twilight** (p33)
the light in the sky just after sunset or just before sunrise

**declaration** (p53)
a formal statement or announcement

**abolitionists** (p53)
people who wanted to end slavery in the United States

**petition** (p53)
a formal written request, often with many signatures, sent to a person or group in authority

# Small Group Reading

📖  Wiseman, David. ***Thimbles***. Boston: Houghton Mifflin, 1982.

A twentieth-century girl is magically transported through time to join the 1819 demonstration that ended in tragedy for Manchester mill workers seeking the right to vote. Grades 4–7.

## Author Information

David Wiseman was born January 13, 1916, in Manchester, England. He attended the British Institute of Adult Education in London, England. His working career has included stints as editor of the *Journal of Adult Education* in London and a high school teacher in Worcestershire, Yorkshire, and Cornwall, England. He was also a high school principal in Doncaster, England from 1959 to 1963 and in Cornwall, England from 1963 to 1975. Wiseman served on the Cornwall Education Board from 1975 to 1977.

Wiseman's grandmother, who was a suffragette in England and was imprisoned for her stand on women's rights, had an influence on his writing. In an interview for *Something About the Author* (volume 43), Wiseman said, "Writing is both a joy and an obsession. I am unhappiest when circumstances prevent me from writing." *Thimbles* was designated as an ALA Notable Book by the American Library Association.

## Activities

1.  On a map of Europe, have students locate:

    Cornwall, England          Manchester, England
    Dartmoor, England          Plymouth, England
    London, England            Teign River

2.  Have students compare the fight for liberty and suffrage for all in England with the same fight in the United States, presenting this comparison orally to the rest of the class.

3.  Have students research the St. Peter's Massacre.

4.  Have students write a letter from Cathy to her great-great-great-grandmother, telling her how things have changed for women today.

## Discussion

Give the small group the following instruction: As your group reads this book, discuss the following.

1.  Why is Catherine being sent away? Where is she going?

2.  How does Catherine feel about what has happened to her father?

3.  What was Catherine's reaction to the red velvet cap that she and her grandmother found in the trunk?

4.  What happened when Catherine picked up the worn and battered thimble?

5.  What did Catherine discover about the golden thimble?

6.  What did Catherine learn about the girl who had made the sampler?

7.  Who is Sophia? What did Sophia's parents tell her about what was going to happen at the Yeomanry?

8.  Why was Catherine's great-great-great-grandmother imprisoned eighty years ago?

From *Teaching U.S. History Through Children's Literature.* © 1998 Wanda J. Miller. Teacher Ideas Press. (800) 237-6124.

9. What does *universal suffrage* mean?

10. What was Kate's red velvet cap used for?

11. What gift did Catherine's grandparents give her for her birthday?

12. What did Kate receive for her twelfth birthday?

13. Why do you think the cavalry attacked at St. Peter's Fields?

14. What happened to Kate's cap of liberty?

15. What does Sophia's father want?

16. What did Stanley bring Sophia? How did she react? Why?

17. How did Catherine feel about her birthday surprise?

18. How was Sophia related to Catherine?

19. Why do you think Catherine chose what she did to keep from Aunt Maisie's things?

## Vocabulary

**union** (p1)
an association of workers organized to improve working conditions and to protect the interests of members

**vigilant** (p2)
watchful

**contemptuous** (p3)
full of contempt or scorn; disdainful

**immersed** (p4)
deeply involved

**dejection** (p4)
lowness of spirits; depression; sadness

**estuary** (p5)
the broad meeting place of a river and sea, where the tide flows in

**heron** (p5)
any of several wading birds having a long bill, a long neck, and long legs

**horizon** (p5)
the line where the earth and sky seem to meet

**silhouette** (p5)
the outline of a person or object against a light or a light background

**eccentric** (p8)
odd; peculiar

**discontent** (p11)
an unhappy, dissatisfied feeling

**hearty** (p12)
healthy and strong

**lass** (p12)
a young woman or girl

**banish** (p17)
to compel to leave a country, such as by political decree

**heed** (p17)
to pay careful attention

**submissive** (p17)
giving in or willing to give in to what is asked or demanded; obedient; docile

**steward** (p18)
a person who manages the property, finances, or other affairs of another person or persons

**damask** (p20)
a rich, reversible silk fabric with an elaborate woven design

**intricate** (p21)
complicated or involved

**christening** (p21)
a Christian baptism, especially of a baby

**revulsion** (p21)
a sudden change of feeling, especially to one of disgust

**crimson** (p21)
deep red

**procession** (p24)
a group of people or cars, arranged one behind the other and moving in a formal way; a parade

**apprehension** (p25)
a worried expectation of something bad; dread or fear

**banter** (p25)
playful teasing; good-natured joking

**dunes** (p26)
hills or banks of loose sand built up by the wind

**compulsion** (p27)
an irresistible, sometimes irrational, urge

**dismay** (p28)
a feeling of alarm, uneasiness, or confusion

**tedious** (p29)
long, dull, and tiresome

**governess** (p29)
a woman who cares for and teaches children in a private home

**finicky** (p29)
hard to please; fussy

**saber** (p30)
a heavy cavalry sword with a curved blade

**scabbard** (p30)
a case or sheath to protect the blade of a weapon, such as a sword or bayonet

**feigned** (p31)
purely imaginary; made up

**vivid** (p38)
creating clear, lifelike, or original images in the mind

**petticoat** (p40)
a skirt, usually hanging from the waist and worn as an undergarment

**corset** (p40)
a close-fitting undergarment, worn to give support and shape to the hips and waist

**forebears** (p44)
ancestors

**staves** (p49)
sticks or poles carried as aids in walking or climbing

**dispersed** (p50)
scattered or spread in many directions

**libertas** (p50)
Latin for "liberty"

**larder** (p50)
a place where food is stored; a pantry

**incoherent** (p52)
unclear; confused; disjointed

**dispel** (p55)
to drive away as if by scattering

**magistrate** (p57)
a highly public official having many executive or legal powers

**radicals** (p57)
people who favor rapid and widespread changes or reforms, especially in politics or government

**demure** (p57)
quiet, modest, and shy, or seeming so

**hearth** (p59)
the floor of a fireplace or furnace

**scones** (p60)
round, flat cakes or biscuits, usually eaten with butter

**suffragette** (p64)
a woman who fought for women's right to vote

**convey** (p64)
to make known; to communicate

**imperious** (p64)
proud and haughty; domineering; arrogant

**mutton** (p69)
the flesh of sheep, especially an adult sheep, used as food

**sustenance** (p69)
something that maintains life or strength; nourishment; food

**provocation** (p74)
the act of making angry or resentful, or causing irritation

**constable** (p74)
a police officer

**loitering** (p74)
lingering or dawdling

**pinafore** (p81)
a sleeveless, apronlike garment, worn as a dress or protective smock by girls and women

**contingent** (p81)
a group making up part of a larger group

**dignified** (p81)
honorable or worthy

**laurel** (p83)
an evergreen shrub of southern Europe with fragrant lance-shaped leaves, used by the ancients to make wreaths for heroes

**orator** (p83)
a person who delivers a serious public speech, usually given at a formal occasion

**nostalgic** (p88)
having, showing, or coming from a longing for some pleasant place, happening, or time that is past

**noble** (p97)
having or showing outstandingly good or moral qualities

From *Teaching U.S. History Through Children's Literature.* © 1998 Wanda J. Miller. Teacher Ideas Press. (800) 237-6124.

**indignant** (p99)
angry at something that is not right, just, or fair

**Parliament** (p99)
the legislature of Great Britain, or any of the self-governing members of the commonwealth

**complacent** (p104)
satisfied with oneself, one's possessions, or one's accomplishments

**shako** (p107)
a high, stiff military hat with an upright plume

**peril** (p111)
exposure to the chance of injury, loss, or destruction; danger; risk

**tunic** (p112)
a close-fitting jacket, often worn as part of a uniform

**succor** (p112)
help or comfort given in danger or distress

**inert** (p112)
lacking the power to move or act

**concourse** (p117)
an open place where crowds gather or through which they pass

**barouche** (p117)
a four-wheeled carriage with a folding top, two seats facing each other, and an outside seat for the driver

**Quaker** (p126)
a member of the Society of Friends, whose name came from their founder's statement to tremble at the word of the Lord

# Bibliography

## Individual Titles

Archer, Jules. *Breaking Barriers: The Feminist Revolution from Susan B. Anthony to Margaret Sanger to Betty Friedan.* New York: Viking, 1991.

This exploration of the women's movement includes biographies of Susan B. Anthony, Margaret Sanger, and Betty Friedan. Grades 6 and up.

Ashby, Ruth, and Deborah Gore Ohrn, eds. *Herstory: Women Who Changed the World.* New York: Viking, 1995.

This book contains biographical sketches of 120 women who helped change the lives of women in America. Grades 6 and up.

Bacon, Margaret Hope. *Valiant Friend: The Life of Lucretia Mott.* New York: Walker, 1980.

This is a biography of Lucretia Mott, who has been called "the most venerated woman in America." She led an active life as a reformer, Quaker minister, anti-slavery leader, wife, mother, grandmother, and mainstay of the women's rights movement. The Equal Rights Amendment was named for her when it was introduced. Grades 8 and up.

Brill, Marlene Targ. *Let Women Vote!* Brookfield, CT: Millbrook Press, 1996.

This book's focus is the ratification of the Nineteenth Amendment. An afterword presents contemporary issues related to women's rights. Grades 5–8.

Bryant, Jennifer Fisher. *Lucretia Mott: A Guiding Light.* Grand Rapids, MI: William B. Eerdmans, 1996.

A biography of the nineteenth-century Quaker leader who dedicated her life to the abolitionist and early feminist movements. Grades 7 and up.

Chafe, William H. *The Road to Equality: American Women Since 1962.* New York: Oxford University Press, 1994.

In the 1960s, American women challenged prejudices about female capabilities. Women sought and continue to seek equality in all areas. This book focuses on the women's movement from 1962 to the present. Grades 5 and up.

Cullen-DuPont, Kathryn. *Elizabeth Cady Stanton and Women's Liberty.* New York: Facts on File, 1992.

This is a biography of one of the first leaders of the women's rights movement, whose work led to the adoption of the Nineteenth Amendment. Grades 8 and up.

Dash, Joan. *We Shall Not Be Moved: The Women's Factory Strike of 1909.* New York: Scholastic, 1996.

Dash describes the harsh working conditions and the courageous fight by young workers called the Shirtwaist Girls to form the Women's Trade Union League in New York's garment industry in the early 1900s. Grades 3–8.

Demos, John. *The Tried and the True: Native American Women Confronting Colonization*. New York: Oxford University Press, 1995.

This book looks at the full range of Native American women's experiences. Grades 5 and up.

Deutsch, Sarah Jane. *From Ballots to Breadlines: American Women 1920–1940*. New York: Oxford University Press, 1994.

This book examines the status of American women from the euphoria of the 1920s to the reality of the 1930s. As women began to vote and bring home wages, their role began to change. Grades 5 and up.

Faber, Doris. *Lucretia Mott: Foe of Slavery*. Champaign, IL: Garrard, 1971.

This is the story of Lucretia Mott, a pioneer in the fight for equal rights for women. Grades 2–4.

———. *Oh, Lizzie! The Life of Elizabeth Cady Stanton*. New York: Lothrop, Lee & Shepard, 1972.

Faber used Elizabeth Cady Stanton's own papers to write this true account of the woman who dared to propose in 1848 that women should be able to vote. Grades 5–8.

Goldberg, Michael. *Breaking New Ground: American Women 1800–1848*. New York: Oxford University Press, 1994.

The years leading up to the first women's rights convention in Seneca Falls, New York in 1848 were a time of awakening for women. Through education, religion, and social reform, women began to assert their influence in the political arena. Grades 5 and up.

Greene, Carol. *Elizabeth Blackwell: First Woman Doctor*. Chicago: Childrens Press, 1991.

This is a biography of the first woman doctor in the United States, who worked in both America and England to open the field of medicine to women. Grades 2–4.

Griffin, Lynne, and Kelly McCann. *The Book of Women: 300 Notable Women History Passed By*. Holbrook, MA: Bob Adams, 1992.

The authors provide brief descriptions of women who have had an impact on society. Grades 5 and up.

Hart, Philip S. *Up in the Air: The Story of Bessie Coleman*. Minneapolis, MN: Carolrhoda Books, 1996.

This is a biography of Bessie Coleman, the first African American woman to obtain a pilot's license. Grades 4–7.

Haskins, James. *Shirley Temple Black: Actress to Ambassador*. New York: Viking Kestrel, 1988.

This is a biography of the child actress who, as an adult, became active in politics and served as the first woman Chief of Protocol at the White House. Grades 4–7.

Hodges, Margaret. *Making a Difference: The Story of an American Family*. New York: Charles Scribner's Sons, 1989.

In the early 1900s in Cornwall, New York, Mary Beattie Sherwood leads her five children in efforts to bring changes for women, especially in higher education and voting rights. Grades 7 and up.

Johnson, Norma. *Remember the Ladies: The First Women's Rights Convention*. New York: Scholastic, 1995.

Johnson gives an account of the first women's rights convention, held in Seneca Falls, New York. Grades 6 and up.

Johnston, Johanna. *They Led the Way: 14 American Women*. New York: Scholastic, 1973.

This book, originally titled *Women Themselves*, contains short biographies of fourteen women, including Elizabeth Cady Stanton, Harriet Beecher Stowe, Clara Barton, and Carrie Chapman Catt. Grades 4–7.

Kamensky, Jane. *The Colonial Mosaic: American Women 1600–1760*. New York: Oxford University Press, 1995.

This book gives readers a view of American women's lives from 1600 to 1760. Grades 5 and up.

Lantham, Jean Lee. *Elizabeth Blackwell: Pioneer Woman Doctor*. New York: Chelsea House, 1991.

This is an easy-to-read account of the life of Elizabeth Blackwell, the first woman doctor in the United States. Grades 2–4.

Levin, Pamela. *Susan B. Anthony*. New York: Chelsea House, 1993.

This is an easy-to-read biography of Susan B. Anthony, a woman who devoted her life to achieving equality for women. Grades 2–5.

Levinson, Nancy Smiler. *The First Women Who Spoke Out*. Minneapolis, MN: Dillon, 1983.

Levinson presents the lives of six women, including Elizabeth Cady Stanton, Lucretia Mott, and Lucy Stone, who were among the first to speak for women's rights. Grades 5 and up.

Lindstrom, Aletha Jane. *Sojourner Truth: Slave, Abolitionist, Fighter for Women's Rights.* New York: Messner, 1980.

This biography of the former slave who became one of the best-known abolitionists of her time describes how she spent her life trying to improve living conditions for blacks. Grades 5 and up.

May, Elaine Tyler. *Pushing the Limits: American Women 1940–1961.* New York: Oxford University Press, 1994.

May uses primary sources to describe the changing roles of women in work and popular culture from Rosie the Riveter through Betty Friedan. Grades 5 and up.

McCully, Emily Arnold. *The Ballot Box Battle.* New York: Alfred A. Knopf, 1996.

Young Cordelia is an eyewitness to Lizzie Stanton's attempt to vote in 1880. Grades 2–4.

Meltzer, Milton. *The American Promise: Voices of a Changing Nation 1945–Present.* New York: Bantam Books, 1990.

Meltzer provides an overview of the women's rights movement in this book, which also looks at the Cold War, the Korean War, the civil rights movement, and the concerns of minority groups. Grades 7–8.

Monsell, Helen Albee. *Susan B. Anthony: Champion of Women's Rights.* New York: Aladdin, 1986.

This book focuses on the childhood of a pioneer in the crusade for human rights, particularly those of women. Grades 4–7.

Rappaport, Doreen, ed. *American Women: Their Lives in Their Words.* New York: Thomas Y. Crowell, 1990.

Through letters, journals, and speeches, Rappaport presents the struggles of American women from Anne Hutchinson to today's teenagers. Grades 8 and up.

Salmon, Marylynn. *The Limits of Independence: American Women 1760–1800.* New York: Oxford University Press, 1994.

Salmon looks at the traditional patterns of women's lives during the time of the American Revolution and the new directions to come as women help to carve a new nation. Grades 5 and up.

San Souci, Robert D. *Cut from the Same Cloth: American Women of Myth, Legend, and Tall Tale.* New York: Philomel, 1993.

This is a collection of twenty stories about legendary American women from various cultural backgrounds taken from folktales, popular stories, and ballads. Grades 3 and up.

Savage, Jeff. *Julie Krone: Unstoppable Jockey.* Minneapolis, MN: Lerner, 1996.

This is a biography of one of the most successful jockeys ever, Julie Krone, who overcame frightening falls and prejudiced racehorse owners and trainers who didn't want to let a woman ride. Grades 4–7.

Sigerman, Harriet. *Laborers for Liberty: American Women 1865–1890.* New York: Oxford University Press, 1994.

This book looks at the many women, well-known and not so well-known, who struggled for women's rights from 1865 to 1890 and sought liberty in the home, on the farm, and in the factory. Grades 5 and up.

———. *An Unfinished Battle: American Women 1848–1865.* New York: Oxford University Press, 1994.

The years 1848 to 1865 were a time of momentous change in the United States. This book looks at women's participation in the events of this time period and their fight for equal rights for all. Grades 5 and up.

Smith, Karen Manners. *New Paths to Power: American Women 1890–1920.* New York: Oxford University Press, 1994.

Smith gives an historical view of women at home, at work, and in public life, and of the conditions that led to their social rebellion in the early part of the twentieth century. Grades 6 and up.

St. George, Judith. *By George, Bloomers!* New York: Coward, McCann & Geoghegan, 1976.

Eight-year-old Hannah's mother disapproves when Hannah wants to wear bloomers, which cause a mild sensation when they are introduced in the mid-nineteenth century. Grades 2–5.

Stalcup, Brenda, ed. *The Women's Rights Movement.* San Diego, CA: Greenhaven Press, 1996.

The topics addressed in this book are still controversial today, raising questions about women's legal and political status. Essays included that either support or oppose the questions are authored by Abigail Adams, Elizabeth Cady Stanton, Antoinette Brown Blackwell, Theodore Roosevelt, and Betty Friedan, among others. Grades 9 and up.

Swain, Gwenyth. *The Road to Seneca Falls: A Story About Elizabeth Cady Stanton.* Minneapolis, MN: Carolrhoda, 1996.

Swain tells the story of how Elizabeth Cady Stanton and her friend Lucretia Mott organized the nation's first women's rights convention, which took place in Seneca Falls, New York, in 1848. Grades 3–6.

Veglahn, Nancy J. *Women Scientists*. New York: Facts on File, 1991.

Veglahn profiles the lives and achievements of ten American women scientists, including Annie Jump Cannon, Margaret Mead, and Rachel Carson. Grades 8 and up.

Wheeler, Marjorie Spruill. *One Woman, One Vote: Rediscovering the Woman Suffrage Movement*. Troutdale, OR: NewSage Press, 1995.

This is a very thorough resource on the women's suffrage movement that could be used by older students for research purposes. Grades 8 and up.

White, Florence Meiman. *First Woman in Congress: Jeannette Rankin*. New York: Messner, 1980.

This is a biography of the first woman elected to Congress, who spent the 92 years of her life as a leader for women's suffrage, a lobbyist, and a social reformer. Grades 5–8.

Whitney, Sharon, and Tom Raynor. *Women in Politics*. New York: Franklin Watts, 1986.

This book traces the history of women's involvement in American politics, with profiles of women candidates, mayors, governors, congressional representatives, and cabinet members. Grades 8 and up.

Wolfe, Rinna Evelyn. *Mary McLeod Bethune*. New York: Franklin Watts, 1992.

Wolfe traces Bethune's life from childhood through her involvement in public service. Grades 3–5.

Woolum, Janet. *Outstanding Women Athletes: Who They Are and How They Influenced Sports in America*. Phoenix, AZ: Oryx Press, 1992.

The author documents many of the contributions made by women for the betterment of sport and society. Grades 6 and up.

## Theme Resources

### *Commercial Resources*

Atherton, Herbert M., and J. Jackson Barlow, eds. *1791–1991 The Bill of Rights and Beyond*. Washington, DC: Commission on the Bicentennial of the United States Constitution, 1991.

This resource describes in detail the first twenty-six amendments to the Constitution. Suggested activities for teachers and librarians are included. For use with students in grades 5 and up.

*Booklinks*. Chicago: Booklist Publications.

The July 1996 issue has an article called "Jean Fritz You Want to Vote, Lizzie Stanton?" by Pat Scales. It includes an interview with Jean Fritz, discussion topics, activities, and research topics. For use with students in grades 4 through 6.

*Cobblestone: The History Magazine for Young People*. Peterborough, NH: Cobblestone.

The title of the March 1985 issue for students in grades 4 and up is "Susan B. Anthony and the Women's Movement." Articles include "The Roots of Women's Rights," "The Birthplace of Women's Rights," and "Testing the Fourteenth Amendment."

The subject of the October 1985 issue for students in grades 4 and up is "American Clothing: Then and Now." It includes an article called "The Bloomer Outfit."

The subject of the June 1994 issue for students in grades 4 and up is "Women Inventors." Articles include "Early Women Inventors," "A Chat with a Nobel Prize Winner: Gertrude Elion," and "The Youngest Female Inventor: Jeanie Low."

The focus of the February 1996 issue for students in grades 4 and up is Mary McLeod Bethune. Articles include "Changing America" and "A Force for Constructive Action."

*Educational Oasis: The Magazine for Middle Grades 5–9*. Carthage, IL: Good Apple.

The March/April 1991 issue for students in grades 5 through 9 includes the article "Amelia Earhart: Famous Woman Flyer."

Fischer, Max W. *American History Simulations*. Huntington Beach, CA: Teacher Created Materials, 1993.

This book includes a simulation called "A Woman's Place," which can be used to help students learn about the treatment and feelings of women during the women's suffrage movement. For use with students in grades 4 through 8.

Keenan, Sheila. *Encyclopedia of Women in the United States*. New York: Scholastic, 1996.

Readers will meet more than 250 women who have shaped the history of the United States from the sixteenth century to the present. Grades 4 and up.

Scriabine, Christine, historian. *Jacdaw: Votes for Women: The Fight for Suffrage.* Amawalk, NY: Jackdaw, 1992.

This is a portfolio of primary source material, including fourteen reproductions of historical documents. Among them are "Votes for Women" full-color postcards and a collection of anti-suffrage publications. Comprehensive notes on the documents, a reading list, and critical thinking questions are also included. This resource is suitable for use with students in grades 5 and up.

## Computer Resources

*Her Heritage: A Biographical Encyclopedia of Famous American Women.* Cambridge, MA: Pilgrim New Media, 1994. (CD-ROM)

This CD-ROM includes information about more than 1,000 extraordinary women from all walks of life. Available for Macintosh and Windows.

## Videos

*Mary McLeod Bethune.* Bala Cynwyd, PA: Schlessinger Video Productions, 1994. (30 minutes)

This video examines Bethune's importance in society today and the inspirational forces that helped shape her life.

*One Woman, One Vote.* Alexandria, VA: Educational Film Center, 1995. (106 minutes)

This video documents the seventy-year battle for women's suffrage, which finally culminated in the passage of the Nineteenth Amendment to the Constitution.

*The Susan B. Anthony Story.* Richardson, TX: Grace Products, 1994. (40 minutes)

The story of the courageous woman and her role in the early women's rights movement is seen through the eyes of a young girl. Upon entering a mysterious library, this young girl finds herself in the past. She meets Susan B. Anthony and learns that the only "lost causes" are the ones we don't fight for.

Warren, Rebecca Lowe, and Mary H. Thompson. *The Scientist Within You: Experiments and Biographies of Distinguished Women in Science.* Eugene, OR: ACI, 1994.

This is an instructor's guide for use with students in grades 3 through 7. It includes twenty-five discovery units with hands-on experiments based on the work of twenty-three women scientists and mathematicians.

*The National American Woman Suffrage Association (NAWSA) Collection, 1860–1920.*

This collection can be accessed on the Library of Congress's World Wide Web homepage at: http://lcweb2.loc.gov/ammemhome.html.

*United States History Video Collection: Post–War U.S.A.* Bala Cynwyd, PA: Schlessinger Video Productions, 1996. (35 minutes)

This video covers post–war prosperity and the roles of women, along with the rise of the consumer society, the Cold War, the Korean War, and the early civil rights movement.

# End-of-Unit Celebration

## Women's Rights Movement
## Research Project

Assign a topic to each student in your class. The student's responsibility is to research that topic and write a summary of important information. These summaries could then be shared orally and hung around the classroom or compiled into a booklet.

Susan B. Anthony

Clara Barton

Catherine Beecher

Mary McLeod Bethune

Dr. Elizabeth Blackwell

Hillary Rodham Clinton

The Declaration of Sentiments

Frederick Douglass

Jocelyn Elders

Geraldine Ferraro

Betty Friedan

The First Women's Rights Convention, held in Seneca Falls, NY on July 19, 1848

The Fourteenth Amendment to the Constitution

William Lloyd Garrison

Angelina Grimke

Sarah Grimke

Dr. Mae Jemison

Barbara Jordan

Abraham Lincoln

Mary Lyon

James Mott

Lucretia Mott

The National-American Woman Suffrage Association (NAWSA)

The Nineteenth Amendment to the Constitution

Rosa Parks

Jeanette Rankin

Janet Reno

Eleanor Roosevelt

Gerrit Smith

Elizabeth Cady Stanton

Gloria Steinem

Lucy Stone

Harriet Beecher Stowe

Title IX of the Higher Education Act of 1972

Sojourner Truth

Mary Wollstonecraft

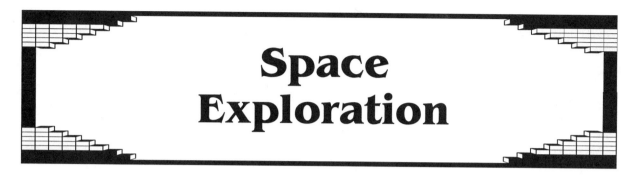

# Chapter 4

# Space Exploration

## Introduction

The age of space exploration began about twelve years before the first human stepped foot on the moon. The Soviet Union launched the first satellite to circle the earth on October 4, 1957, named *Sputnik* (Russian for "traveler"). It went on to launch nine more *Sputniks*, each designed to gather information for manned space flight. Satellites circling the earth today are commonplace, serving many purposes. They transmit television programs from around the world, they make it possible for us to talk to people from around the world on telephones, and they help scientists to make maps of the earth and gather weather information.

The first space vehicles were tested using animals. On November 2, 1957, the Soviet Union launched a dog named Laika into orbit. The first United States space traveler was a four-year-old chimpanzee named Ham in late 1957.

The first human to travel in space was Russian Yuri Gagarin. He blasted off in his *Vostok 1* spacecraft on April 12, 1961. *Vostok 1* made one full orbit of the earth. His mission lasted 108 minutes. Alan B. Shepard, a 37-year-old Navy commander, was the first American sent into space. Shepard's flight lasted only fifteen minutes, reaching a height of 115 miles. On February 20, 1962, Marine Corps Major John Glenn became the first American to orbit the earth in his *Friendship 7* spacecraft.

On June 3, 1965, astronauts Edward White and James McDivitt lifted off from Cape Kennedy in a *Gemini 4* spacecraft. White became the first American astronaut to perform a space walk. Three months earlier, a Soviet astronaut named Aleksei Leonov had done the same.

Astronauts Gus Grissom, Ed White, and Roger Chaffee were selected for the first of the manned *Apollo* test flights. While participating in a routine rehearsal on January 27, 1967 for their flight, a fire broke out in the capsule. Heat and smoke built up so quickly that the three astronauts were unable to escape and soon died. The precise cause of this human tragedy was never determined. However, it is thought that a spark, possibly caused by a short circuit, started the fire. An investigation led to the discovery of several problems with the design of the capsule.

Twenty-two months after the *Apollo 1* disaster, the Apollo program was ready to resume. The eleven-day earth-orbital flight of *Apollo 7* on October 11, 1986, which held astronauts Walter Schirra, Donn Eisele, and Walter Cunningham, was a success.

The flight of *Apollo 11* on July 16, 1969, carrying astronauts Neil Armstrong, Edwin Aldrin, Jr., and Michael Collins, was one of major historic proportions. On July 20, Armstrong and Aldrin landed on the moon aboard a lunar landing craft named *Eagle*. The words "Houston, Tranquility Base here. The *Eagle* has landed" from Armstrong prompted cheers at Mission Control in Houston. These two astronauts became the first humans to walk on the moon. The first words spoken on the moon by Neil Armstrong were the historic, "That's one small step for man, one giant leap for mankind." There were six moon landings between 1969 and 1972.

The flight of *Apollo 13* on April 11, 1970 began with a normal liftoff. Two days later, when the crew was nearly five-sixths of the way to the moon, disaster struck. A sharp bang and vibrations were felt by the crew, which included Jim Lovell, Fred W. Haise, Jr., and John L. Swigert, Jr. Swigert, who had replaced Ken Mattingly at the last minute as command module pilot, radioed, "Houston, we've had a problem here." It was soon discovered that an oxygen tank in the service module had exploded. In addition, two of the three electricity-producing fuel cells were inoperable. Another oxygen tank was leaking. When the tank was empty, the last fuel cell would be useless, leaving *Apollo 13* without power.

In order for *Apollo 13* to return to Earth it needed to use the moon's gravity and the thrust from the lander. The crew raced to abandon ship before the cockpit went cold, dead, and airless. They took refuge in the attached lunar lander that was built and equipped to keep two men alive for two days. However, there were three of them and they were four days from Earth. All unnecessary electrical devices were turned off and water was rationed. Cabin temperature plunged to thirty-eight degrees Fahrenheit. Six days after *Apollo 13*'s liftoff, it splashed down in the Pacific Ocean with all three members of the crew alive. Lovell, Haise, and Swigert were greeted with a celebration that included parades, speeches, and medals. However, the celebration soon ended and the press and public looked upon the *Apollo 13* mission as a failure.

In the early 1970s, the Soviet Union and the United States began experimenting with manned space stations, which orbited the earth. *Skylab*, the first United States space station, was sent into orbit in 1973. Astronauts aboard *Skylab* performed numerous experiments. Their main goal was to study the effects of weightlessness on humans over long periods of time.

The space shuttle *Columbia* made history on April 14, 1981, when it became the first reusable space vehicle to come back to Earth and land like an airplane. Space shuttles are officially known as Space Transportation Systems. NASA (the National Aeronautics and Space Administration) had developed four space shuttles by the late 1980s. *Columbia* was named after a Navy frigate launched in 1836. *Challenger* was named in honor of a Navy vessel that explored the Pacific and Atlantic Oceans from 1872 to 1876. *Discovery* was named after two ships: Henry Hudson's and James Cook's. *Atlantis* was named after a sailing ship from Woods Hole Oceanographic Institute.

The first United States female astronaut, Sally Kristen Ride, made history in June 1983 aboard the *Challenger*.

On January 28, 1986, the space shuttle launch of *Challenger* ended in disaster when it exploded soon after liftoff, killing the crew: Francis R. Scobee, Michael J. Smith, Judith A. Resnik, Ellison S. Onizuka, Ronald E. McNair, Gregory B. Jarvis, and Christa McAuliffe, the first teacher in space. This tragedy put a stop to space shuttle flights for almost three years while an investigation into the disaster was conducted and new safety features added to the remaining space shuttles.

Frequent space shuttle flights have taken place since 1988. One major international project that NASA is currently involved in is to build and operate a permanent manned space station. This orbiting facility will be ready for use early in the twenty-first century. Until then, NASA astronauts are working as guest scientists aboard the Russian space station *Mir*. The future of space exploration appears to be limitless. The trade books recommended in this chapter were chosen to assist teachers in widening students' knowledge of both the history of space flight and future space exploration. Begin your study of space history by reading aloud *One Giant Leap* by Mary Ann Fraser to your class.

## Whole Group Reading

Sullivan, George. *The Day We Walked on the Moon: A Photo History of Space Exploration*. New York: Scholastic, 1990.

Sullivan traces the technological advances that have made it possible to explore outer space and walk on the moon. He also discusses the training of astronauts and the future of space exploration. Grades 5–8.

## Author Information

George Sullivan was born August 11, 1927, in Lowell, Massachusetts. Sullivan has worked in public relations, as an adjunct professor of nonfiction writing from 1969 to 1972 at Fordham University in Bronx, New York, as well as working as a freelance writer since 1962.

Sullivan has written more than 100 nonfiction books, including *Mathew Brady, His Life and Photographs*; *Slave Ship: The Story of Henrietta Marie*; and *Black Artists As Photographers, 1840–1940*. In addition to writing the text, Sullivan also takes many of the photographs for his books. Several of his books are about sports, particularly baseball and football. Sullivan has written books for adults, but prefers to write for young people.

Getting ideas for his books has never been a problem for Sullivan. He says, "The ideas spring from my curiosity about people, places, and events."

## Activities

1. Have students research the following astronauts:

| | |
|---|---|
| Edwin "Buzz" Aldrin, Jr. | Gregory Jarvis |
| Joseph Allen | James Lovell, Jr. |
| William Anders | Christa McAuliffe |
| Neil Armstrong | James McDivitt |
| Frank Borman | Ronald McNair |
| Michael Collins | Ellison Onizuka |
| Robert Crippen | Judith Resnick |
| Ronald Evans | Sally Ride |
| John Fabian | Dr. Harrison Schmitt |
| Yuri Gagarin | Francis Scobee |
| Dale Gardner | Alan B. Shepard |
| John Glenn | Michael Smith |
| Robert Goddard | Valentina Tereshkova |
| Frederick Hauck | Dr. Norman Thagard |
| Steven Hawley | Edward White |
| Eugene Herman | John Young |

2.  Have students interview family members and teachers to find out what they remember about the first walk on the moon. Students could audiotape their responses and play them back for the rest of the class.

3.  Photocopy and enlarge as much as possible the front pages of *The New York Times* shown on pages 9, 15, 19, 36, 51, and 55, then display them in your classroom. Have students read these articles and write short summaries of them.

4.  Have students write an essay that answers the following questions: If you were an astronaut and landed on the moon, what would you want to leave there? Why?

5.  On a world map, have students locate:

    Australia                    Houston, TX
    China                        Los Angeles, CA
    Concord, NH                  Mojave Desert, CA

6.  Have students interview family members and teachers about the *Challenger* disaster on January 28, 1986. What do they remember about it?

7.  If your budget allows, purchase freeze-dried ice cream sandwiches for students to try. Students could also contribute money to pay for them. These are available at many science stores.

8.  The activity book *Space* by Mary Kay Carson contains a read-aloud play titled "Neil Armstrong: To the Moon!" This play is about the first moon landing of *Apollo 11* in 1969. Divide your class into two or three groups to read this play.

## Discussion

Give the class the following instruction: As we read this book, we will be discussing the following.

1.  What did Neil Armstrong say when he first set foot on the moon? When did this take place?

2.  Who joined Armstrong for the first walk on the moon?

3.  How do you think Michael Collins felt in the command ship while the other two astronauts walked on the moon?

4.  What chores did the astronauts have to do on the moon?

5.  How much time did the astronauts spend on the moon's surface?

6.  When did the space age begin?

7.  What country was the first to launch an artificial satellite? What was the name of the satellite?

8.  What was the purpose of artificial satellites?

9.  How do satellites help us today?

10. What did scientists have to do before humans could be sent into space?

11. What living beings were first sent into space? What experiments were conducted on these flights?

12. Who was the first human to travel in space? How long did his mission last?

13. Who was the first American astronaut to travel in space?

14. What type of food did the first astronauts eat in space?

15. What did astronaut John Glenn do after retiring from the space program?

16. Who was the first woman in space? Why was she seen as an inspiration to women around the world?

17. What was the purpose of *Intelstat 1*?

18. Who was the first American to walk in space?

19. What was the mission of *Apollo 8*?

20. How long did it take *Apollo 11* to reach the moon?

21. What happened when *Apollo 11* went behind the moon?

22. What did the plaque that *Apollo 17* astronauts left on the moon say?

23. What was life like aboard *Skylab*?

24. Why is it difficult to stay in shape in space? What did astronauts do to keep fit?

25. What is the jack-in-the-box effect?

26. How do astronauts take showers?

27. What was the main goal of *Skylab*? How long was it in space?

28. What are the three main stages of a space shuttle?

29. What new advantages did space shuttles provide?

30. What are the responsibilities of the shuttle commander or pilot?

31. What responsibilities does a payload specialist have?

32. What does a mission specialist do?

33. Discuss the training that astronauts receive before going into space.

34. Who was the first American woman astronaut?

35. What was the purpose of the November 1984 mission of the shuttle *Discovery*?

36. What types of scientific experiments have been conducted on *Space Lab*?

37. What happened to the space shuttle *Challenger* on January 28, 1986?

38. What had Christa McAuliffe planned to do in space?

39. What caused the explosion aboard *Challenger*?

40. Discuss the effect the *Challenger* disaster had on the space program.

41. What changes were made before the September 1988 flight of the shuttle *Discovery*?

42. What was the mission of the unmanned *Voyager 2*?

43. What is the Hubble Space Telescope?

44. What future projects are anticipated for the space program?

# Vocabulary

**clad** (p8)
an alternative past tense and past participle of clothe

**lunar** (p8)
of or having to do with the moon

**adheres** (p8)
sticks to

**gravity** (p8)
in physics, gravitation, especially as shown by the tendency of objects to fall toward the center of the earth

**barren** (p8)
empty; lacking

**orbit** (p8)
the path taken by a celestial body or artificial satellite as it moves around its center of attraction

**voyage** (p10)
a journey, such as one through air or space

**satellite** (p12)
an object launched by means of a rocket into an orbit around Earth or another celestial body

**alloys** (p12)
mixtures of two or more metals or of a metal and some other substance

**meteorite** (p12)
> a part of a meteor that is not burned up and strikes the earth as a lump of stone or metal

**space shuttle** (p13)
> a reusable space vehicle

**atmosphere** (p13)
> the air surrounding the earth

**hostile** (p14)
> of, having to do with, or belonging to an enemy

**radiation** (p14)
> the sending out of radiant energy, such as from radioactive substances

**venture** (p14)
> to expose to chance or risk; to place in danger; to hazard

**air pressure** (p14)
> the pressure of air in a confined space

**meteors** (p14)
> small fragments of matter from outer space that are heated white-hot by friction with the earth's atmosphere and appear briefly as streaks of light; shooting stars

**spherical** (p17)
> shaped like a sphere; round; globular

**horizon** (p17)
> the line where the earth and the sky seem to meet

**transition** (p17)
> the act or condition of changing from one form, place, type, or existence to another

**immortal** (p17)
> living, lasting, or remembered forever

**lob** (p17)
> to throw or toss slowly

**capsule** (p20)
> a compartment of a spacecraft designed to separate from the rocket during flight

**amateur** (p22)
> a person who practices any art, study, or sport for enjoyment but not for money

**sensation** (p22)
> great interest or excitement

**republic** (p22)
> a government in which the power is given to officials elected by and representing the people

**geologist** (p28)
> a person who specializes in the study of the origin, history, and structure of the earth, especially recorded in rocks

**cosmic** (p37)
> of or having to do with the universe or cosmos

**universe** (p37)
> the whole that is made up of everything that exists, including the earth, sun, stars, planets, and outer space

**physicist** (p37)
> a student of or a specialist in the science dealing with matter, energy, motion, and their interrelations, including the study of mechanics, heat, sound, light, electricity, and magnetism

**probe** (p37)
> to investigate or examine thoroughly

**deploy** (p38)
> to put in appropriate positions for use

**meteorology** (p38)
> the science that studies the atmosphere, winds, and weather

**immerse** (p41)
> to dip into liquid so as to cover completely

**salvage** (p46)
> to save

**astronomy** (p48)
> the study of the stars, planets, and other heavenly bodies, including information on their makeup, positions, and motions

**biology** (p48)
> the science of life and the ways in which living things grow, develop, and reproduce

**veteran** (p57)
> a person who has had much experience in doing something

# Small Group Reading

📖 Cohen, Daniel, and Susan Cohen. *Heroes of the Challenger*. New York: Pocket Books, 1986.

This book gives an account of the *Challenger* disaster on January 28, 1986, and information about each of the seven astronauts who were aboard. Grades 6 and up.

## Author Information

Daniel Cohen was born March 12, 1936, in Chicago, Illinois. Cohen attended the University of Illinois, where he received a degree in journalism in 1959.

Cohen has worked at Time, Inc. and at *Science Digest*, where he was assistant editor from 1960 to 1965 and managing editor from 1965 to 1969. He has been a full-time writer since 1969. He also speaks at universities, colleges, secondary schools, and elementary schools in the United States and Canada.

Cohen has written dozens of books for young adults and children. He and his wife, Susan, have written many books together.

Susan Cohen was born March 27, 1938, in Chicago, Illinois. She attended the University of Illinois from 1957 to 1959. She received a bachelor of arts degree from the New School for Social Research in 1960. In 1962 she received a master's degree in social work from Delphi University.

Susan Cohen's career has included stints as a social worker at Foster Care Riverdale Children's Association in New York City and the Travelers Aid Society.

Besides the books she has written with her husband, Daniel, she has also written several gothic novels and mysteries under the pseudonym Elizabeth St. Claim.

## Activities

1.  The authors state that most people will probably remember for the rest of their lives where they were and what they were doing when the *Challenger* exploded. Have students interview family members or teachers to find out what they remember.

2.  At the time the Cohens' book was written, the exact cause of the *Challenger* tragedy was unknown. Have students locate other sources to find out what was subsequently discovered about the explosion.

3.  On a world map, have students locate:

| | | |
|---|---|---|
| Akron, OH | Concord, NH | Philadelphia, PA |
| Annapolis, MD | Detroit, MI | Pittsburgh, PA |
| Arizona | Framingham, MA | Queens, NY |
| Atlanta, GA | Hawaii | Sacramento, CA |
| Auburn, WA | Houston, TX | San Antonio, TX |
| Beaufort, NC | Illinois | Seattle, WA |
| Bedford, NH | Kingsville, TX | Senegal, Africa |
| Bethesda, MD | Lake City, SC | Commonwealth of |
| Boston, MA | Lanham, MD | Independent States |
| Boulder, CO | Los Angeles, CA | (formerly the |
| Buffalo, NY | Malibu, CA | Soviet Union) |
| Cape Canaveral, FL | Miami, FL | Springfield, VA |
| Charlotte, NC | Mohawk, NY | Tacoma, WA |
| Cle Elum, WA | Morningside, MD | Utah |
| Cleveland, OH | New York City | Washington, DC |

4.  In chapter 15, the authors make some predictions about the future of the space program. Since this book was written in 1986, have students do some research to discover which of the predictions have come true and what further advances have been made.

## Discussion

Give the small group the following instruction: As your group reads this book, discuss the following.

1.  Who were the seven astronauts aboard the *Challenger* when it exploded?

2.  Why were many people taking space shuttle flights for granted by 1986?

3.  What made the *Challenger* shuttle flight special to the youth of America?

4.  Why were there delays of the launch of the *Challenger*?

5.  Describe what people saw when the *Challenger* exploded.

6.  What did television anchor Peter Jennings mean when he said, "We all shared in this experience in an instantaneous way because of television. I can't recall any time or crisis in history when television has had such an impact."?

7.  What plans did President Ronald Reagan change because of the *Challenger* tragedy?

8.  How did the nation react to the news of the explosion?

9.  What did the former Soviet Union do as a tribute to *Challenger* astronauts?

10. Describe Christa McAuliffe. What kind of person was she?

11. What made Christa McAuliffe a kind of ambassador in space?

12. Why did McAuliffe's death bring the *Challenger* disaster home to the world?

13. What was Gregory Jarvis like?

14. Why was Gregory Jarvis chosen as an astronaut candidate?

15. What experiments was Jarvis scheduled to complete on the *Challenger* mission?

16. How did Francis "Dick" Scobee surprise family and friends?

17. What led up to Dick Scobee becoming an astronaut?

18. What hobby did Michael J. Smith pursue as a high school student?

19. Who was Smith's hero?

20. What training did Smith receive prior to becoming an astronaut?

21. What awards and honors did Ronald McNair win in college?

22. What obstacles did McNair have to overcome where he grew up?

23. What did McNair do to promote educational opportunities?

24. Why did Judith Resnik decide to become an astronaut?

25. What were Resnik's duties aboard *Discovery* on her first shuttle flight?

26. What was Resnik to do on the *Challenger* mission?

27. Describe Ellison Onizuka.

28. Why did Onizuka feel that he had no chance of becoming an astronaut?

29. What "firsts" did Onizuka achieve by becoming an astronaut?

30. What caused the *Challenger* to explode?

31. What did engineers from the company that made the rocket boosters tell space agency officials the night before the *Challenger* liftoff?

32. What questions have been asked about how the disaster occurred?

33. What happened aboard *Apollo 13* on April 13, 1970?

34. Discuss other tragedies that have occurred in the United States and Soviet space programs.

35. Why was the launching of *Sputnik* by the Soviet Union a shock to Americans?

36. What effect did *Sputnik* have on the United States space program?

37. What did *Sputnik II* carry into space? Why?

38. Who were the seven original *Mercury* astronauts?

39. What made John Glenn's *Mercury* flight a major triumph?

40. Who was the first astronaut to walk in space? Who was the first American to walk in space?

41. What was the goal of project Apollo?

42. Discuss the achievement of *Apollo 11*. What made this mission so spectacular?

43. After the Apollo program, why did the space shuttle become the only active space project?

44. What are the advantages of the space shuttle? What has it been used for?

45. Who was the first American woman to go into space?

46. What have critics said about the space shuttle program?

47. Why was the *Voyager 2* mission so successful?

48. Why do some people argue against manned space flights?

## Vocabulary

**catastrophically** (p2)
    caused by, resulting in, or like a sudden and widespread misfortune, calamity, or disaster

**precaution** (p2)
    something done to avoid a possible danger

**amiss** (p2)
    out of order; wrong; imperfect

**remote** (p3)
    distant in relationship

**identify** (p3)
    to associate closely

**NASA** (p4)
    National Aeronautics and Space Administration

**deteriorated** (p5)
    made worse

**ultimately** (p6)
    in the end; at last; finally

**trivial** (p7)
    of little value or importance; insignificant

**ominous** (p7)
    threatening or foreboding, like a bad omen

**ascent** (p8)
    the act of rising or climbing

**nautical mile** (p9)
    a measure of distance equal to about 6,706 feet

**velocity** (p9)
    speed

**malfunction** (p11)
    a failure to work properly

**horizons** (p16)
    the limits of observation, knowledge, or experience

**exploits** (p16)
    brave or daring acts

**stoic** (p16)
    unaffected by pleasure or pain

**adversaries** (p17)
    opponents, such as in a contest; enemies

**tribute** (p17)
    something, such as a speech, compliment, or gift, given to show admiration, gratitude, or respect

**dignified** (p18)
    having dignity; proud; calm and stately

**admire** (p21)
    to regard or look on with wonder, pleasure, and approval

From *Teaching U.S. History Through Children's Literature.* © 1998 Wanda J. Miller. Teacher Ideas Press. (800) 237-6124.

**idealize** (p21)
  to regard or represent as perfect

**robust** (p21)
  strong; sturdy; vigorous

**ecstatic** (p21)
  full of or marked by a feeling of great
  happiness or delight

**prestige** (p22)
  fame, importance, or respect based on
  a person's reputation, power, or past
  achievements

**morale** (p22)
  state of mind, especially in terms of confidence, courage, or hope

**optimism** (p22)
  the tendency to see things on their bright
  side

**conventional** (p23)
  established by custom; customary; usual

**feminism** (p23)
  the principle that women should have the
  same political, social, and economic rights
  and opportunities as men

**pioneer** (p25)
  to lead the way, such as into new territory

**ambassador** (p28)
  any representative or messenger

**anticipation** (p28)
  expectation

**epitaph** (p28)
  the writing on a monument or gravestone in
  remembrance of the person who has died

**suburb** (p29)
  a place, such as a town, village, or district,
  that is close to a large city

**astonishing** (p33)
  amazing

**hectic** (p33)
  marked by or full of excitement, confusion,
  or haste

**moderation** (p33)
  the condition or quality of being not extreme
  or excessive

**persistence** (p36)
  the act of continuing firmly or stubbornly in
  spite of opposition, warning, or difficulty

**essential** (p43)
  extremely important or necessary; vital

**magna cum laude** (p47)
  Latin for "with great praise or high honor,"
  used to indicate a person who is graduating
  from a college or university with an excellent
  record

**physics** (p47)
  the science dealing with matter, energy,
  motion, and their interrelations, including
  the study of mechanics, heat, sound, light,
  electricity, and magnetism

**doctorate** (p47)
  the university degree or status of a doctor

**prestigious** (p47)
  having or giving prestige; honored or
  esteemed

**Ku Klux Klan (KKK)** (p48)
  a secret organization, founded in the southern United States after the Civil War, that
  advocates white supremacy

**rural** (p48)
  of or having to do with the country or with
  country things or people

**initiative** (p48)
  the first step in starting or doing something

**rustic** (p48)
  roughly or simply made

**segregation** (p48)
  the practice of separating a racial or religious
  group from the rest of society, such as in
  schools, housing, or parks

**decreed** (p48)
  formally ordered

**aspirant** (p50)
  a person who aspires, or tries to achieve
  honors or high position

**legacy** (p53)
  something left to others by a person who has
  died

**distinction** (p54)
  exceptional merit; honor

**intrigued** (p56)
  interested; fascinated

**maiden** (p56)
  of or having to do with the first use, trial, or
  experience

**bas mitzvah** (p56)
  a Jewish religious ceremony in which a
  thirteen-year-old girl is recognized as having
  reached the age of religious responsibility

**sorority** (p57)
    a social club for girls or women, often organized nationally and having local chapters in many schools, colleges, and universities

**pride** (p60)
    someone or something of which one is proud

**ancestor** (p61)
    a person from whom one is descended, generally further back than a grandparent; forebear

**modest** (p61)
    not boastful; humble

**lofty** (p63)
    very high

**elite** (p64)
    the social or professional group considered to be the best

**volatile** (p69)
    fickle; changeable

**debris** (p71)
    scattered fragments or remains; rubble

**revelation** (p73)
    something made known, especially something surprising

**inevitable** (p76)
    unavoidable; certain

**dehydration** (p79)
    the condition of losing water from the body

**perspective** (p82)
    a way of seeing and judging things in relation to one another; a point of view; an outlook

**primitive** (p83)
    simple or crude, like that of early ages

**astray** (p84)
    away from the right path

**erratically** (p87)
    unevenly or irregularly

**maneuver** (p90)
    any skillful move or action

**flagging** (p91)
    falling behind

**versatile** (p96)
    having many uses

**placid** (p100)
    calm; peaceful

**astronomer** (p103)
    a person who is an expert in the study of the stars, planets, and other heavenly bodies, including information on their makeup, positions, and motions

**skeptical** (p105)
    not believing readily; inclined to question or doubt

**rendezvous** (p110)
    a planned meeting

**deploy** (p110)
    to put in appropriate positions for use

## Small Group Reading

📖 Fichter, George S. *The Space Shuttle*. New York: Franklin Watts, 1990. This revised edition covers the history of the space shuttle's development, with information on its functions and on the flights of individual spacecraft. Grades 4–8.

## Author Information

George S. Fichter was born September 17, 1922, in Hamilton, Ohio. Fichter's career has included stints as an instructor in zoology at Miami University in Oxford, Ohio, editor of *Fisherman* magazine from 1950 to 1956, and writer and editor of natural history books for young people.

Fichter has written dozens of books, including *Rocks and Minerals*, *Reptiles and Amphibians* and *Cells*. He has also written several hundred articles that have been published in *Reader's Digest*, *Coronet*, *Science Digest*, and other magazines.

## Activities

1. On a world map, have students locate:

   Alabama
   Atlantic Ocean
   Concord, NH
   Florida
   Germany
   Houston, TX

   Indian Ocean
   Kitty Hawk, NC
   Los Angeles, CA
   Mojave Desert
   Palmdale, CA
   Commonwealth of Independent States
   (formerly the Soviet Union)

2. Have students in this group make a poster listing the uses of satellites, then hang the poster in the classroom.

3. The author talks about the future of the Hubble Space Telescope. Have students research this telescope, including its problems and how they were fixed and what the Hubble has been used for. They can then present their findings to the rest of the class.

4. Have students research which space stations are in operation. What experiments have been completed aboard these space stations? Have there been any problems with them? Students can outline the information they obtain on a poster to be hung in the classroom.

## Discussion

Give the small group the following instruction: As your group reads this book, discuss the following questions.

1. Why is the space shuttle sometimes called the "sky truck"?

2. What are space shuttles used for?

3. What do scientists predict about the future in space?

4. Who made the first powered flight by airplane? When did it take place?

5. Who is considered the "Father of American Rocketry"?

6. What country began the "Space Age"? What did it send into space?

7. When did the United States active space program begin?

8. Who was the first person to go into space?

9. Who became the first American in space?

10. Why do you think that many Americans believed that the United States's reputation was at stake based on the space program?

11. What was astronaut John Glenn, Jr.'s accomplishment in space?

12. What mission made the United States the leader in the space race? What took place on this mission?

13. Why did people begin to question the space program?

14. When was the first space shuttle transportation system developed?

15. What problems were found in the testing of the space shuttle *Columbia*?

16. When was the first space shuttle transportation system launched?

17. Who were the astronauts aboard the first shuttle flight?

18. What were the goals of that first flight?

19. How did the space shuttle *Columbia* earn money for NASA?

20. Who was the first American woman to travel in space?

21. What experiments were conducted aboard the first flight of *Challenger* in 1983?

22. Who was the first black American to travel in space?

23. What did astronauts Bruce McCandless and Robert Stewart do during *Challenger's* February 1984 mission? What nicknames did they receive?

24. Why was the Long Duration Exposure Facility left in space? How did schoolchildren become involved in its experiments?

25. Who was aboard *Challenger* on January 28, 1986? Why was there so much publicity surrounding this flight?

26. What caused the explosion aboard *Challenger*?

27. How did the *Challenger* disaster affect the space program?

28. How was the flight of *Discovery* on September 29, 1988, like that of the first flight of *Columbia*?

29. What plans did NASA make after the *Discovery* flight?

30. What space shuttle was built to replace the *Challenger*?

31. How do metals react differently in space than they do on Earth?

32. What experiments were planned for completion aboard *Spacelab*?

33. What are satellites used for?

34. How do space stations operate?

35. What does the author predict about space colonization?

36. What is the objective of colonizing space?

37. What are some of the possible dangers space colonies would face?

## Vocabulary

**orbit** (p9)
the path taken by a celestial body or artificial satellite as it moves around its center of attraction

**glider** (p9)
a light aircraft like an airplane but without an engine (it is kept aloft by air currents)

**astronomer** (p11)
a person who is an expert in the study of the stars, planets, and other heavenly bodies, including information on their makeup, positions, and motions

**visionary** (p11)
idealistic but not practical

**skeptics** (p11)
people who doubt or disbelieve things that many people accept as fact or truth

**conquest** (p12)
something conquered, such as territory

**gravity** (p13)
in physics, gravitation, especially as shown by the tendency of objects to fall toward the center of the earth

**primitive** (p13)
simple or crude, like that of early ages

**missile** (p14)
an object, especially a weapon, intended to be thrown or shot, such as a bullet, arrow, stone, or guided missile

**emigrate** (p14)
to move from one country or section of a country to settle in another

**NASA** (p14)
National Aeronautics and Space Administration

**cosmonaut** (p14)
a Russian astronaut

**decade** (p17)
a period of ten years

**reputation** (p17)
the general estimation in which a person or thing is held by others

**sentiment** (p19)
an attitude, opinion, or feeling

**drastically** (p19)
severely

From *Teaching U.S. History Through Children's Literature*. © 1998 Wanda J. Miller. Teacher Ideas Press. (800) 237-6124.

**authorized** (p19)
approved

**cargo** (p19)
freight carried by a vehicle such as a ship or aircraft

**subcontract** (p21)
an agreement between a person who has already agreed to do some work and another person, whereby the second person agrees to do some or all of the work

**friction** (p22)
the rubbing of one object against another

**astonishing** (p22)
surprising

**delicate** (p23)
weak or easily damaged

**subjected** (p23)
affected by

**endure** (p23)
to bear up under; to stand firm against

**welding** (p23)
the process of uniting pieces of metal by softening them with heat and pressing them together

**synchronization** (p26)
the condition of moving together or occurring at the same time or speed

**altitude** (26)
the height above any given point, especially above sea level

**descent** (p26)
the action of going or coming down to a lower point

**disintegrating** (p26)
breaking apart into small pieces or fragments; crumbling

**atmosphere** (p26)
the air surrounding the earth

**spacious** (p28)
having much space; large

**verify** (p29)
to prove to be true or accurate; to confirm

**anxious** (p29)
causing or marked by anxiety; worrying

**enthusiasm** (p30)
keen interest or liking

**transcontinental** (p31)
going from one side of the continent to the other

**potential** (p31)
possible, but not yet actual

**donned** (p32)
put on

**astrophysicist** (p32)
a person who is an expert in the science dealing with the physical properties and chemical composition of celestial bodies

**versatile** (p32)
having many uses

**payload** (p34)
the load of a spacecraft that includes people, scientific instruments, and other things directly related to the purpose of the flight, as distinguished from things needed to operate the spacecraft

**orientation** (p36)
the act of placing, setting, or adjusting in some position, especially in relation to the points of the compass

**ambitious** (p39)
requiring great skill or much effort for success; challenging; difficult

**synthetic** (p39)
in chemistry, produced artificially by synthesis rather than occurring naturally

**fragile** (p44)
easily shattered or broken; delicate

**debris** (p44)
scattered fragments or remains; rubble

**conservative** (p44)
moderate; cautious

**sphere** (p52)
a surface that has all its points the same distance from its center; a ball

**alloy** (p52)
a mixture of two or more metals or of a metal and some other substance

**cyclone** (p54)
a storm in which winds whirl spirally toward a center of low pressure, which also moves

**hurricane** (p54)
a storm with heavy rains and whirling winds of 75 miles per hour or more, usually beginning in the tropics, often the West Indies

**agriculture** (p54)
the art or science of cultivating the soil; the raising of crops, livestock, or both; farming

**cosmic** (p54)
of or having to do with the universe or cosmos

**universe** (p54)
the whole that is made up of everything that exists, including the earth, sun, stars, planets, and outer space

**surveillance** (p54)
the act of watching or supervising closely

**ultimate** (p54)
last, final, or eventual

**arrays** (p54)
large or impressive displays

**fusion** (p57)
the union at very high temperatures of nuclei of light atoms, forming nuclei of heavier atoms and releasing enormous energy

**perimeter** (p57)
outer boundary

**ample** (p58)
abundant; liberal

**habitat** (p58)
a place where someone or something lives; a dwelling

**objective** (p60)
a goal or an end

**physics** (p60)
the science dealing with matter, energy, motion, and their interrelations, including the study of mechanics, heat, sound, electricity, and magnetism

**adequate** (p60)
equal to what is needed; good enough or sufficient

**artificial** (p61)
made by a person or persons; unnatural

**catastrophic** (p61)
caused by, resulting in, or like a sudden widespread misfortune, calamity, or disaster

## Small Group Reading

📖 Mikaelsen, Ben. *Countdown*. New York: Hyperion Books for Children, 1996.

In two parallel stories, a fourteen-year-old boy who is NASA's first Junior Astronaut and a fourteen-year-old Maasai boy in Kenya both face maturity while questioning their family traditions. Grades 5 and up.

## Author Information

Ben Mikaelsen was born November 24, 1952 in La Paz, Bolivia. He attended Concordia College in Moorhead, Minnesota and Bemidji State University in Bemidji, Minnesota.

Mikaelsen owned an awards and office supply business from 1980 to 1984. From 1984 to 1985 he owned a woodworking business. He has worked as a writer since 1985.

Mikaelsen and his wife live in Bozeman, Montana, where they adopted and raised a black bear cub named Buffy. The Fish and Game Department in Bozeman learned about their success with Buffy and brought them other orphaned black bear cubs to raise. Some of these cubs were later destroyed because no home could be found for them. Mikaelsen used this experience for the premise of his book *Rescue Josh McGuire*.

Of his writing, Mikaelsen says, "The secret to happiness has been described to me as doing whatever you do with a passion, to the best of your ability, and for others. Writing has given me this happiness."

# Activities

1.  On a world map, have students locate:

    Allentown, PA
    Argentina
    Big Timber, MT
    Canada
    Colorado
    Florida
    France
    Germany
    Houston, TX
    Huntsville, AL
    Indian Ocean
    Israel

    Kenya, Africa
    Maryland
    Morocco
    Nairobi
    New Zealand
    Pasadena, CA
    Saudi Arabia
    Senegal, Africa
    Spain
    Virginia
    Washington
    Washington, DC

2.  Have students research astronaut Neil Armstrong, then write a short biography and present it to the rest of the class.

3.  The following similes and metaphors were used by the author of this book.

    **Similes:**

    "Moving as silently as a cheetah, he walked to the edge of the corral and crouched in the dark."

    "The boys' chants rose like the howling of the wind."

    "As clever as a four-legged chair that does not walk."

    "After declaring an emergency, the Shuttle swarmed with activity like a beehive smacked with a stick."

    **Metaphor:**

    "A coward is the hyena that growls with a tail between its legs."

    Have students write five similes and five metaphors of their own.

4.  Divide the small group into two smaller groups. One group should research the Andromeda Galaxy and the other should research the Milky Way. The information they gather can be placed on posters to display in the classroom.

# Discussion

Give the small group the following instruction: As your group reads this book, discuss the following.

1.  What is Elliot's dream?

2.  What was the announcement made by NASA that Elliot is so excited about?

3.  Why doesn't Vincent go to school any longer?

4.  Why do you think Elliot decided not to shoot Old Crow Leg?

5.  How does Vincent feel about the infirmary?

6.  Why does Vincent have a large hole in his lower ear?

7.  When Vincent attended school, why was he only allowed to speak English?

8.  Discuss Elliot's reaction to the announcement from NASA. How would you feel if you were Elliot?

9.  How does Vincent feel about becoming a warrior? Why?

10. What did Elliot learn about what his job would be on the space shuttle mission?

11. Why is Vincent's father angry with him?

12. According to Vincent, how are humans different from animals?

13. During orientation, what did the guide tell Elliot and Mandy about their mission?

14. Why did it rain during the test firing of the space shuttle?

15. What was Vincent's punishment for the loss of three cows?

16. What is the secret of survival?

17. What else did Mandy and Elliot learn about wilderness survival?

18. How does Vincent feel about the white man?

19. What should Elliot and Mandy have done differently in the wilderness?

20. What did Elliot and Mandy learn in the classroom sessions?

21. How do astronauts go to the bathroom in space?

22. What did Vincent mean when he told his father, "Papa, if truth needs proof, there is no honor"?

23. What is Vincent's dream?

24. How were Elliot and Mandy tested for motion sickness?

25. Mandy and Elliot were told that they are part of a search for secrets. What does this mean?

26. Why doesn't Vincent trust the white man?

27. What did Mandy and Elliot learn to do during the orientation to the Orbiter simulator?

28. How is space food different than it used to be?

29. What do you think Elliot learned from the problems he faced in the altitude chamber?

30. Following the ceremony Embolata Olketeng, what did the elder say about bravery? Do you agree?

31. Discuss your feelings about Elliot's admission to Mandy, Mr. Boslow, and Ms. Lopex.

32. Why did the astronaut review board decide to keep Elliot as the first Junior Astronaut?

33. Why did Vincent decide to kill a lion? Do you think he will follow through with his decision?

34. In what ways does the human body physically change in space?

35. What happened to Leboo?

36. What did Elliot and Mandy learn about the atmosphere?

37. How have Vincent's feelings about the Maasai changed?

38. Discuss Elliot's feelings as it gets closer to launch time. How would you feel?

39. When Elliot had finished setting up the radio equipment on the space shuttle, from whom did he hear?

40. Discuss the difference in the cultures from which Vincent and Elliot come.

41. How are Elliot's and Vincent's fathers alike?

42. Why do you think people around the world are interested in Elliot's conversations with Vincent?

43. Why didn't Sambeke call Vincent Dreamer Boy when he and Peninah left the infirmary?

44. When Commander Beaman told Elliot, "Boundaries exist only in our minds," what did he mean?

45. According to Commander Beaman, why is the earth on a countdown?

46. What is the problem aboard the *Endeavor*?

47.   Why do you think NASA wants Elliot and Vincent to meet?

48.   Discuss your feelings about the meeting between Elliot and Vincent.

49.   Reread the last paragraph of the novel, on page 246. What did the author mean?

# Vocabulary

**sagebrush** (p1)
a bitter herb or small shrub with white or yellow flowers, found on the dry plains of the western United States

**gunnysack** (p1)
a sack made from a coarse, heavy material such as burlap

**NASA** (p2)
National Aeronautics and Space Administration

**aptitude** (p3)
natural ability or capacity

**ludicrous** (p4)
causing laughter, scorn, or ridicule; ridiculous; absurd

**revitalize** (p4)
to give life, energy, or vigor to again

**wildebeest** (p6)
another name for a gnu, a large antelope of South Africa with a head like an ox's, curved horns, a mane, and a long tail

**ravine** (p10)
a long, narrow, deep depression in the earth that has steep sides and was usually cut out by a flow of water; a gorge

**instinctively** (p10)
done with a natural tendency or impulse

**majestic** (p10)
having great beauty; stately; royal

**infirmary** (p12)
a place for treating the sick

**toga** (p13)
a loose outer garment

**honor** (p15)
fairness, rightness, and honesty

**pride** (p15)
a proper sense of one's own dignity and worth; self-respect

**stethoscope** (p15)
a small, portable instrument by which doctors can hear sounds produced in the chest, especially in the lungs and heart

**proverbs** (p19)
old and often repeated sayings of advice or wisdom

**mongoose** (p20)
a small animal of Asia and Africa that resembles the ferret and preys on snakes and rats

**jackal** (p22)
a doglike mammal of Asia and Africa that feeds on small animals and decaying carcasses

**ghetto** (p27)
any section of a city or town crowded with a minority or the very poor

**corral** (p28)
an enclosed space or pen for livestock

**taunted** (p30)
insulted, provoked, or made fun of with scornful, mocking, or sarcastic remarks

**cockpit** (p34)
a compartment in an airplane where the pilot sits

**adrenaline** (p35)
a hormone produced by the adrenal glands that raises blood pressure, quickens breathing, and prepares the body for activity or defense

**altimeter** (p36)
an instrument for measuring height, used in aviation to determine how high a plane is flying

**vultures** (p38)
large birds that feed mostly on decaying flesh

**tarmac** (p39)
an airport runway

**physiology** (p40)
the study of the activities of a living organism or of the functions of any of its organs, parts, or systems

**lariat** (p45)
a long rope having a loop with a slip knot at one end, used for catching horses and cattle; a lasso

**calabash** (p47)
a bowl made from the gourdlike fruit of a calabash tree

**perspective** (p54)
a way of seeing and judging thoughts in relation to one another; a point of view; an outlook

**atmosphere** (p55)
the air surrounding the earth

**jargon** (p81)
the special words or terms used by the members of a particular profession

**egress** (p81)
the act of going out

**ocher** (p84)
an earthy material containing iron that varies in color from light yellow to deep orange or red and is used as a pigment

**toga** (p85)
a loose outer garment

**queasy** (p90)
sick to the stomach

**g forces** (p90)
gravitational forces

**gait** (p91)
a way of walking, stepping, or running

**astronomy** (p92)
the study of the stars, planets, and other heavenly bodies, including information on their makeup, positions, and motions

**conjunction** (p92)
combination; association

**mystical** (p92)
having a quality or meaning that is spiritual and beyond human reason

**prism** (p92)
a transparent glass object, triangular in cross section, that can break up white light into rainbow colors

**cosmos** (p93)
the universe thought of as a complete and harmonious system

**quasar** (p94)
a very distant celestial object that emits radio waves and light whose spectrum indicates that it is moving at very high speeds away from the earth

**black holes** (p94)
stars that have contracted under their own gravitation and become so dense that nothing, not even light, can escape their gravitational field

**bullock** (p96)
a steer or ox

**ingress** (p99)
the act of going in or the right to go in

**nominal** (p99)
small

**acquisition** (p99)
the act of coming into possession of; obtaining

**abort** (p100)
to end (the project or mission of a space vehicle or missile) before it is completed

**stabilize** (p100)
to steady the motion of (an aircraft or ship) by means of a stabilizer

**deploy** (p100)
to put in appropriate position for use

**decompression** (p101)
the lowering or removing of air pressure

**buoyancy** (p110)
the ability to keep afloat

**metabolism** (p119)
all the processes by which a plant or animal converts materials taken from its environment into the energy required to maintain itself, grow, and carry on all vital activities

**urgency** (p125)
the need or demand for prompt action or attention

**ozone** (p126)
an unstable form of oxygen having a sharp odor, produced by electric sparks in the air

**quarantine** (p130)
the keeping of persons or things that have been infected by or exposed to contagious diseases away from other people or things

**stratosphere** (p141)
a layer of the atmosphere beginning about seven miles up, in which temperatures are more or less uniform and clouds are rare

**trajectory** (p149)
> the curved path followed by a projectile or comet in its flight

**sporadically** (p152)
> occasionally

**aurora borealis** (p162)
> a richly colored display of lights seen in the night sky near the North Pole; the northern lights

**folklore** (p162)
> the beliefs, stories, and customs preserved among a people or tribe

**custom** (p181)
> something that has become an accepted practice by many people

**exotic** (p197)
> strangely different and fascinating

**typhoon** (p199)
> a violent hurricane originating over tropical waters in the western Pacific Ocean and the China Seas

**ambient** (p201)
> surrounding

**turbulent** (p233)
> being in violent agitation or commotion; disturbed

**sonic boom** (p234)
> a disturbance in the atmosphere, heard as a loud clap of thunder, made by an airplane flying faster than the speed of sound

# Bibliography

## Individual Titles

Allen, Joseph P., with Russell Martin. *Entering Space: An Astronaut's Odyssey*. New York: Stewart, Tabori & Chang, 1986.
Joseph Allen, an astronaut, shares with readers his firsthand insights into traveling in space. He describes a shuttle flight, the challenges of working in space, the emotional impact of seeing Earth from space, and the drama of the descent and landing. Included are more than 200 color photographs taken by astronauts. Grades 5 and up.

Asimov, Isaac. *Isaac Asimov's Library of the Universe: Piloted Space Flights*. Milwaukee, WI: Gareth Stevens, 1990.
Asimov gives a brief history of the human experience in space, including circling the earth and landing on the moon. Grades 4 and up.

Baird, Anne. *Space Camp: The Great Adventure for NASA Hopefuls*. New York: Morrow Junior Books, 1992.
Test and photographs follow young campers as they experience NASA-style astronaut training at the United States Space Camp in Huntsville, Alabama. Grades 4–8.

Baker, Wendy. *America in Space*. New York: Crescent Books, 1986.
Through text and photographs, the author covers America's first ventures in space exploration and our future in space. Grades 6 and up.

Barrett, N. S. *The Picture World of Space Shuttles*. New York: Franklin Watts, 1990.
Barrett discusses how space shuttles work and looks at selected space shuttle missions. Grades 3–6.

Belew, Leland F., ed. *Skylab, Our First Space Station*. Washington, D.C.: National Aeronautic and Space Administration, 1977.
This book contains a wealth of information about *Skylab*, as well as many photographs. Grades 5 and up.

Bendick, Jeanne. *Artificial Satellites: Helpers in Space*. Brookfield, CT: Millbrook Press, 1991.
Bendick answers children's questions about artificial satellites. What are they? What do they do? How do they work? How do they get up into space? Grades 3–5.

——. *Space Travel*. New York: Franklin Watts, 1982.
Bendick describes space, the planets in our solar system, and what it would be like to travel and live in space. Grades 5–8.

Benford, Timothy B., and Brian Wilkes. *The Space Program Quiz & Fact Book*. New York: Harper & Row, 1985.
This book is full of questions and answers concerning the United States and Russian space programs. It includes a comprehensive appendix of information and more than fifty photographs from the files of the National Aeronautics and Space Administration. Grades 4–8.

Berliner, Don. *Living in Space*. Minneapolis, MN: Lerner, 1993.

Berliner describes spacecraft design features, the preparation and eating of food, personal hygiene, exercise, safety, and relationships between astronauts living in space. Grades 5 and up.

———. *Our Future in Space*. Minneapolis, MN: Lerner, 1991.

Berliner examines current space research and future space projects such as a permanent space station, an observatory and research base on the moon, and the search for extraterrestrial life. Grades 5 and up.

Blocksma, Mary, and Dewey Blocksma. *Easy to Make Spaceships That Really Fly*. Englewood Cliffs, NJ: Prentice-Hall, 1983.

The authors provide directions for spaceships that can be made without adult supervision from paper plates, straws, styrofoam cups, and other materials. Suggestions are included for designing one's own spaceships. Grades 3–7.

Blumberg, Rhoda. *The First Travel Guide to the Moon*. New York: Scholastic, 1980.

This book provides information about the moon for future travelers. Grades 4–7.

Boyne, Walter J. *The Smithsonian Book of Flight for Young People*. New York: Aladdin Books, 1988.

This book traces the history of flight with text and photos from the first unmanned balloon flights through the record-breaking, around-the-world flight of the *Voyager*. Grades 5 and up.

Branley, Franklyn M. *Columbia and Beyond: The Story of the Space Shuttle*. New York: William Collins, 1979.

Branley discusses the space shuttle *Columbia*, *Spacelab*, and other proposed space projects. Grades 5–8.

———. *From Sputnik to Space Shuttles: Into the New Space Age*. New York: Thomas Y. Crowell, 1986.

Branley provides information on the history of artificial satellites from the launching of *Sputnik* to developments in the mid-1980s and discusses how these satellites have aided in communications, weather forecasting, and scientific experiments. Grades 6 and up.

———. *Space Colony: Frontier of the 21st Century*. New York: Elsevier/Nelson Books, 1982.

Branley discusses the future in space, particularly that of space colonies. Grades 6 and up.

Briggs, Carole S. *Women in Space: Reaching the Last Frontier*. Minneapolis, MN: Lerner, 1988.

The author profiles the lives of many of the women who have participated in space programs in the United States, Russia, Canada, and Japan; describes their training; and highlights their achievements. Grades 4–8.

Burleigh, Robert. *Flight: The Journey of Charles Lindbergh*. New York: Philomel, 1991.

Burleigh tells the story of Charles Lindbergh's solo flight across the Atlantic Ocean in 1927. Grades 2–6.

Burns, Khephra, and William Miles. *Black Stars in Orbit: NASA's African-American Astronauts*. San Diego, CA: Harcourt Brace, 1995.

This is the inspiring story of African Americans who have taken their place in space exploration and discovery. Grades 5 and up.

Butterfield, Moira. *Look Inside Cross-Sections: Space*. New York: Dorling Kindersley, 1994.

Detailed drawings show the insides of every spacecraft, from the early *Mercury* capsules to the multileveled space shuttle and the Hubble telescope. The book includes a glossary, a time line, an index, and large illustrations of eleven different spacecrafts. Grades 4 and up.

Cassutt, Michael. *Who's Who in Space: The First 25 Years*. Boston: G. K. Hall, 1987.

This book contains short biographies of astronauts involved during the first 25 years of space exploration. Grades 5 and up.

Chadwick, Roxane. *Amelia Earhart: Aviation Pioneer*. Minneapolis, MN: Lerner, 1987.

Chadwick traces the life of the pilot who became the first woman to fly across the Atlantic Ocean. Grades 4–6.

Cole, Joanna. *The Magic School Bus Lost in the Solar System*. New York: Scholastic, 1990.

On a special field trip in the magic school bus, Ms. Frizzle's class goes into outer space and visits each planet in the solar system. Grades 2–4.

Cole, Michael D. *John Glenn: Astronaut and Senator*. Hillside, NJ: Enslow, 1993.

Cole describes the life of John Glenn, from his childhood in Ohio, through his days as an astronaut, to his political career. Grades 4–8.

Collins, Michael. *Liftoff: The Story of America's Adventure in Space*. New York: Grove Press, 1988.

A history of space exploration from *Apollo 11* to the space shuttle program and beyond. Grades 8 and up.

Cross, Wilbur, and Susanna Cross. *Space Shuttle*. Chicago: Childrens Press, 1985.

This book discusses the history and development of the space shuttle, and how our lives will be affected by it. Grades 5–8.

Dunham, Montrew. *Neil Armstrong: Young Flyer*. New York: Aladdin, 1996.

Dunham presents the childhood of the man who would be the first person to walk on the moon. Grades 3–7.

Dwiggins, Don. *Flying the Space Shuttles*. New York: Dodd, Mead, 1985.

Dwiggins describes the history and uses of the space shuttle, how it works, and the details of a typical flight. Grades 4–8.

Earhart, Amelia. *Last Flight*. New York: Harcourt Brace, 1937.

In her own words, Earhart describes her career. Part of the book was written before her final flight, and the rest was sent by cable and telephone as she flew around the world. Grades 7 and up.

Embury, Barbara. *The Dream Is Alive: A Flight of Discovery Aboard the Space Shuttle*. New York: Harper & Row, 1990.

Through text and numerous photographs, Embury documents the experiences of those who have participated in space shuttle flights. Grades 4 and up.

English, June A., and Thomas D. Jones. *Mission: Earth: Voyage to the Home Planet*. New York: Scholastic, 1996.

When the *Endeavour* space shuttle lifted off in April 1994, its mission was to give the Space Radar Lab a look at Earth. The combination of three different radar echoes would provide scientists a complete picture of Earth, as they would be able to see through clouds, underneath sand, and beneath dense forests. Coauthor Thomas D. Jones was an astronaut aboard this flight. This book chronicles the mission through text, photographs, and radar images. Grades 5 and up.

Fox, Mary Virginia. *Women Astronauts Aboard the Shuttle*. New York: Messner, 1984.

Fox describes the June 1983 flight of the space shuttle with emphasis on the experiences of Sally Ride, the first American woman to fly in space. She also includes brief biographies of eight women astronauts who discuss their training and their future participation in space flights. Grades 5 and up.

Fraser, Mary Ann. *One Giant Leap*. New York: Henry Holt, 1993.

This book, full of realistic paintings and diagrams, gives an account of the expedition of *Apollo 11* to the moon. Grades 4–7.

Freedman, Russell. *The Wright Brothers: How They Invented the Airplane*. New York: Holiday House, 1991.

This book traces the lives of the Wright brothers and describes how they developed the first airplane. Grades 4–8.

Gaffney, Timothy R. *Grandpa Takes Me to the Moon*. New York: Tambourine Books, 1996.

A child whose grandfather was an astronaut always asks Grandpa for a bedtime story in which the two of them blast off to the moon together. Grades 1–3.

———. *Kennedy Space Center*. Chicago: Childrens Press, 1987.

Gaffney describes the history and work of the John F. Kennedy Space Center located on Merritt Island on the east coast of Florida. Grades 2–4.

Gold, Susan Dudley. *To Space and Back: The Story of the Shuttle*. New York: Crestwood House, 1992.

Gold examines the history, uses, and accomplishments of the space shuttle program. Grades 5 and up.

Hart, Philip S. *Flying Free: America's First Black Aviators*. Minneapolis, MN: Lerner, 1992.

Hart presents the history of black aviators, from the early black aviation communities in Los Angeles and Chicago in the 1920s through World War II to the present day. Grades 5–8.

———. *Up in the Air: The Story of Bessie Coleman*. Minneapolis, MN: Carolrhoda, 1996.

Hart presents the story of Bessie Coleman, an American who in 1920 traveled to France to become the first black woman to earn a pilot's license. Grades 4–7.

Hartmann, William K., Ron Miller, and Pamela Lee. *Out of the Cradle: Exploring the Frontiers Beyond Earth*. New York: Workman, 1984.

Astronomer William Hartmann and his coauthors explore the new landmarks within our reach and the possibilities for space exploration in the future. Grades 7 and up.

Haskins, Jim, and Kathleen Benson. *Space Challenger: The Story of Guion Bluford*. Minneapolis, MN: Carolrhoda Books, 1984.

This is a biography of Guion Bluford, the first black American in space, and a crew member of the space shuttle *Challenger* August 1983 flight. Grades 4–7.

Hawkes, Nigel. *New Technology: Space and Aircraft.* New York: Twenty-First Century Books, 1994.
Hawkes gives detailed information regarding the technology of flight, including helicopters, space probes, supersonic jets, balloons, and space shuttles. Grades 4 and up.

Hurwitz, Jane, and Sue Hurwitz. *Sally Ride: Shooting for the Stars.* New York: Fawcett Columbine, 1989.
This is a biography of Sally Kristen Ride, the first U.S. woman astronaut to be sent into space. Grades 5-8.

Kerrod, Robin. *Living in Space.* New York: Crescent Books, 1986.
This book provides information on training for spaceflight, space stations and laboratories, colonization of the solar system, and space stations of the future. More than 140 photographs are included. Grades 5 and up.

Kettlekamp, Larry. *Living in Space.* New York: Morrow Junior Books, 1993.
This is the story of living in space, of achievements, goals, and dreams for the future in space exploration. Grades 5 and up.

Kluger, Jeffrey. *The Apollo Adventure: The Making of the Apollo Space Program and the Movie* Apollo 13. New York: Pocket Books, 1995.
This book gives readers an inside look at the Apollo space program, starting with *Apollo 1* in 1967. In particular, the author provides an account of the *Apollo 13* flight, which nearly ended in tragedy. An inside view of the making of the movie *Apollo 13*, which depicts this event, rounds out the book. Grades 6 and up.

Larsen, Anita. *Amelia Earhart: Missing, Declared Dead.* New York: Crestwood House, 1992.
Larsen reviews the mystery surrounding Amelia Earhart's disappearance in 1937 while attempting a flight around the world. Grades 4–7.

Lauber, Patricia. *Journey to the Planets.* New York: Crown, 1993.
Lauber explores the planets of our solar system, highlighting the prominent features of each. Photographs and information gathered by the *Voyager* and *Magellan* explorations are included. Grades 4–7.

———. *Lost Star: The Story of Amelia Earhart.* New York: Scholastic, 1988.
Lauber traces the life of the pilot who became the first woman to fly across the Atlantic Ocean and mysteriously disappeared in 1937 while attempting to fly around the world. Grades 4–6.

———. *Meteors and Meteorites: Voyagers from Space.* New York: Thomas Y. Crowell, 1989.
Lauber discusses asteroids, comets, and meteorites, explaining where they come from, how they were formed, and what effect these missiles from space have when they streak past Earth or plummet to its surface. Grades 4–8.

Livingston, Myra Cohn. *Earth Songs.* New York: Holiday House, 1986.
A poetic tribute to the earth, its continents, hills, forests, and seas. Grades 2–5.

———. *Space Songs.* New York: Holiday House, 1988.
An illustrated collection of poems about outer space. Grades 2–5.

Long, Kim. *The Astronaut Training Book for Kids.* New York: Lodestar, 1990.
Long discusses the history and potential of astronautics and provides information about the education and training necessary to become an astronaut. Grades 3 and up.

Lopez, Donald S. *The National Air and Space Museum: A Visit in Pictures.* Washington, DC: Smithsonian Institution Press, 1989.
Text and photographs take readers on a tour through the National Air and Space Museum. Grades 4–7.

Markle, Sandra. *Pioneering Space.* New York: Atheneum, 1992.
Markle describes how spacecrafts work, how space stations function, and how people live in these environments. Grades 4 and up.

Mason, Robert Grant, ed. *Life in Space.* Alexandria, VA: Time–Life Books, 1983.
This book chronicles each space mission through the *Challenger* flight on April 9, 1983. Grades 5 and up.

Maurer, Richard. *The NOVA Space Explorer's Guide: Where to Go and What to See.* New York: Clarkson N. Potter, 1991.
Maurer brings the reader on board various rockets as they explore the nine planets of our solar system. Grades 5 and up.

Moser, Barry. *Fly! A Brief History of Flight Illustrated.* New York: Willa Perlman Books, 1993.
Moser highlights sixteen episodes in the development of aviation, ranging from balloons to the space shuttle. A time line and historical notes are included. Grades 3–7.

Nahum, Andrew. *Eyewitness Books: Flying Machine.* New York: Alfred A. Knopf, 1990.

This photo essay traces the history and development of aircraft from hot air balloons to jetliners. It includes information on the principles of flight and the inner workings of various flying machines. Grades 4 and up.

NASA Space Center. *Skylab Explores the Earth.* Washington, DC: National Aeronautics and Space Administration, 1977.

Photos and text give readers an exciting view of Earth. Grades 8 and up.

Neal, Valerie, Cathleen S. Lewis, and Frank H. Winter. *Spaceflight: A Smithsonian Guide.* New York: Macmillan, 1995.

This book gives a thorough history of space flight from early rockets to present-day space exploration. Grades 7 and up.

Pearce, Carol A. *Amelia Earhart.* New York: Facts on File, 1988.

Pearce traces the life of the American pilot who became the first woman to fly across the Atlantic Ocean. Grades 6–12.

Pogue, William R. *How Do You Go to the Bathroom in Space?* New York: Tom Doherty Associates, 1991.

Colonel William R. Pogue was selected as an astronaut in 1966. He served in the support crew of the *Apollo 7* and *Apollo 11* missions, and was the pilot for *Skylab 4.* In this book, Pogue answers many of the questions students have asked about living in space. Grades 4–9.

Poynter, Margaret, and Arthur L. Lane. *Voyager: The Story of a Space Mission.* New York: Atheneum, 1981.

The authors discuss the planning, development, and launching of the *Voyager* spacecrafts and what happens to the data they transmit to Earth. Grades 5–8.

Randolph, Blythe. *Amelia Earhart.* New York: Franklin Watts, 1987.

A biography of the woman pilot who, among other achievements, became the first woman to fly across the Atlantic Ocean. Grades 7 and up.

Ride, Sally, with Susan Okie. *To Space & Back.* New York: Lothrop, Lee & Shepard, 1986.

Text and photographs show what it is like to be an astronaut aboard the space shuttle. Grades 4 and up.

Robson, Pam. *Air, Wind & Flight.* New York: Gloucester Press, 1992.

Robson examines flight, propulsion, and power and applies basic principles of aerodynamics to explore and experiment with the properties of air. Grades 3–7.

Schulke, Flip, Debra Schulke, Penelope McPhee, and Raymond McPhee. *Your Future in Space: The U.S. Space Camp Training Program.* New York: Crown, 1986.

Topics include rocket power, living in space, the space shuttle, gravity, mission training, your mission in space, the next step, and tomorrow and beyond. This book includes a foreword by astronauts Bruce McCandless and Kathryn Sullivan. Grades 5 and up.

Scott, Elaine, and Margaret Miller. *Adventure in Space: The Flight to Fix the Hubble.* New York: Hyperion Books for Children, 1995.

On December 2, 1993, the space shuttle *Endeavor* carried seven astronauts on a mission to repair the Hubble telescope. Through text and photographs, this book details how the problem with the telescope was solved. Grades 4 and up.

Shorto, Russell. *How to Fly the Space Shuttle.* Santa Fe, NM: John Muir, 1992.

Shorto explains how space shuttles work and what astronauts do during the course of a shuttle mission. Grades 4–7.

Simon, Seymour. *Galaxies.* New York: Morrow Junior Books, 1988.

Simon identifies the nature, locations, movement, and different categories of galaxies. Grades 3–6.

———. *Jupiter.* New York: William Morrow, 1985.

This book describes the characteristics of the planet Jupiter and its moons as revealed by photographs sent back by two unmanned *Voyager* spaceships—spaceships that took one and one-half years to reach the distant planet. Grades 3–6.

———. *Mars.* New York: William Morrow, 1987.

Through text and photographs, Simon describes the features of the red planet. Grades 3–6.

———. *Mercury.* New York: Morrow Junior Books, 1992.

Simon describes what is known about Mercury from the photographs taken by *Project Mariner.* Grades 3–6.

———. *Saturn.* New York: William Morrow, 1985.

This book describes the sixth planet from the sun, including its rings and its moons, and features photographs taken in outer space. Grades 3–6.

——. *Space Words: A Dictionary*. New York: HarperCollins, 1991.

Simon defines words commonly used in discussing outer space. Grades 3–6.

——. *Stars*. New York: William Morrow, 1986.

Simon describes the stars, their composition, and their characteristics with actual photographs. Grades 3–6.

——. *The Sun*. New York: William Morrow, 1986.

Simon describes the nature of the sun, its origin, source of energy, layers, atmosphere, sunspots, and activity. Grades 3–6.

——. *Uranus*. New York: William Morrow, 1987.

Simon introduces, through text and photographs, the characteristics of the seventh planet in the solar system. Grades 3–6.

——. *Venus*. New York: Morrow Junior Books, 1992.

Simon describes the movements and physical features of the planet Venus and recent findings about its climate and surface. Grades 3–6.

Skurzynski, Gloria. *Zero Gravity*. New York: Bradbury Press, 1994.

Text and full-color photographs give readers an understanding of gravity's effects by comparing and contrasting what happens in zero gravity on a space shuttle flight with gravity on Earth. Winner of the American Institute of Physics Science Writing Award. Grades 3–6.

Smith, Elizabeth Simpson. *Breakthrough: Women in Aviation*. New York: Walker, 1981.

Stories of several women give readers a glimpse of several careers in aviation. Grades 6–12.

Stille, Darlene R. *Spacecraft*. Chicago: Childrens Press, 1991.

Stille describes a variety of spacecraft from the past, present, and future, including the early rockets, the space shuttle, and possible space stations. Grades 2–4.

Tames, Richard. *Amelia Earhart*. New York: Franklin Watts, 1989.

Tames traces the life of the pilot who became the first woman to fly across the Atlantic Ocean and mysteriously disappeared in 1937 while attempting to fly around the world. Grades 5 and up.

Taylor, L. B., Jr. *Gifts from Space: How Space Technology Is Improving Life on Earth*. New York: John Day, 1977.

Taylor surveys the benefits received through the use of space technology, including medical advances, satellite communication, and weather predictions. Grades 7 and up.

——. *Space Shuttle*. New York: Thomas Y. Crowell, 1979.

Taylor describes the reasons for and the design and operation of NASA's space shuttle. Grades 5–8.

VanMeter, Vicki, with Dan Gutman. *Taking Flight: My Story by Vicki VanMeter*. New York: Viking, 1995.

This is the story of the twelve-year-old female airplane pilot who flew across the Atlantic in 1994. Grades 4–7.

Vogt, Gregory. *The Hubble Space Telescope*. Brookfield, CT: Millbrook Press, 1992.

Color photographs accompany the description of the Hubble telescope's design, problems, and repairs. Grades 4–8.

——. *A Twenty Fifth Anniversary Album of NASA*. New York: Franklin Watts, 1983.

This is a brief history of NASA's development, from its early stages of research, through the space shuttle program, to possibilities for future projects in space research and travel. Grades 5 and up.

Vogt, Gregory L. *The Solar System: Facts and Exploration*. New York: Twenty First Century Books, 1995.

Vogt provides readers with an abundance of information on the planets in our solar system, asteroids, comets, and meteoroids. Grades 4 and up.

Wilford, John Noble. *We Reach the Moon*. New York: Grosset & Dunlap, 1973.

This book traces step-by-step development of the United States space program and the Apollo program's journey to the moon. Grades 4–9.

Yenne, Bill. *The Encyclopedia of US Spacecraft*. New York: Exeter Books, 1985.

This book, produced in cooperation with the National Aeronautics and Space Administration (NASA), examines thoroughly all of the space vehicles developed by the United States before 1985. Grades 7 and up.

# Theme Resources

## *Commercial Resources*

Carson, Mary Kay. *Space*. New York: Scholastic, 1996.

This resource contains a variety of activities and reproducible pages on the following topics: "What's Out in Space?," "The Journey to Space," "Surviving in Space," "The Astronauts," and "Future Journeys." Suitable for use with students in grades 3 through 6.

Challenger Center for Space Science Education.

This is a privately funded, non-profit organization founded as a living memorial to the *Challenger* crew. For information regarding the services offered by the Center, write to:

> Challenger Center for Space Science
> Education
> 1101 King Street, Suite 700
> Alexandria, VA 22314
> (703) 683-9740

*Cobblestone, The History Magazine for Young People*. Peterborough, NH: Cobblestone.

The July 1990 issue for grades 4 and up is titled "Amelia Earhart: Heroine of the Skies." Articles include "Teach Me to Fly," "World Flight, Last Flight," and "The Continuing Search for Amelia Earhart."

*Creative Classroom*. New York: Children's Television Workshop.

The March/April 1997 issue contains a poem about thirteen women aviators called "Women in the Skies." Suitable for use with students in grades 2 through 5.

Freeze-dried space foods. Information regarding the purchase of space-type freeze-dehydrated foods may be obtained by writing to any of the following companies:

> Action Products, Inc.
> 344 Cypress Road
> Ocala, FL 32672

> G. Armanio & Sons, Inc.
> 1970 Carroll Avenue
> San Francisco, CA 94124

> Freeze Dry Products
> 321 Eighth Street, NW
> Evansville, IN 47708

> GEWA Visitor Gift Shop
> Goddard Space Flight Center
> Greenbelt, MD 20771

> Oregon Freeze-Dry, Inc.
> PO Box 1048
> Albany, OR 97321

> Sky-Lab Foods, Inc.
> 177 Lake Street
> White Plains, NY 16040

> Sam-Andy Foods
> PO Box 1120
> Colton, CA 92324

> Spaceland Enterprises
> PO Box 775
> Merrit Island, FL 32952

Johnson Space Center.

Teachers can borrow NASA science and space videos by mail from the Johnson Space Center. There is no charge except for return postage. Video catalogs can be obtained by calling (713) 483-4231 or faxing (713) 483-2848. Or you may write to:

> NASA Johnson Space Center
> Media Resource Center
> Building 423/AP42
> Houston, TX 77058-3696

*Kids Discover*. New York: Kids Discover.

The subject of the January 1993 issue of *Kids Discover* for students in grades 4 through 7 is "Space." Articles include "Major Moments in Space," "Getting into Space," and "Would You Like to Be an Astronaut?"

The subject of the October 1995 issue of *Kids Discover* for students in grades 4 through 7 is "Solar Systems." Articles include "A Spin Around the Solar System" and "Planet Earth."

Kozloski, Lilian D. *U.S. Space Gear: Outfitting the Astronaut*. Washington, DC: Smithsonian Institution Press, 1994.

Kozloski gives detailed descriptions of the various space suits that have been used over the course of space exploration. For use with grades 8 and up.

*The Mailbox: The Idea Magazine for Teachers*. Greensboro, NC: The Education Center.

The December/January 1995–1996 issue for use with students in grades 4 through 6 contains the article "Space: The Final Fun-tier." This article includes many activities, reproducibles, and literature suggestions.

NASA Teacher Resource Centers.

NASA Teacher Resource Centers are established to provide educators with NASA-related materials for classroom use. These materials, which may be referenced or duplicated at the Center, include classroom activities, lesson plans, teacher guides, slides, and audio- and videotapes.

Contact the NASA Center that serves your state for Teacher Resource Center material or information about other available services.

| NASA Center | States Served |
| --- | --- |
| **NASA Ames Research Center**<br>Teacher Resource Center<br>Mail Stop TO-25<br>Moffett Field, CA 94035-1000<br>(415) 604-3574 | Alaska, Arizona, California, Hawaii, Idaho, Montana, Nevada, Oregon, Utah, Washington, Wyoming |
| **NASA Goddard Space Flight Center**<br>Teacher Resource Laboratory<br>Mail Code 130.0<br>Greenbelt, MD 20771<br>(301) 286-8570 | Connecticut, Delaware, District of Columbia, Maine, Maryland, Massachusetts, New Hampshire, New Jersey, New York, Pennsylvania, Rhode Island, Vermont |
| **NASA Jet Propulsion Laboratory**<br>Teacher Resource Center<br>Attn: JPL Educational Outreach<br>Mail Stop CS-530<br>Pasadena, CA 91109<br>(818) 354-6916 | Responds to nationwide inquiries related to space exploration and other JPL activities |
| **NASA Lyndon B. Johnson Space Center**<br>Teacher Resource Room<br>2101 NASA Road One<br>Code AP-4<br>Houston, TX 77058<br>(713) 483-8696; (713) 483-8618 | Colorado, Kansas, Nebraska, New Mexico, North Dakota, Oklahoma, South Dakota, Texas |
| **NASA John F. Kennedy Space Center**<br>Educators Resource Laboratory<br>Mail Code ERL<br>Kennedy Space Center, FL 32899<br>(407) 867-4090 | Florida, Georgia, Puerto Rico, Virgin Islands |
| **NASA Langley Research Center**<br>Teacher Resource Center<br>Mail Stop 146<br>Hampton, VA 23665<br>(804) 864-3297 | Kentucky, North Carolina, South Carolina, Virginia, West Virginia |
| **NASA Lewis Research Center**<br>Teacher Resource Center<br>Mail Stop 8-1<br>Cleveland, OH 44135<br>(216) 433-2017 | Illinois, Indiana, Michigan, Minnesota, Ohio, Wisconsin |

(List continues on page 112.)

| NASA Center | States Served |
| --- | --- |
| **NASA George C. Marshall**<br>**Space Flight Center**<br>Teacher Resource Center at Alabama<br>Space and Rocket Center<br>One Tranquility Drive<br>Huntsville, AL 35807<br>(205) 544-5812 | Alabama, Arkansas, Iowa,<br>Louisiana, Mississippi,<br>Missouri, Tennessee |
| **NASA John C. Stennis Space Center**<br>Teacher Resource Center<br>Building 1200<br>Stennis Space Center, MS 39529-6000<br>(601) 688-3338 | Mississippi |

The National Air and Space Museum's Education Resource Center.

This center is open to teachers of all disciplines and levels and offers access to materials that relate to science, space, and aviation. For further information, write to:

Education Resource Center
Office of Education P-700
National Air and Space Museum
Smithsonian Institution
Washington, DC 20560
(202) 786-2106

*National Geographic World*. Washington, DC: The National Geographic Society.

The March 1997 issue of *World* contains the article "International Space Station." It chronicles a preview that students from Seabrook Intermediate School had of the International Space Station at the Johnson Space Center in Houston, Texas. Another article in this issue is "Would Space Suit You?" It includes several flight simulator activities for your students to try. Suitable for use with students in grades 4 through 7.

The Young Astronaut Council.

This is a private-sector educational program, created by President Ronald Reagan in 1984, which focuses on improving the math and science skills of elementary and junior high school students. For further information, write to:

Young Astronaut Council
1211 Connecticut Avenue, NW
Suite 800
Washington, DC 20036
(202) 682-1986

## Computer Resources

*Eyewitness Encyclopedia of Space and the Universe*. New York: Dorling Kindersley, 1996. (CD-ROM)

This CD-ROM is a reference guide to astronomy and space exploration. It is full of information on the planets, stars, galaxies, astronauts, spacecrafts, satellites, and probes. Students can compete in interactive activities for one or two players to test their knowledge of space. Students can even spend time aboard the *Mir* space station to discover how astronauts live in space. Available for Windows.

*Space Shuttle Physics: Newton's Laws of Motion*. Huntsville, AL: Britt Communications, 1993. (CD-ROM)

This is a multimedia atlas on the space shuttle, space history, and Newton's laws of motion. Available for Macintosh.

*Voyage Through the Solar System*. Hollywood, CA: Palo/Haklar Multimedia, 1994. (CD-ROM)

This CD-ROM is filled with up-close images, full-motion action, and dynamic music. It uses actual video and film of our solar system from the Jet Propulsion Lab and NASA.

## Videos

*Apollo 13*. Universal City, CA: Universal City Studios, 1995. (140 minutes)

Tom Hanks, Kevin Bacon, Bill Paxton, Gary Sinise, Ed Harris, and Kathleen Quinlan star in this reenactment of the near fatal disaster aboard *Apollo 13*.

*The Dream Is Alive: A Window Seat on the Space Shuttle*. Whittier, CA: Finley-Holiday Film Corp., 1985. (37 minutes)

This video is part of the space and science series narrated by Walter Cronkite. Viewers will be able to look back at the earth from aboard a space shuttle, witness a satellite being repaired, and see a space walk.

*The Space Shuttle*. Bethesda, MD: Discovery Communications, 1994. (100 minutes)

This video profiles the people who work behind the scenes in the space shuttle program.

*We Remember: The Space Shuttle Pioneers, 1981–1986*. Whittier, CA: Finley-Holiday Film Corp., 1988. (60 minutes)

This video is a tribute to the adventurers who pioneered new frontiers in the space shuttle program. It presents the historical record of twenty-five missions from the official NASA archives.

*Women in Space: A Ride to Remember*. Bill Gibson Productions, 1983. (60 minutes)

This video profiles women astronauts through flight clips and interviews.

## End-of-Unit Celebration

## Space Exploration Research Project

Assign a topic to each student in your class to research. When completed, hold a presentation day.

| | |
|---|---|
| Edwin Aldrin, Jr. | James Lovell, Jr. |
| *Apollo 1* Disaster | Christa McAuliffe |
| *Apollo 11* Mission | Bruce McCandless |
| *Apollo 13* Near Disaster | James McDivitt |
| Neil Armstrong | Ronald E. McNair |
| Guion Bluford | Ellison S. Onizuka |
| Roger Chaffe | Judith A. Resnik |
| *Challenger* Explosion, January 28, 1986 | Sally Kristen Ride |
| Michael Collins | Walter Schirra |
| Walter Cunningham | Francis R. Scobee |
| Don Eisele | Alan Shepard |
| Yuri Gagarin | Skylab |
| John Glenn | Michael J. Smith |
| Gus Grissom | The Soviet Union Space Program |
| Fred W. Haise, Jr. | Robert Stewart |
| How Space Technology Has Improved Life on Earth | John L. Swigert, Jr. |
| The Hubble Space Telescope | The U.S. Space Shuttle Program |
| Gregory B. Jarvis | Edward White |

## Space Exploration Crossword Puzzle

Have students work individually or in groups to solve the "Space Exploration" crossword puzzle below.

**Fig. 4.1.** Space exploration.

### Across

1. a compartment of a spacecraft designed to separate from the rocket

4. of or having to do with the moon

6. an unstable form of oxygen produced by electric sparks

7. the height above any given point, especially above sea level

8. a Russian astronaut

11. a reusable space vehicle

### Down

2. the study of the stars, planets, and other heavenly bodies

3. the tendency of objects to fall toward the center of the earth

5. a part of a meteor that is not burned up and strikes the earth

9. the air surrounding the earth

10. National Aeronautics and Space Administration

**WORD LIST:**

| | | |
|---|---|---|
| ALTITUDE | COSMONAUT | NASA |
| ASTRONOMY | GRAVITY | OZONE |
| ATMOSPHERE | LUNAR | SPACESHUTTLE |
| CAPSULE | METEORITE | |

**ANSWERS:**

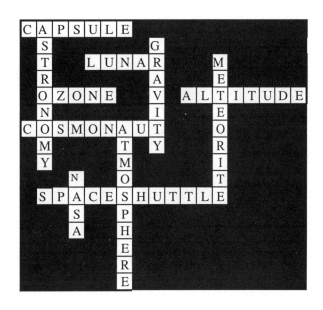

# Chapter 5

# The Vietnam War

## Introduction

After the end of World War II, Vietnam fought for independence from France. In 1954, the French army was defeated at Dien Bien Phu. Following this defeat, a conference was held in Geneva, Switzerland. Several representatives of different countries, including the United States, attended the conference. The decision was made to divide Vietnam into Communist North Vietnam and Nationalist South Vietnam. National elections were supposed to be held to decide whether South Vietnam would have a communist or non-communist government. However, the South Vietnamese regime refused to hold the elections and in 1955 declared South Vietnam an independent republic. North Vietnam began to provide support to the Vietcong—a Communist guerrilla group in South Vietnam.

In 1955 the United States began to help South Vietnam by supplying advisors, war equipment, and economic aid. The Vietcong continued to be a threat, and in 1965 President Lyndon Johnson sent the first U.S. troops to South Vietnam.

The Vietnam War divided the United States. Many believed that the support of non-Communist South Vietnam was necessary, while others believed the United States had no business becoming involved in another country's dispute.

By late 1965, 200,000 Americans were fighting in Vietnam. By 1966, the number doubled. Within one year, the number reached half a million. By 1967, antiwar demonstrations were taking place all over the United States.

President Johnson admitted his failure in ending the war and did not seek reelection. Richard Nixon was elected president of the United States in 1968. The war continued for another four years. In 1973 a cease-fire agreement was signed by South Vietnam, the United States, and the communists. However, North Vietnam ignored the cease-fire and in April of 1975 invaded South Vietnam. The remaining American forces and embassy personnel were airlifted out of Vietnam. The war finally ended in 1975. It was the longest war in U.S. history.

The Vietnam War was fought at a tremendous cost to the United States. More than 58,000 men and women were killed or declared missing in action. The wounded numbered more than 300,000, with 74,000 suffering from a more than fifty percent disability. It is estimated that the United States spent 150 billion dollars in direct expenses and another 150 billion dollars in indirect expenses related to the war.

The Vietnam War had an extremely negative impact on the American public and the soldiers in particular. Many citizens continued to believe that the United States should never have gone to war. Although veterans of earlier wars had been treated as heroes upon their return home, Vietnam veterans were treated with hostility or ignored. This treatment contributed to the significant emotional problems of countless returning veterans. Many who sought professional help were misdiagnosed and mistreated because mental health professionals had no diagnosis or treatment for post-traumatic stress disorder at the time.

The trade books in this chapter were chosen to assist teachers in helping students understand what took place before, during, and after the Vietnam War, and the effects it had on the lives of Vietnam veterans.

The following are excerpts from letters written home from my good friend Direct Procurement Officer Third Class (PO3) David W. Reilly to his parents and two brothers when he was stationed in Vietnam. He was with Mobile Construction Battalion 3 (MCB3). He was a Seabee. Seabees are the construction division of the Navy. Read these excerpts to your class to begin your study of the Vietnam War.

**Fig. 5.1.** Photograph taken at the Greater Rochester Vietnam Veterans Memorial in Rochester, New York.

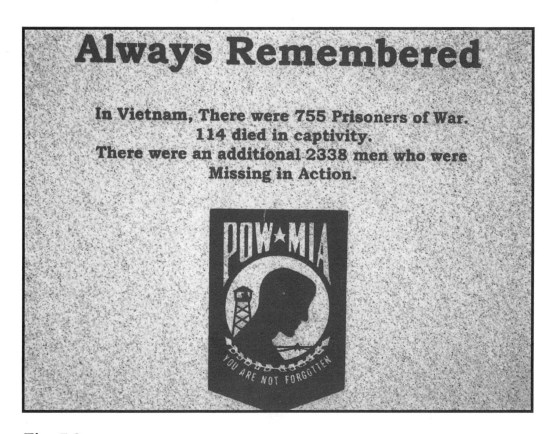

**Always Remembered**

In Vietnam, There were 755 Prisoners of War.
114 died in captivity.
There were an additional 2338 men who were
Missing in Action.

POW★MIA
YOU ARE NOT FORGOTTEN

**Fig. 5.2.** Photograph taken at the Greater
Rochester Vietnam Veterans Memorial
in Rochester, New York.

**Fig. 5.3.** Photograph taken at the Greater
Rochester Vietnam Veterans Memorial
in Rochester, New York.

**Fig. 5.4.** Direct Procurement Officer Third Class (PO3) David W. Reilly.

*14 July 68*

*Hi,*

*Here we are 30 hours ahead of your time. The first night I had a hard time sleeping, jets & helicopters are flying over us all the time. We are about 2 or 3 miles east of Da Nang. From here I can see the air strip & helicopter pads, and they are constantly flying over us night and day. During the night we can hear machine gun fire, mortars and bombs going off. From what I understand our camp is pretty secure.*

*Last night we were alerted of a possible ambush, the marines set up out in front of us, but nothing happened. We figured they would try something with a new battalion just arriving.*

*The heat here is something else. I'd say it's about 110 or 115 right now. The water just pours off of yourself. But the nights aren't bad, it cools down pretty good. The food here isn't the greatest but either eat or starve.*

*Love,*

*Dave*

*8/16/68*

*Hi Everybody,*

*Just got back from a 1½ mile hike. They just took us (the reactionary force) to show us the terrain of the country around us. They are expecting trouble around here and Hue sometime between now and Sept. 1. They are expecting mainly another hit on Hue like the one that took the city apart last February. I think every house there has a bullet hole in it or it's been blown to pieces, you wouldn't believe it.*

*A couple of army guys got it last night. Their camp is a couple of miles down the road and a couple of miles up in the hills next to MCB8 camp. It's the 101st airborne division. It was a sniper, but from what I heard they got him too.*

*I guess today is about the first day no one has seen any dead V.C. along the roadside.*

*I've heard the V.C. want to have a big push in this area, but they can't all muster in one place because of too many military forces in the area.*

*Love,*

*Dave*

———————

*8/17/68*

*Hi,*

*Had some more excitement south of here last night. They tried to blow up a bridge on the Tray River last night, plus they overran a marine camp, 25 marines got killed. That camp is about 15 miles south of us, but last week I took some cement down there, and what I had left over from the job, I gave to them. I got to know some of them pretty good (commanding officer too). I am wondering how those guys I knew made out. I think there is only about 100 or 125 in the whole camp!*

*Love,*

*Dave*

8/24/68

*Hi,*

*How's everything in Sauquoit? Had quite a bit of excitement around here. I'll start from the beginning.*

*Last Wednesday I was working out on a bridge with some guys from MCB8 pouring concrete and about noon there was an explosion, by an army bunker. Three kids threw a clayman mine into a fire, two of them got killed, they were really torn apart, what a mess. The third one got away. Guess who put them up to that? V.C.*

*Then Thursday night at 3:00 A.M. we got called out. We took a couple mortar rounds into our camp, nobody got hurt. I heard they hit the Marine camp across the street from us pretty hard.*

*Then last night, I got in about 6:00 A.M., got out of my truck walking to the dispatch office and heard a whistling sound out my head. Guess what, a mortar round hit right in the center of the Marine camp again. I made a bee line for the bunker. So once again we hit the lines. Nobody in our camp got hurt, but down the street from us 4 army men got killed and 7 injured.*

*Today has been quiet and I hope it stays this way tonight, I am dead tired. In fact last night was the first night since I have been in Vietnam I have slept through the whole night without waking up from hearing shooting, bombs, or helicopters going over.*

*Tell everybody I said hi & I'm fine here (but I hate the place).*

*Love,*

*Dave*

—————————————

9/16/68

*Hi,*

*Things are still quiet around here, but the night before last we watched the helicopters shoot tracer rounds. Tracers are bullets, used at night, they have a red flash so you can see where they go. You ought to see it, it's really something. About every morning from 4 A.M. to about 5:30 we can hear light artillery fire. I'm so used to it I usually sleep right through it. When I get home I probably won't be able to sleep nights, it will be too quiet, and when I hear the fire siren go off I'll probably run outdoors looking for a mortar hole.*

*Love,*

*Dave*

*11/18/68*

*Hi,*

*Well we've had some excitement around here last night. Da Nang got hit twice. The first time was at 1 a.m. and the second was at 5 a.m. Our camp didn't take any rounds in but across the street at a marine base I heard that a squad of guys (around 14 or 15) got killed and at a place called Deep Water Pier, where the ships bring in supplies. 2 guys got killed and 17 wounded. I think they blew up one bridge also, I'm not sure about that. We are expecting to hit the holes again tonight.*

*Love,*

*Dave*

———

*23 Nov. 68*

*Hi,*

*You probably heard about Da Nang area getting hit. Well it's true. Our camp hasn't been hit, but the Marines across the road from us have. Last Wed. night they had an officer killed when a rocket hit a helicopter. You ought to see the helicopter. I heard they also hit downtown Da Nang. The Marines (4 companies) are having a sweep of the Da Nang area on a search & destroy mission. They are killing anyone who acts like a V.C. There are too many terrorists around. Two days ago the O.C. (South Vietnamese Military Police) killed a man and a woman for not stopping at a checkpoint, shot them right in the back. The gooks have to stop at the checkpoints to show their papers, if they don't, well sorry about that. We've hit the holes about every night this week, except for 2 nights.*

*One night we were in the chow hall at 11 P.M., eating and the siren went off. You should have seen the chow hall, tables tipped over, cups & plates broken, food & trays on the floor. When that siren goes off you just drop everything you got and find the nearest bunker.*

*I've heard that this is the start of the 3rd Tet offensive. This is supposed to be the worst one. The V.C. usually don't bother the Seabees, they want the marine & army, but we are on the lookout. If I ever hear the siren when I get home I'll probably run out the door looking for a bunker! (Ha, Ha)*

*Love,*

*Dave*

# Whole Group Reading

📖 Boyd, Candy Dawson. *Charlie Pippin*. New York: Macmillan, 1987.
Eleven-year-old Charlie seeks to understand her father by learning everything she can about the Vietnam War. Her father survived the war, but it put an end to his dreams. Sybil Steinberg wrote in her *Publishers Weekly* review of *Charlie Pippin*: "A strong black protagonist makes this a rare YA book, the finesse with which Boyd ties its many themes into a very moving, unified whole turns this into a stellar offering." Grades 4–8.

## Author Information

Candy Dawson Boyd was born August 8, 1946, in Chicago, Illinois. Her full name is Marguerite Dawson Boyd.

Boyd received her bachelor's degree from Northeastern Illinois State University. She received her master's degree and her Ph.D. from the University of California at Berkeley.

Boyd worked as a teacher at Overton Elementary School in Chicago, Illinois from 1968 to 1971 and at Longfellow School in Berkeley, California from 1971 to 1973. From 1972 to 1979 she was an extension instructor at the University of California at Berkeley. She was the district teacher trainer in reading and communication skills from 1973 to 1976 at Berkeley Unified School District in Berkeley, California. Since 1972, Boyd has filled several positions at St. Mary's College of California in Morgana, including extension instructor in language arts, lecturer, assistant professor, tenured associate professor, professor of education, director of reading leadership and teacher effectiveness programs, and director of elementary education.

Boyd has won many awards for her writing. Her book *Circle of Gold* was named a Notable Children's Trade Book in the field of Social Studies by the National Council for the Social Studies and the Children's Book Council in 1984, and a Coretta Scott King Award Honor Book by the American Library Association in 1985. *Charlie Pippin* was nominated for the Mark Twain Award and the Dorothy Canfield Fisher Children's Book Award in 1988, and was chosen by the International Reading Association and Children's Book Council for the Children's Choices for 1988 List.

Boyd decided to become a writer while teaching elementary school in California. While searching for books for her students, she found that there was a disturbing lack of children's literature from the diverse cultural background of her students. In an interview for *Something About the Author* (volume 72), Boyd said, "I never saw children of color in realistic fiction depicted as children whose culture, embedded within them as a part of who they were, came out in ways that were ordinary and regular. That enraged me and I decided to become a writer."

## Activities

1. On a world map, have students locate:

   | | |
   |---|---|
   | Afghanistan | Indochina |
   | Atlanta, GA | Iran |
   | Bangalore, India | Iraq |
   | Berkeley, CA | Ireland |
   | Chicago, IL | Israel |
   | China | Japan |
   | El Salvador | Kampuchea (formerly Cambodia) |
   | England | Laos |
   | Ethiopia | Lebanon |
   | France | Los Angeles, CA |

| Monterey, CA | San Francisco, CA |
| Nicaragua | Seattle, WA |
| North Carolina | South Africa |
| North Korea | South China Sea |
| Portland, OR | South Korea |
| Reno, NV | Vietnam |
| Russia | Washington, DC |
| Saigon, South Vietnam (renamed Ho Chi Minh City in 1975) | West Africa |

2. Have students research President Johnson and the building of the Vietnam Veterans Memorial.

3. Hold your own peace demonstration. Students could create banners and posters advocating the value of peace and warning about the dangers of war.

4. Ask a student volunteer to recite Charlie's oratory speech, which begins on page 130.

5. Using a simple questionnaire, have students interview family members and teachers to find out how the Vietnam War affected them and their families. Then have the students bind the questionnaires into a booklet titled "Effects of the Vietnam War."

6. Ask your school art teacher to make origami golden cranes with your class. These symbols of peace can be hung in your classroom as a reminder of the importance of peace.

# Discussion

Give the class the following instruction: As we read this book, we will be discussing the following.

1. What does Charlie do to earn money?

2. Discuss the discipline code that Charlie's school has. Does your school have a similar policy?

3. In what current events project does Charlie want to participate? Why?

4. What is Charlie's relationship with her father like?

5. How did Charlie's father react to the note from Mrs. Hayamoto?

6. According to Charlie's mother, how did the Vietnam War change her father?

7. Why did the principal, Mr. Rocker, call Charlie's father at work?

8. Describe Charlie's grandmother.

9. When talking about Charlie's Vietnam project, Mama Bliss told Charlie, "Reading books is only going to give you a certain kind of information. The rest has to come from people." Do you agree? Why or why not?

10. What do you think Uncle Ben meant when he told Charlie's dad, "The sooner you realize that you're still fighting that war, the better off you will be"?

11. How does Charlie's dad feel about the U.S. involvement in the Vietnam War?

12. How does Uncle Ben feel about the U.S. involvement in the Vietnam War?

13. How many American soldiers served in Vietnam?

14. What did Charlie learn about communism? Discuss your feelings about it.

15. How did Charlie's father injure his leg?

16. Discuss the incident at the airport when Charlie's father returned from Vietnam.

17. How were World War II veterans treated differently upon their return to the United States?

18. What did Chris tell the class that he had learned by working on the war and peace project?

From *Teaching U.S. History Through Children's Literature.* © 1998 Wanda J. Miller. Teacher Ideas Press. (800) 237-6124.

19. Discuss Charlie's speech about the Vietnam War.

20. Why does Mrs. Pippin believe that people protesting is important? Do you agree?

21. What was the speech that Charlie gave in the school oratory contest about?

22. What happened at the district oratory contest?

23. Where did Charlie go with her Uncle Ben? Why?

24. Describe Charlie's homecoming.

25. What did Charlie bring home for her father? Why?

26. How did Mr. Pippin react to the gift?

27. Discuss your feelings about the Vietnam War and what you have learned from reading *Charlie Pippin*.

## Vocabulary

**efficiency** (p1)
the ability to produce results without any waste, such as of time, effort, or money

**origami** (p2)
the Japanese art of folding paper to form a decorative object, such as a flower or an animal

**plummet** (p2)
to fall straight down; to plunge

**hefty** (p3)
heavy

**sympathetic** (p4)
sharing the feelings of another

**hubbub** (p5)
a loud, confused noise; an uproar

**aroma** (p5)
a pleasant fragrance or smell, such as of food or a plant

**symmetrical** (p5)
having an arrangement in which each feature on one half of a figure or object has a matching feature in the other half

**vegetarian** (p6)
a person who eats mostly fruits and vegetables and no meat

**frantic** (p16)
wild with fear, worry, pain, or rage

**contentment** (p17)
calm satisfaction; peaceful happiness

**scornful** (p17)
full of contempt

**niche** (p17)
a position or situation that is suitable

**affectation** (p18)
an artificial way of acting or talking meant to create an effect

**retorted** (p18)
replied sharply

**connoisseur** (p19)
an expert qualified to judge in some field of art or taste

**meditation** (p21)
the act or process of thinking quietly and deeply over a period of time

**tumbleweed** (p24)
a plant that, when withered, breaks from its roots and is blown about by the wind, scattering its seed

**sarcasm** (p25)
an unpleasant remark that mocks or makes fun of something or someone

**berating** (p30)
scolding sharply and severely

**infraction** (p31)
an act or instance of breaking a rule or law; a violation

**pungent** (p32)
sharp or piercing to the taste or smell

**rigid** (p33)
not giving or bending; stiff or firm

**quips** (p36)
clever or witty remarks that are sometimes sarcastic

**racism** (p37)
prejudice in favor of a particular race

**apartheid** (p37)
the governmental policy of racial segregation and social, economic, and educational discrimination in the Republic of South Africa

From *Teaching U.S. History Through Children's Literature.* © 1998 Wanda J. Miller. Teacher Ideas Press. (800) 237-6124.

**rebel** (p39)
a person who refuses to submit to authority and fights against it instead

**flourish** (p41)
a showy display of doing something

**edicts** (p43)
official rules or laws that are made known to the public by a formal announcement

**Communist** (p48)
a person who supports a political organization in which a single political party controls the state and manages the production and distribution of goods

**maimed** (p48)
crippled

**infantry** (p49)
soldiers or a branch of the army, trained and equipped to fight on foot

**litany** (p52)
a prayer consisting of a series of readings by the minister with responses by the people

**clique** (p54)
a small group whose members stick together and shut out outsiders

**monotonous** (p57)
boring because of lack of variety or change

**pneumonia** (p57)
a disease caused by a bacterial or virus infection and marked by inflammation of one or both lungs

**fatigue** (p61)
a tired condition resulting from hard work, effort, or strain; weariness

**sulk** (p61)
to be cross or ill-humored

**senile** (p67)
failing in body and mind because of old age

**solitude** (p73)
the condition of being away from others

**tumultuous** (p76)
full of commotion or noise, such as that made by a large, disorderly crowd

**shrapnel** (p78)
fragments scattered when a shell explodes

**exuberance** (p81)
joy and energy; high spirits

**furtively** (p81)
done secretly

**enclave** (p82)
a distinctly separate area within another

**chaotic** (p88)
completely disordered and confused

**proliferation** (p89)
the condition of increasing or reproducing rapidly

**ludicrous** (p91)
causing laughter, scorn, or ridicule; ridiculous; absurd

**hospitality** (p103)
friendly, welcoming treatment of guests or strangers

**oratory** (p106)
the art of speaking before an audience

**initiative** (p108)
the first step in starting or doing something

**inalienable rights** (p108)
rights that cannot be taken away or transferred

**enunciate** (p123)
to pronounce words; to speak

**elaborate** (p126)
to add more details

**civil war** (p131)
a war between groups of citizens of the same country

**entrepreneurship** (p141)
a business venture started by a business person

**capitalist** (p141)
a person who believes in a system in which the factories, materials, and equipment for making and distributing goods are privately owned and operated for a private profit rather than being owned and controlled by a state or government

**apparition** (p155)
a ghost; a spirit

**ambience** (p156)
a surrounding atmosphere; an aura

**incredulous** (p159)
feeling, having, or showing doubt or disbelief

**desolate** (p167)
dreary

**ingenuity** (p177)
skill or cleverness, such as shown in inventing or solving things

# Small Group Reading

📖 Antle, Nancy. *Tough Choices: A Story of the Vietnam War*. New York: Viking, 1993.

Samantha finds herself torn between her loyalty to her two brothers, one a soldier who recently returned from the war in Vietnam and the other a war protester. Grades 4–7.

## Author Information

Nancy Antle well remembers the Vietnam War. Doing research for *Tough Choices: A Story of the Vietnam War* brought back many memories for her. She says, "Vietnam was always on our minds. My friends and I talked about the men we knew who were already there. We wondered how much longer the war would last. We worried about who would be called to go next."

Nancy Antle is also the author of *Hard Times*. She lives in Connecticut with her husband and two children.

## Activities

1. On a world map, have students locate North and South Vietnam and North Carolina.

2. Have students research Ho Chi Minh and the Vietcong.

3. Have students write letters from Mitch to Samantha after his return to Vietnam. In the letter, students should explain Mitch's decision and his feelings about the war.

4. Have students write essays comparing the treatment of Vietnam veterans with the treatment of World War II veterans, then share these essays with the class.

## Discussion

Give the small group the following instruction: As your group reads this book, discuss the following.

1. Why doesn't Samantha like Lee Ann Wilkerson?

2. Who were Samantha and her family waiting for at the airport?

3. Why do Samantha and other students in her fifth-grade class wear silver bracelets?

4. How does Samantha feel about the war protesters?

5. Why did Samantha's mother fear that she would never see her son again?

6. How did the protesters react to seeing Mitch? How do you think Mitch felt?

7. How does Emmett feel about the war?

8. Why do you think Mitch said he might never be ready to talk about the war?

9. What is the "Die-In" that Emmett plans to attend?

10. According to Mitch, what do the Vietcong do with villagers who won't help the communist movement in Vietnam?

11. Discuss the tension between Mitch and Emmett. Share your opinions in your group.

12. What is Mitch's worst nightmare?

13. What happened when a car backfired in front of Mitch and Samantha's house?

14. Samantha met a wounded man at the Die-In. He said that Mitch probably misses Vietnam. How could that be?

15. What is Samantha's favorite television show?

16. Why is Lee Ann worried about Mitch?

17. What news did Mitch receive in a letter? How did he react?

18. What decision did Mitch make about what to do with his life?

19. Discuss your feelings about the war in Vietnam.

20. What happened to Major Jack Tomes, the POW soldier whose name was on Samantha's bracelet?

21. Why were soldiers who fought in Vietnam treated so badly when they returned to the United States? Compare their treatment with the treatment of soldiers who fought in World War II.

## Vocabulary

**terminal** (p3)
the station at the end of a route, such as of a train or a bus

**drafted** (p4)
selected for service in the armed forces

**POW** (p5)
prisoner of war

**MIA** (p5)
missing in action

**tarmac** (p7)
an airport runway

**hippie** (p9)
a person who adopts an alternative, often rebellious lifestyle characterized by liberal or radical politics, casual and colorful dress, and indifference to the values of work and career

**decent** (p12)
kind or kindhearted; generous

**groovy** (p15)
a slang word used in the 1960s and 1970s which means "cool," "neat," or "great"

**Viet Cong** (p19)
a Communist group in South Vietnam

**grenade** (p20)
a small bomb thrown by hand or fired from a rifle

**Communism** (p20)
a political organization in which a single political party controls the state and manages the production and distribution of goods

**deserter** (p37)
a person who leaves his or her military post without permission and without intending to return

**land mine** (p44)
a hidden explosive buried in shallow earth and designed to go off when troops approach or pass over it

**grunts** (p49)
new soldiers

## Small Group Reading

📖 Ashabranner, Brent. *Always to Remember: The Story of the Vietnam Veterans Memorial*. New York: Dodd, Mead, 1988.

Ashabranner discusses the building of the Vietnam Veterans Memorial, the controversies that have surrounded it, and some human interest stories connected with it. Grades 5 and up.

## Author Information

Brent Ashabranner was born November 3, 1921 in Shawnaw, Oklahoma. He received a bachelor of science degree in 1948 and a master's degree in 1951 from Oklahoma State University.

Ashabranner was an English instructor at Oklahoma State University from 1952 to 1955, and acting director of a program in Nigeria for the Peace Corps from 1961 to 1962.

In 1988, *Always to Remember: The Story of the Vietnam Veterans Memorial* was selected as an American Library Association Notable Book and as an American Library Association Best Books for Young Adults.

## Activities

1.  On a world map, have students locate:

    | | |
    |---|---|
    | Athens, OH | Laos |
    | Barre, VT | Memphis, TN |
    | Bowie, MD | New Haven, CT |
    | Cambodia | Paris, France |
    | Dien Bien Phu, Vietnam | Philippines |
    | Geneva, Switzerland | Thailand |
    | Indonesia | Vietnam |
    | Lanham, MD | Washington, DC |

2.  Have students research the following presidents and the roles they played in the Vietnam War:

    Jimmy Carter
    Lyndon B. Johnson
    Richard Nixon

3.  Have students write an essay titled "What the Vietnam Veterans Memorial Stands For." A volunteer from this group could read his or her essay to the rest of the class.

4.  Try to acquire a copy of the CD-ROM *Beyond the Wall: Stories Behind the Vietnam Wall* for students in this group to use to learn more about the war and the Wall.

## Discussion

Give the small group the following instruction: As your group reads this book, discuss the following.

1.  Where is Constitution Gardens and the Vietnam Veterans Memorial?

2.  What was the average age of the men who died in Vietnam?

3.  What message does the Vietnam Veterans Memorial have for its visitors?

4.  Why was Memorial Day once called Decoration Day?

5.  Why did the author decide that it is okay to read messages left at the Wall?

6.  How can a memorial encourage healing following a war?

7.  Up until the mid-1950s, of what country was Vietnam a colony? What happened when Vietnam wanted to become independent?

8.  What caused the Vietnam War?

9.  Why did the United States become involved in the Vietnam War?

10. How did the Vietnam War divide people in the United States?

11. Discuss your own feelings about the U.S. involvement in the Vietnam War.

12. Why did President Lyndon Johnson decide not to run for reelection?

13. What were the costs of United States involvement in the war?

14. What was the cost in human lives to North and South Vietnam?

15. Who were the "hawks" and the "doves"?

16. How were Vietnam veterans treated upon their return to the United States? Why?

17. Why did presidential candidate George McGovern say that the psychological needs of the Vietnam veterans were greater than those of veterans of any other war in which the United States had participated?

18. Why did Jan Scruggs decide that a Vietnam veterans memorial was needed?

19. Why did the jurors choose the design for the memorial that they did?

20. Why were people surprised to learn the identity of the designer of the winning entry?

21. How are the names of soldiers declared dead or missing in action arranged on the Wall? Why?

22. Why did some people find it hard to believe that a salute to Vietnam veterans would ever become a reality?

23. What kinds of things do people who visit the Wall leave there?

24. Consider the age of Jan Scruggs, who seriously pursued his idea of a Vietnam veterans memorial, and the age of Maya Lin, who designed the memorial. How does this make you feel about the possibilities in your own life?

# Vocabulary

**infantrymen** (p6)
   soldiers in the army who are trained and equipped to fight on foot

**comrade** (p6)
   a close companion or friend

**litany** (p6)
   a prayer consisting of a series of readings by the minister with responses by the people

**battalion** (p11)
   two or more companies of soldiers led by a lieutenant colonel or major

**impaled** (p12)
   pierced with something sharp or pointed

**solemn** (p12)
   serious

**controversy** (p12)
   an argument or debate on an issue for which opinions differ

**Communists** (p18)
   people who support a social system in which the means for producing economic goods belong to the entire community or the state, not to individuals

**faction** (p19)
   a distinct group of people within a larger group, working against other parts of the main group to gain its own ends

**regime** (p19)
   a system of government

**Vietcong** (p19)
   a Communist group in South Vietnam

**contrary** (p20)
   entirely different; opposite

**tacit** (p21)
   understood or meant without being said or spoken

**dissension** (p23)
   conflict

**defoliants** (p23)
   chemical sprays or dust used to strip the leaves of a plant or tree

**napalm** (p23)
   gasoline and chemicals mixed together to form a flammable jelly that is used in bombs and flamethrowers

**atrocities** (p23)
   wicked, criminal, vile, or cruel acts

**shrapnel** (p28)
   fragments scattered when a shell explodes

**mortar** (p28)
   a short cannon, loaded through the muzzle
   and fired at a high angle

**credentials** (p31)
   something, such as a letter or certificate, that
   identifies the owner and shows the person's
   position, authority, or right to be trusted

**unanimously** (p32)
   in total agreement

**distinguished** (p36)
   having the look of a notable person;
   dignified

**architect** (p36)
   a person who designs and draws up plans
   for buildings or other structures, then oversees their construction by the builders

**harmonious** (p37)
   free from disagreement

**dignity** (p44)
   the quality of character, worth, or nobility
   that commands respect

**nobility** (p44)
   a group of people who have hereditary titles
   and rank, such as kings, queens, duchesses,
   dukes, countesses, and earls

**abstract** (p45)
   not dealing with anything specific or particular; general

**prophetic** (p45)
   of, having to do with, or like a person who
   speaks as if with a divine message

**endorsement** (p48)
   approval, especially formal approval

**divisive** (p52)
   causing people to disagree sharply

**vigil** (p60)
   the act of staying awake to observe or
   protect; a watch

**poignancy** (p63)
   the quality of being poignant; keenly felt;
   painfully affecting

**memorabilia** (p69)
   things worth remembering or keeping

**zealous** (p69)
   filled with or caused by great interest and
   devotion, such as when working for a cause

**anthropologist** (p69)
   an expert in the science that studies the
   physical, social, and cultural development of
   human beings

**melancholy** (p75)
   very gloomy; sad; dejected

**glorification** (p80)
   the condition of being honored or exalted;
   worshipped

**revered** (p82)
   regarded with great respect

**somber** (p89)
   gloomy and melancholy; sad

**metaphor** (p89)
   a figure of speech that suggests, without saying so, that one thing is like another

# Small Group Reading

📖 Hahn, Mary Downing. *December Stillness*. New York: Avon Books, 1988.

Fifteen-year-old Kelly McAllister becomes involved with the plight of a homeless Vietnam vet-eran, Mr. Weems, who takes refuge in the library every day. She attempts to befriend him and interview him for a social studies project, but the attempt backfires. Kelly's father is also a Vietnam veteran who never talks about his experiences in the war. When Kelly and her father visit the Viet-nam Veterans Memorial in Washington, D.C., though, he begins to talk about his experiences. As a result, they become closer than ever. Grades 7 and up.

## Author Information

Mary Downing Hahn was born December 9, 1939, in Washington, D.C. Hahn was a junior high school art teacher from 1969 to 1971 in Greenbelt, Maryland. She has also worked as a store clerk, as a correspondence clerk for a credit union, and as a children's librarian associate. She has been writing full-time since 1991.

*December Stillness* received the Child Study Association Book Award in 1989, the Jane Addams Children's Book Award Honor Book citation in 1990, and the California Young Reader's Medal in 1991.

Hahn's books include *The Sara Summer, Wait Till Helen Comes: A Ghost Story, Stepping on the Cracks*, and *Look for Me by Moonlight*. Her books have been translated into Danish, Swedish, Italian, German, Japanese, and French.

In an interview for *Something About the Author* (volume 81), Hahn said that by the time she was in high school she had decided she wanted to write and illustrate children's books: "I loved to draw, and I always looked forward to embellishing my book reports and term papers with illustrations—they were my sure A's."

## Activities

1.  On a map of the United States, have students locate Baltimore, Maryland and Washington, D.C.

2.  Have students call a social services agency in your county to find out what services are available for Vietnam veterans.

3.  Have students contact your local Veterans of Foreign Wars (VFW) post to find out the names of those who fought in Vietnam from your town. They should post the names in your classroom.

4.  Have students write a letter from Kelly's father to Kelly. They should include in the letter his feelings about the war, what he saw in Vietnam, and how he felt when he came home. Students can then read their letters to the rest of the class.

5.  Have students research post-traumatic stress disorder. How does it affect men and women who have fought in a war? What treatments are available to them? Students can then present their findings to the rest of the class.

## Discussion

Give the small group the following instruction: As your group reads this book, discuss the following.

1.  What type of paper does Kelly have to write on current issues?

2.  What does Kelly's mom do for a living?

3.  What does Kelly want to be when she is older?

4.  Describe Kelly's relationship with her father.

5.  What topic did Kelly choose for her paper? Why?

6.  Whom does Kelly plan to interview for her paper?

7.  How did Kelly's teacher, Mr. Hardy, compare the Vietnam War with the Trojan War?

8.  Why do you think it bothers Kelly's father that she painted a peace sign on the back of his army jacket that she wears?

9.  Why did the poem by Shel Silverstein make Kelly think of Mr. Weems?

10. How did Kelly's parents meet?

11. What was Kelly's father like before he finished law school? Why do you think he changed?

From *Teaching U.S. History Through Children's Literature.* © 1998 Wanda J. Miller. Teacher Ideas Press. (800) 237-6124.

12. What things did Kelly take to Mr. Weems? What did Mr. Weems do with them?

13. How did Kelly defend Mr. Weems at the library?

14. Discuss your own feelings about war. Do you agree with Kelly or with Brett?

15. Why do you think Mr. Weems refused help from Mr. Walker?

16. How did Kelly finally get Mr. Weems to talk to her? What did he tell her about Vietnam?

17. How is Kelly and Julie's relationship changing? Why?

18. Why do so many Vietnam veterans have post-traumatic stress disorder?

19. Do you agree with Kelly that people like Mr. Weems need help?

20. What happened to Mr. Weems? Why does Kelly feel responsible?

21. What did Kelly mean about the war not being over yet?

22. How does Kelly plan to make sure that Mr. Weems is remembered?

23. What is success to Kelly? Discuss your own definitions of success.

24. Why did Kelly feel that the Vietnam Veterans Memorial was like the war itself?

25. How did Kelly's father react to seeing the Vietnam Veterans Memorial?

26. How did you feel when Kelly placed Mr. Weems's name on the memorial?

## Vocabulary

**concrete** (p1)
actually existing; real

**controversial** (p1)
tending to stir up argument

**impudence** (p3)
offensive boldness; lack of shame; rudeness

**underachiever** (p3)
a student who performs at a lower level than expected

**suburbs** (p5)
the area surrounding a large city

**cul-de-sac** (p6)
a dead-end street or passageway

**betrothed** (p8)
engaged to be married

**algebra** (p8)
a branch of mathematics that deals with the relations between numbers

**jovial** (p11)
possessing or showing good nature; jolly; happy

**modest** (p14)
not boastful; humble

**composition** (p14)
the act of putting together

**sarcastic** (p16)
mocking; taunting

**trivial** (p17)
of little value or importance; insignificant

**euthanasia** (p18)
the merciful killing of a person or animal suffering severely from a condition that cannot be cured or relieved

**capital punishment** (p18)
a penalty of death for a crime

**fumigate** (p19)
to subject to or disinfect with fumes or smoke

**antic** (p20)
a prank or funny act

**subtly** (p22)
not directly or obviously

**Achilles' heel** (p23)
one's weak point

**patron** (p26)
a person who supports, defends, or champions a person or thought

**instigator** (p27)
a person who spurs or urges others to do something

**civilization** (p28)
>   the society and culture of a particular people, place, or period

**plume** (p28)
>   a long ornamental feather

**epic** (p28)
>   a long poem that tells of the wanderings and adventures of a great person or persons

**exotic** (p33)
>   strangely different and fascinating

**contemplate** (p34)
>   to look at or consider thoughtfully for a long time

**veteran** (p35)
>   a former member of the armed forces

**acid rain** (p36)
>   rain containing high levels of sulfuric and nitric acid caused mainly by smoke from the burning of fossil fuels

**rancid** (p37)
>   having the bad taste or smell of spoiled fat or oil

**draft** (p38)
>   to select for service in the armed forces

**hippie** (p45)
>   a person who adopts an alternative, often rebellious lifestyle characterized by liberal or radical politics, casual and colorful dress, and indifference to the values of work and career

**graffiti** (p50)
>   inscriptions, slogans, drawings, or other graphic images painted or scrawled on a public surface, such as on the wall of a building

**indignant** (p52)
>   angry because of something that is not right, just, or fair

**conceited** (p56)
>   having too high an opinion of oneself or one's accomplishments; vain

**futile** (p61)
>   done in vain; useless

**idealist** (p63)
>   a person who tends to see things as they would like to have them rather than as they are

**sedately** (p64)
>   calmly and steadily in manner

**berth** (p67)
>   to keep safely out of the way

**chariot** (p71)
>   a two-wheeled vehicle pulled by horses, used in ancient times for racing, in war, and in processions

**carnage** (p73)
>   a bloody killing of great numbers of people, such as in war

**ardent** (p75)
>   very enthusiastic and eager; fervent

**atomic bomb** (p80)
>   a powerful bomb using the energy suddenly released when the nuclei of atoms or uranium or plutonium are split

**perspective** (p82)
>   the effect of distance on spatial relationships and the appearance of objects

**infantry** (p88)
>   soldiers or a branch of the army, trained and equipped to fight on foot

**naive** (p93)
>   not carefully thought out

**tenant farmer** (p96)
>   a farmer who lives on land owned by someone else and pays rent either in cash or in farm produce

**liberal** (p98)
>   favoring progress, reform, and the use of governmental power to achieve social or political goals

**squalor** (p119)
>   filth, wretched poverty, or degradation

**extol** (p122)
>   to praise highly

**virtues** (p122)
>   good qualities or features

**vitality** (p124)
>   physical or mental energy; vigor; liveliness

**vagrant** (p125)
>   a person without a settled home or regular job; a vagabond

**altruistic** (p125)
>   concerned with the welfare of others; unselfish

**idealist** (p128)
>   a person who has high ideals of conduct and tries to live according to them

**pneumonia** (p134)
    a disease caused by a bacterial or viral infection and marked by inflammation of one or both lungs

**digress** (p158)
    to turn aside from the main subject

**platoon** (p180)
    a subdivision of a company, troop, or other military unit, commanded by a lieutenant

# Small Group Reading

📖 Nelson, Theresa. *And One for All*. New York: Orchard, 1989.
Geraldine's close relationship with her older brother Wing and his friend Sam changes when Wing joins the Marines and Sam leaves for Washington, D.C., to join a peace march during the Vietnam War. Grades 6 and up.

## Author Information

Theresa Nelson was born August 15, 1948, in Beaumont, Texas. Nelson has worked as an actress, teacher of creative dramatics, and Glee Club director. Since 1983 she has worked as a free-lance writer and as a speaker in schools, libraries, and literary groups.

*And One for All* has won numerous awards and honors. Among them are a Notable Children's Book citation and Best Book for Young Adults citation from the American Library Association; Best Book of the year citation from *School Library Journal*; Editor's Choice selection from *Booklist*; and a Teacher's Choice citation from the International Reading Association.

## Activities

1.  On a world map, have students locate:

    Guadal Canal          Pacific Ocean
    Hudson River, NY      Parris Island, SC
    Korea                 South Vietnam
    Mississippi River     Virginia
    North Vietnam         Washington, DC
    Okinawa

2.  Have students research President Lyndon Johnson and the Tet Offensive.

3.  Have students write a position paper explaining how they feel about the way Vietnam veterans were treated upon their return to the United States. They can then read their papers to the rest of the class.

4.  At the end of each chapter of *And One for All*, have students write diary entries from Geraldine's, Wing's, or Sam's point of view.

## Discussion

Give the small group the following instruction: As your group reads this book, discuss the following questions.

1.  On her trip to Washington, D.C., what is Geraldine homesick for?

2.  How does Geraldine's father feel about the peace march in Washington, D.C.? Why?

3. What is the difference in Wing's and Sam's feelings about war? What do you think caused them to feel differently?

4. What does Geraldine like to do in her spare time?

5. Why did Wing get kicked off the basketball team? How did his parents react when they found out?

6. Why does Geraldine think her mother is afraid for Wing?

7. What did Wing give Dub for Christmas?

8. In President Johnson's State of the Union address, he said, "Let us remember that those who expect to reap the blessings of freedom must, like men, undergo the fatigues of supporting it." What did he mean? Do you agree?

9. How did Sam and Wing react to President Johnson's speech?

10. Why was Wing suspended from school?

11. What did Wing tell Sam and Geraldine during his surprise party?

12. Why didn't Wing want his parents to see his report card?

13. What did Sam do that made Geraldine's father think of him as a traitor?

14. Why does Geraldine wish the Vietnam War was like World War II? What difference would this make in her life?

15. What do you think happened between Wing and Sam when Wing came home on leave?

16. How do you think Geraldine felt when she got a letter of her own from Wing?

17. What happened to Wing's friend Hopkins? Do you think Wing has changed because of it?

18. How did Geraldine react to the news she and her family received from the Marine officers?

19. Why did Geraldine decide to go to Washington, D.C.?

20. What did Geraldine learn from Sam on their way home from Washington, D.C.?

21. What do you think will become of Sam and Geraldine?

## Vocabulary

**sophisticated** (p4)
wise and experienced in worldly things

**assassination** (p4)
the murder of someone by a secret or surprise attack

**reservoir** (p5)
a basin, either natural or constructed, for collecting and storing a large supply of water

**formaldehyde** (p9)
a colorless gas used in a liquid solution to kill germs and to preserve dead animals for study

**prosperous** (p9)
successful; flourishing; thriving

**solitary** (p14)
single

**adage** (p15)
an old, much-used saying generally thought to be true; a proverb

**sporadic** (p15)
occasional

**draft age** (p16)
the age when a person is old enough (age 18) to be selected for service in the armed forces

**Purple Heart** (p18)
a decoration given to members of the United States armed services who have been wounded in action against an enemy

**morose** (p21)
gloomy or sullen

**dilapidated** (p21)
half ruined by neglect; falling to pieces

From *Teaching U.S. History Through Children's Literature*. © 1998 Wanda J. Miller. Teacher Ideas Press. (800) 237-6124.

**chlorophyll** (p26)
>   the green substance found in most plants, which in the presence of sunlight converts water and carbon dioxide from the air into sugars and starches

**decipher** (p28)
>   to translate into plain language; to decode

**patriot** (p30)
>   a person who loves his or her country and loyally defends and supports it

**redcoat** (p30)
>   a British soldier during the American Revolution and the War of 1812

**civil war** (p35)
>   a war between groups of citizens of the same country

**Communists** (p35)
>   people who support a social system in which the means for producing economic goods belong to the entire community or the state, not to individuals

**foyer** (p36)
>   an entrance room or hall

**inconspicuous** (p40)
>   not very noticeable; not attracting attention

**deceitful** (p42)
>   tending to deceive; lying or treacherous

**anguished** (p43)
>   feeling, showing, or caused by great suffering of mind or body

**pneumonia** (p48)
>   a disease caused by a bacterial or viral infection and marked by inflammation of one or both lungs

**crèche** (p56)
>   a group of figures representing the scene in the stable when Jesus was born

**hearth** (p56)
>   the floor of a fireplace or furnace

**specter** (p63)
>   a ghost

**unprecedented** (p65)
>   having no earlier example

**melancholy** (p66)
>   very gloomy; sad; dejected

**aggression** (p66)
>   an attack, especially an unprovoked attack

**persist** (p68)
>   to continue firmly or stubbornly in spite of opposition, warning, or difficulty

**propaganda** (p115)
>   a group of facts or ideas used in an effort to persuade a group of people to adopt or support certain ideas, attitudes, or actions

**platoon** (119)
>   a subdivision of a company, troop, or other military unit, commanded by a lieutenant

**tarmac** (p120)
>   an airport runway

**rosary** (p129)
>   a series of prayers recited by Roman Catholics

**mortar** (p130)
>   a short cannon, loaded through the muzzle and fired at a high angle

**guerrilla** (p142)
>   one of a group of fighters, usually not part of a regular army, who harasses the enemy with surprise raids and sabotage

**catechism** (p143)
>   a short book in the form of questions and answers for teaching the principles of a religion

**fascist** (p162)
>   a person who supports a form of government in which a dictator and the dictator's party support private property but strictly control industry and labor and ruthlessly suppress criticism or opposition

**throng** (p165)
>   a great crowd; a multitude

**placards** (p165)
>   posters that are publicly displayed

**perpetual** (p177)
>   continuing indefinitely; eternal

# Small Group Reading

Paterson, Katherine. *Park's Quest*. New York: E. P. Dutton, 1988.
Eleven-year-old Park travels to his grandfather's farm in Virginia to learn about his father, who died in the Vietnam War. Grades 5–8.

## Author Information

Katherine Paterson was born October 31, 1932 in the Jiangsu Province of China in the city of Qing Jiang. She spent her first four years in the nearby city of Hwaian. In the summer of 1937, she and her family went to the mountains of Jiangxi for a vacation. While there, war broke out between China and Japan. Her father crossed through combat zones to return to work in Hwaian, but Katherine, her mother, and her three sisters never saw their home again. Since then, Paterson has lived in more than thirty homes in three countries.

Of her early years, she says, "My mother read to us regularly, and because it opened up such a wonderful world, I taught myself to read before I entered school. Soon afterwards I began to write. I can't remember wanting to become a writer, but I loved stories and poems so much that it was only natural to try my hand at them. My first published work appeared in the Shanghai American School newspaper when I was seven years old."

Following college, Paterson taught sixth grade in rural Virginia. She returned to school to study Bible and Christian Education before going to Japan in 1957. She studied the Japanese language for two years and then worked on the island of Shikoku as an assistant for Christian education.

Paterson's writing career began in 1964 after her first son was born. It was nine years before her first novel, *The Master Puppeteer*, was published. Since then, Paterson has won the Newbery Medal twice and has received many other awards in children's literature.

## Activities

1. On a map of the United States, have students locate:
   Bethany Beach, DE                  Strathaven, VA
   Roanoke, VA                        Washington, DC

2. Have students illustrate the scene depicted on page 23.

3. Have students write an epilogue that takes place ten years after the end of *Park's Quest*, focusing on how Park's, Park's mother's, Park's grandfather's and Thanh's lives have changed.

4. Have students write a review of this novel. It should include a summary and reasons why other students should read this book. Then display these reviews in your school's hallway.

## Discussion

Give the small group the following instruction: As your group reads this book, discuss the following.

1. What does Park want to do?

2. Why do you think Park's mother finds it difficult to call him Park?

3. How does Park feel about his father?

4. How can Park find out what he wants to know about his father?

5.  What does Park daydream about?

6.  What do you think the two poems that Park found in a book with his father's picture meant?

7.  What did Park mean when he said, "Books tell you about the person who chose them." Do you agree?

8.  What do you think Park's mother's thoughts were when she took Park to Bethany Beach?

9.  How do you think Park felt when he saw his father's name on the Vietnam memorial?

10.  Why does Park want to meet his father's family?

11.  How would you feel if you were Park, about to meet your grandfather for the first time?

12.  Describe Park's grandfather's home.

13.  Who do you think the girl was that Park met at the springhouse?

14.  Why do you think Park daydreams so often?

15.  What does Park want his Uncle Frank to teach him?

16.  How did Park feel the first time he saw his grandfather?

17.  What news did Uncle Frank tell Park about Park's mother and father? How did it make Park feel?

18.  What happened when Park first met his grandfather?

19.  What did Park find out while looking for Thanh in her room?

20.  Why does Park's mother feel she is to blame for Park's father's death?

21.  What did Park discover about what made his grandfather cry?

## Vocabulary

**naught** (p5)
  nothing

**scullion** (p5)
  a servant who washes dishes, pots, and kettles

**presume** (p5)
  to take for granted; to assume; to suppose

**arrogant** (p6)
  too proud and disdainful of others

**quest** (p6)
  an expedition, such as by a knight seeking adventure

**mercy** (p6)
  kind treatment or mildness where severity is expected or deserved

**perfidious** (p6)
  treacherous

**indulgent** (p6)
  very kind and lenient; not strict or critical

**mortification** (p6)
  a feeling of loss of self-respect or pride; humiliation

**drudge** (p7)
  a person whose work is hard and boring

**veteran** (p7)
  a former member of the armed forces

**inauguration** (p8)
  a ceremony installing a person in an office

**ordinance** (p10)
  an order, law, or decree, especially one made by a city government

**insignia** (p11)
  badges or emblems used as special marks of membership, office, or honor

**solemnly** (p11)
  seriously

**enchantment** (p12)
  the use or effect of charms, or spells' magic

**threshold** (p12)
  the bar of wood, stone, or other material placed under a door

**thrall** (p14)
  slavery; bondage

From *Teaching U.S. History Through Children's Literature*. © 1998 Wanda J. Miller. Teacher Ideas Press. (800) 237-6124.

**resemblance** (p19)
similarity; likeness

**immortality** (p20)
life or fame lasting forever

**exuberant** (p20)
full of high spirits, joy, and energy

**inscription** (p22)
something, such as words or letters, that are written or engraved

**fathom** (p24)
to understand

**servitude** (p26)
slavery

**quest** (p26)
to seek or look for something

**ebony** (p30)
black

**jaunty** (p32)
dashing; perky

**ancient** (p38)
very old

**bitterly** (p39)
resentfully

**calculate** (p40)
to think out; to form an estimate of

**slum** (p40)
a shabby, dirty, run-down section of a city where the poor live crowded together

**stroke** (p43)
the bursting of a blood vessel in the brain

**agitated** (p43)
excited or stirred up

**humid** (p44)
damp, moist

**clapboard** (p47)
a thin board having one edge thinner than the other, used as a siding on wooden buildings

**cupola** (p47)
a small tower built on a roof and having a dome-shaped top

**obsequiously** (p48)
eagerly ready to please, praise, or obey

**dignity** (p48)
the quality of character, worth, or nobility that commands respect

**bureau** (p51)
a chest of drawers, usually with a mirror

**conjure** (p52)
to bring to mind as if by magic

**trough** (p53)
a long, narrow, open container for holding food or water for animals

**vigil** (p54)
the act of staying awake to observe or protect; a watch

**contemplation** (p54)
the act of looking at or considering thoughtfully for a long time

**chalice** (p54)
a goblet

**dishevelment** (p55)
the condition of being rumpled and untidy, such as hair or clothing

**contemptuous** (p57)
full of contempt or scorn

**seemly** (p59)
decent or proper; fitting; suitable

**countenance** (p59)
the expression of the face

**ordained** (p61)
ordered; decreed

**chivalry** (p62)
the ideal qualities of knighthood, such as gallantry, courtesy, bravery, and kindness

**refugee** (p63)
a person who flees from persecution or danger

**pasteurize** (p64)
to treat a liquid, such as milk, by heating it to 145 degrees Fahrenheit for 30 minutes and then rapidly chilling it to 50 degrees Fahrenheit to destroy bacteria

**peril** (p67)
to expose to danger

**colander** (p69)
a kitchen utensil with holes, used for draining off liquids from foods

**tenants** (p71)
people who rent a house or an apartment from someone else

**seneschal** (p79)
in the residence of a medieval noble, an official in charge of the household; a steward

**sympathy** (p80)
loyalty, support, or agreement

**homogenize** (p85)
   to mix the cream throughout the milk so that
   it cannot separate

**blight** (p98)
   anything that harms or destroys

**assent** (p120)
   to agree or consent

**hermit** (p123)
   a person who lives alone and apart from
   others

**ominous** (p133)
   threatening or foreboding

**amicably** (p146)
   in a friendly manner

# Small Group Reading

📖 Paulsen, Gary. *The Monument*. New York: Dell, 1991.
Thirteen-year-old Rocky's life is changed by an artist who comes to her small town in Kansas to design a Vietnam veteran's war memorial. Grades 7 and up.

## Author Information

Gary Paulsen was born on May 17, 1939 in Minneapolis, Minnesota. Paulsen has been a writer since the 1960s. He has also worked as a teacher, field engineer, editor, soldier, director, farmer, rancher, truck driver, and trapper.

*The Monument* was designated an American Library Association Best Book for Young Adults. In addition, *Dogsong* (1986), *Hatchet* (1988), and *The Winter Room* (1990) have all received Newbery Honor Book citations. Many of Paulsen's other books have been selected as American Library Association (ALA) Best Books for Young Adults, ALA Notable Children's Books, as well as awarded other prestigious honors. His books are definite favorites among middle school students.

Paulsen writes from firsthand knowledge of the outdoors—and from his experiences as a hunter, trapper, and even as a dogsledder in the Alaska Iditarod race.

In an interview for *Something About the Author* (volume 79), Paulsen tells of a turning point in his life, when on a subzero winter day he went into a library to warm himself. "To my absolute astonishment the librarian walked up to me and asked if I wanted a library card. When she handed me the card, she handed me the world. I can't even describe how liberating it was."

## Activities

1. On a map of the United States, have students locate Bolton, Kansas; Kansas City, Kansas; and Westfalia, Texas.

2. Following the reading of *The Monument*, involve your school's art teacher with this group. Ask him or her to visit with the students to discuss the art of designing monuments.

3. Have students contact your town historian to find out the names of people from your town who died during the Vietnam War.

4. Have students design a monument to honor soldiers from your town. It could be made out of construction paper or cardboard, depending on the time frame for completion of this project. Students can then present this monument to the class and hold a short memorial service for these soldiers.

# Discussion

Give the small group the following instruction: As your group reads this book, discuss the following.

1. Why was Rachael nicknamed Rocky?

2. Why doesn't Rachael have any friends?

3. How do you think Rachael felt when the Hemesvedts decided to adopt her?

4. What was Rachael's new life with Fred and Emma like?

5. How did Python get his name?

6. Describe Rocky's relationship with Python.

7. Why did the people feel that the town needed a monument?

8. What did Rocky think of Mick when she first met him?

9. Why did Rocky decide she wants to be an artist like Mick?

10. Why didn't Mick sleep at Carlson's bed and breakfast?

11. How do you think Rocky felt about Mick wanting her help?

12. Why did Mick tell Rocky that Mr. Jennings is a hero?

13. Why did Mick want to visit the grain elevator?

14. What do you think Mick meant when he said the grain elevator "is the cosmic center of the universe"?

15. Why do you think Mick told Rocky that there would be an explosion at the courthouse?

16. How did Rocky react to the book that Mick gave her?

17. What was the reaction of the townspeople when they saw Mick's drawings at the courthouse?

18. What do you think of Mick's ideas for Bolton's monument?

19. Why did Mick decide that he and Tru should leave before the official showing of the monument?

20. Discuss Rocky's feelings on discovering that Mick was leaving Bolton.

21. What did Katherine Anne Porter mean when she once said, "Art is what we find when the ruins are cleared away"?

22. How did reading *The Monument* affect you? Have your feelings about art changed in any way?

# Vocabulary

**microcosm** (p4)
   a smaller version of the rest of the world

**cubicle** (p8)
   any small room or partly enclosed section of a room

**auger** (p32)
   a tool for boring holes in the earth or in wood

**civic minded** (p39)
   concerned with a city or citizenship

**merits** (p43)
   marks for someone, showing high quality

**demerits** (p43)
   marks against someone for poor work or bad conduct

**scrutiny** (p43)
   a searching look or close, careful examination

**gnome** (p55)
   in folklore, a dwarf who lives in a cave and guards a treasure

**ambience** (p77)
   a surrounding atmosphere

**crude** (p84)
   lacking refinement or good taste

From *Teaching U.S. History Through Children's Literature.* © 1998 Wanda J. Miller. Teacher Ideas Press. (800) 237-6124.

**crux** (p85)
 the most important

**dysentery** (p94)
 a disease of the intestines

**cosmic** (p98)
 having to do with the universe or cosmos

**universe** (p98)
 made up of everything that exists, including the earth, sun, stars, planets, and outer space

**Impressionist Movement** (p108)
 a time in the late nineteenth century when the style of painting depicted its subject matter by using small strokes of paint to simulate real, reflected light

**avenging** (p134)
 getting revenge for

**horde** (p134)
 a great crowd; a swarm

**platoon** (p138)
 a subdivision of a company, troop, or other military unit, commanded by a lieutenant

**cunning** (p145)
 clever or tricky

# Small Group Reading

📖 Talbert, Marc. *The Purple Heart*. New York: Willa Perlman Books, 1992. When his injured father is sent home early from Vietnam, Luke finds it difficult to adjust to the troubled, emotionally shaken man who seems so unlike his courageous father. Grades 6–8.

## Author Information

Marc Talbert was born July 21, 1953, in Boulder, Colorado. He received his bachelor's degree in 1976 from Iowa State University.

Talbert taught fifth and sixth grade at Marshalltown Public Schools in Marshalltown, Iowa, from 1976 to 1977. From 1977 to 1981, he taught fifth grade at Ames Public Schools in Ames, Iowa. Since 1981, Talbert has worked as a speech writer, editor, and instructor of children's literature at the University of New Mexico.

In an interview for *Something About the Author* (volume 68), Talbert said, "I was always torn between wanting to work with children and wanting to write. I feel lucky to be able to combine these loves in children's books."

## Activities

1. On a world map, have students locate:
 Clifton, IA
 Des Moines, IA
 New Mexico

 Saigon, South Vietnam (renamed Ho Chi Minh City in 1975)
 Tokyo, Japan

2. Have students research President Johnson's role in the Vietnam War.

3. After the students finish reading *The Purple Heart*, have them write essays about what they believe courage is, then read their essays to the rest of the class.

4. Have the students work cooperatively to create a large Purple Heart on construction paper. Beneath the design, students can write an explanation of why soldiers receive a Purple Heart. This Purple Heart should then be hung in your classroom.

# Discussion

Give the small group the following instruction: As your group reads this book, discuss the following.

1.  Why were Luke and his mother sleeping in the basement?

2.  How did Luke's feelings about his father change?

3.  How did Luke's mother feel about her husband being in Vietnam?

4.  Discuss Luke's father's homecoming from Vietnam, along with Luke's reaction.

5.  How did Luke's father react to seeing people protesting the Vietnam War on television? Why?

6.  Why do you think Luke's father is having nightmares?

7.  Why didn't Luke want his friend Mike to see his father's Purple Heart?

8.  What happened to Luke's father's Purple Heart?

9.  Why were Luke's father and mother excited when Luke saw them after returning home from Mrs. Pederson's?

10. What did Luke have to do to make up for scaring Mrs. Pederson? Do you think it was fair?

11. How would you have felt if you were Luke when Mrs. Pederson told him the story about her husband and the bell?

12. How did Luke's father feel after his first day at college? Why?

13. How did Luke's father compare the Vietnam War with World War II?

14. Why did Luke's father receive the Purple Heart?

15. How do you think Luke feels about Mrs. Pederson now?

16. Discuss Luke and his father's talk about courage. Do you agree with Luke's father about what courage really is? Why or why not?

17. How did the Vietnam War affect Luke, his mother, and his father?

18. What does the Purple Heart symbolize to soldiers who receive it?

# Vocabulary

**tornado** (p3)
a violent, destructive wind forming a funnel-shaped cloud that extends downward from a mass of cloud and moves along in a narrow path

**eerie** (p4)
causing or arousing fear; strange

**mortar** (p6)
a short cannon, loaded through the muzzle and fired at a high angle

**shrapnel** (p6)
fragments scattered when a shell explodes

**recuperating** (p8)
regaining health or strength

**sulk** (p9)
to be sullen or ill-humored

**tarmac** (p10)
an airport runway

**quiver** (p10)
to make a slight trembling motion; to vibrate

**profile** (p14)
the outline of a human face as seen from the side

**idling** (p17)
operating without transmitting power

**bellow** (p18)
a loud cry or roar

**despair** (p19)
 the feeling that comes when all hope is lost or given up

**beckoned** (p20)
 summoned or signaled by a movement of the hand or head

**gnarled** (p21)
 knotty or twisted

**fanatic** (p23)
 a person whose exaggerated enthusiasm leads to unreasonable beliefs

**audible** (p24)
 heard or capable of being heard

**siege** (p25)
 the surrounding of a fortified place, town, or structure by a military force trying to capture it

**grimaced** (p26)
 expressed pain, annoyance, distrust, or other feelings by twisting the face

**peasant** (p26)
 in Europe, a country person of humble birth, such as a small farmer

**bewildered** (p26)
 confused or puzzled

**hippie** (p27)
 a person who adopts an alternative, often rebellious lifestyle characterized by liberal or radical politics, casual and colorful dress, and indifference to the values of work and career

**Vietcong** (p28)
 a Communist group in South Vietnam

**callus** (p31)
 a thickened and hardened part of the skin, such as on the foot

**chaos** (p32)
 complete disorder and confusion

**grim** (p35)
 stern or forbidding

**gaunt** (p36)
 very thin, such as from illness or hunger

**private** (p37)
 in the United States Army, the lowest-ranking soldier

**sergeant** (p37)
 in the United States Army, a noncommissioned officer ranking above a corporal

**hammerlock** (p42)
 in wrestling, a hold in which an opponent's arm is pulled behind his or her back and twisted upward

**cringe** (p48)
 to shrink or to cower in fear

**apparition** (p50)
 a ghost or spirit

**admiration** (p53)
 a feeling of wonder, approval, and satisfaction for someone or something of quality

**fraud** (p63)
 a person who is not what he or she seems to be

**mines** (p64)
 hidden explosives set to go off when an enemy comes near

**defiance** (p74)
 bold opposition to power or authority; refusal to submit or obey

**misery** (p81)
 a condition of great suffering

**knickers** (p88)
 loose-fitting, short pants, gathered in below the knee

**Formica** (p93)
 a durable and glossy laminated plastic used as a surface for tabletops and countertops

**fidelity** (p94)
 faithfulness in carrying out one's duties or responsibilities; loyalty

**ornery** (p103)
 mean

**saunter** (p104)
 to walk along in a slow, casual way; to stroll

**ominous** (p115)
 threatening or foreboding, like a bad omen

**eddy** (p120)
 a current of water moving against a main current, often in circles; a whirlpool

**forlorn** (p122)
 sad or pitiful due to being alone or neglected

**debris** (p123)
 scattered fragments or remnants; rubble

**gallantry** (p135)
 bravery and nobility

# Bibliography

## Individual Titles

Barr, Roger. *The Vietnam War*. San Diego, CA: Lucent Books, 1991.

This book gives an account of the Vietnam War, how the United States became involved in it, and the war's legacy. Grades 5 and up.

Brown, Tricia. *Lee Ann: The Story of a Vietnamese-American Girl*. New York: G. P. Putnam's Sons, 1991.

A young Vietnamese-American girl describes her family and school life, Saturday activities, and the celebration of TET, the Vietnamese New Year. Grades 2–5.

Bunting, Eve. *The Wall*. New York: Clarion Books, 1990.

A boy and his father come from far away to visit the Vietnam Veterans Memorial in Washington, D.C., and find the name of the boy's grandfather, who was killed in Vietnam. Grades 2–4.

Devaney, John. *The Vietnam War*. New York: Franklin Watts, 1992.

This book illustrates the horror and the politics of this controversial war, from the French withdrawal after the Battle of Dien Bien Phu to the fall of Saigon in 1975. Grades 6–9.

Dolan, Edward F. *America After Vietnam: Legacies of a Hated War*. New York: Franklin Watts, 1989.

This book examines the physical, emotional, and social effects of the Vietnam War on those who survived it, both the veterans and the refugees who came to the United States. Grades 7 and up.

———. *MIA: Missing in Action*. New York: Franklin Watts, 1989.

Dolan discusses the mysterious disappearance of thousands of American servicemen serving in Vietnam and other areas of Southeast Asia during the Vietnam War. He examines the issue of government reluctance to support the efforts to rescue and help find these missing men. Grades 7 and up.

Donnelly, Judy. *A Wall of Names: The Story of the Vietnam Veterans Memorial*. New York: Random House, 1991.

Donnelly provides readers with information on the history of the Vietnam War and the construction of the Vietnam Veterans Memorial, and discusses what the memorial means to many Americans. Grades 2–5.

Dunn, Mary Lois. *The Man in the Box: A Story from Vietnam*. New York: McGraw-Hill, 1968.

Chau Li's father had been the village chief, until the Vietcong came and put him in a small wooden box and left him there to die. An American soldier was put in the box with him. This book tells the story of these two strangers. Grades 8 and up.

Edelman, Bernard. *Dear America: Letters Home from Vietnam*. New York: Pocket Books, 1985.

The letters included in this book tell the stories of more than 100 men and women stationed in Vietnam. Grades 7 and up.

Edwards, Richard. *The Vietnam War*. Vero Beach, FL: Rourke Enterprises, 1986.

The author discusses the origins, events, conclusion, and aftermath of the war in Vietnam, as well as the reactions and attitudes of the American public. Grades 7 and up.

Green, Carl R., and William R. Sanford. *The Vietnam War Soldier at Con Thien*. Mankato, IL: Capstone Press, 1991.

The authors tell the story of the experiences of an army nurse who served in Vietnam. Grades 4–7.

Hoobler, Dorothy, and Thomas Hoobler. *Vietnam, Why We Fought: An Illustrated History*. New York: Alfred A. Knopf, 1990.

The authors examine the history of Vietnam, the involvement of the United States in the Vietnam War, and the effects of the war. Grades 7 and up.

Isserman, Maurice. *The Vietnam War: America at War*. New York: Facts on File, 1992.

This book discusses the historical and political background, military strategies, and battles of the Vietnam War. Grades 7 and up.

Lawson, Don. *An Album of the Vietnam War*. New York: Franklin Watts, 1986.

An illustrated history of the war in Vietnam from Ho Chi Minh's declaration of independence to the withdrawal of U.S. troops. Grades 5 and up.

———. *The United States in the Vietnam War*. New York: Thomas Y. Crowell, 1981.

The author explains the political, social, economic, and military aspects of the Vietnam War, the longest war in U.S. history. Grades 7 and up.

———. *The War in Vietnam*. New York: Franklin Watts, 1981.

Lawson describes the events leading up to the Vietnam War, American involvement, opposition at home, the end of the conflict, and the aftermath of the war. Grades 6–9.

Lifton, Betty Jean, and Thomas C. Fox. *Children of Vietnam.* New York: Atheneum, 1972.

The authors illustrate through words and photographs the lives of Vietnamese children and the horrors that war can inflict on the lives of children. Grades 7 and up.

Marrin, Albert. *America and Vietnam: The Elephant and the Tiger.* New York: Viking, 1992.

Marrin examines the political history, military events, social impact, and long-term effects of the Vietnam War. Grades 8 and up.

McCloud, Bill. *What Should We Tell Our Children About Vietnam?* Norman, OK: University of Oklahoma Press, 1989.

The author wrote to Vietnam veterans, political decisionmakers, authors of books on the Vietnam War, leading opponents of the war, and current public figures, seeking answers to the question, "What should we tell our children about Vietnam?" Their responses are included in this book. Grades 7 and up.

Nhuong, Huynh Quang. *The Land I Lost: Adventures of a Boy in Vietnam.* New York: Harper & Row, 1982.

This is a collection of Nhuong's personal reminiscences of his childhood in a hamlet on the central highlands of Vietnam. Grades 4–7.

Nickelson, Harry. *Vietnam.* San Diego, CA: Lucent Books, 1989.

This is an account of the Vietnam War and its aftermath, with information on its origins and on how the war affected American foreign policy and attitudes. Grades 7 and up.

Palmer, Laura. *Shrapnel in the Heart: Letters and Remembrances from the Vietnam Veterans Memorial.* New York: Random House, 1987.

This is a collection of letters and poems that have been left at the Vietnam Veterans Memorial in Washington, D.C. Grades 8 and up.

Rabinowitz, Richard. *What Is War? What Is Peace?: 50 Questions and Answers for Kids.* New York: Avon Books, 1991.

This book answers many of the questions that students have about war. It includes a glossary and an appendix that tells what students themselves can do in the quest for world peace. Grades 4–7.

Smith, Nigel. *The United States Since 1945.* New York: Bookwright Press, 1990.

This book of two-page essays describing events since 1945 includes the Vietnam War, along with the Korean battles, the Eisenhower presidency, McCarthyism, segregation, and the growing affluence of the middle class. Grades 4–7.

Smith, Winnie. *American Daughter Gone to War: On the Front Lines with an Army Nurse in Vietnam.* New York: William Morrow, 1992.

Winnie Smith gives an account of her experiences as an Army nurse during the Vietnam War. Grades 7 and up.

Spencer, Duncan. *Facing the Wall: Americans at the Vietnam Veterans Memorial.* New York: Macmillan, 1986.

The stories in this book were assembled over a period of more than a year. They were taped to the Wall or are the results of interviews with people visiting the Wall. These are personal, very real stories of soldiers who went to Vietnam. Grades 6 and up.

Warren, James A. *Portrait of a Tragedy.* New York: Lothrop, Lee & Shepard, 1990.

Warren discusses the causes, events, and aftermath of the Vietnam War. Grades 7 and up.

Wormser, Richard L. *Three Faces of Vietnam.* New York: Franklin Watts, 1993.

Wormser examines the Vietnam War from the perspectives of antiwar protesters, the Vietnamese people, and the American soldiers who fought in the war. Grades 7 and up.

Wright, David K. *Enchantment of the World: Vietnam.* Chicago: Childrens Press, 1989.

Wright discusses the geography, history, people, economy, and customs of Vietnam. Grades 5 and up.

———. *War in Vietnam: Book I—Eve of Battle.* Chicago: Childrens Press, 1989.

This is a review of the Vietnam War beginning with its history and presenting biographical sketches of prominent political figures of the time and a glossary of words and phrases connected to Vietnam. Grades 5 and up.

———. *War in Vietnam: Book II—A Wider War.* Chicago: Childrens Press, 1989.

This is the second in a four-book series. It discusses the Vietnam War from 1965 to the Tet Offensive in 1968. Grades 5 and up.

———. *War in Vietnam: Book III—Vietnamization.* Chicago: Childrens Press, 1989.

This third volume follows the conflict in Vietnam from the period of intensification at the time of Richard Nixon's election to its conclusion and the withdrawal of American troops. Grades 5 and up.

———. *War in Vietnam: Book IV—Fall of Vietnam.* Chicago: Childrens Press, 1989.

This final book in the series examines the conflict in Vietnam, with an emphasis on the final few years, the withdrawal of American troops, and the fall of South Vietnam. Grades 5 and up.

# Theme Resources

## Commercial Resources

*American History Illustrated.* Harrisburg, PA: Cowles Magazines.

The March/April 1993 issue for use with students in grades 8 and up contains an article titled "Khe Sanh." This article details one of the most controversial battles of the Vietnam War, in which 6,000 Marines defended a remote highland outpost.

The April 1995 issue, for use with students in grades 8 and up, includes an article titled "Final Days of South Vietnam." Colonel Harry G. Summers, Jr. was one of the last Americans out of Saigon on April 30, 1975. He looks back twenty years to the aftermath of the Vietnam War. Grades 8 and up.

*Educational Oasis: The Magazine for Middle Grades 5–9.* Carthage, IL: Good Apple.

The May/Summer 1993 issue, for use with students in grades 5 through 9, includes the following articles: "Wall of Remembrance," "War and Language: A Unit Plan for English Class," and "Memorial Day."

Jefferies, David. *Jacdaw: The Vietnam War.* Amawalk, NY: Jackdaw, 1997.

This is a portfolio of primary source material including sixteen reproduction historical documents. Among them are the Vietcong policy toward POWs, a newspaper story on the marine landing at Da Nang, and the April 30, 1975 front page of the *San Francisco Chronicle.* Comprehensive notes on the documents, a reading list, and critical thinking questions are also included. This resource can be used with students in grades 5 and up.

Marsh, Norma. *Novel Ties: Park's Quest.* Hyde Park, NY: Learning Links, 1996.

This resource contains prereading and postreading activities, vocabulary skills, comprehension questions, and writing activities in a chapter-by-chapter format for *Park's Quest.* Use with students in grades 5 through 8.

## Computer Resources

*Beyond the Wall: Stories Behind the Vietnam Wall.* (CD-ROM) Washington, DC: Magnet Interactive, 1995.

This CD-ROM has three main sections. "About the War" uses photographs, brief articles, video clips, audio narration and recordings, and letters home from soldiers to show what life was like on the front lines and to provide background information of U.S. involvement in the war. "About the Wall" chronicles the Vietnam Veterans Memorial's beginnings and construction. "Tour the Wall" is a three-dimensional journey along the monument. Included are the stories of some of the real people behind the names on the Wall. Available for Macintosh and Windows.

*Passage to Vietnam.* (CD-ROM) Redmond, WA: Medio Multimedia, 1994.

This CD-ROM contains more than forty minutes of ABC News video detailing key battles, evacuations, the Tet offensive, and protests in Washington, D.C. More than 300 photographs of events and key people are also included, as well as the full text of *America's Longest War* by George Herring.

*The War in Vietnam: A Multimedia Chronicle from CBS News and The New York Times.* (CD-ROM) New York: Simon & Schuster Macmillan Digital USA, 1995.

Nearly 1,000 *New York Times* articles are included, along with CBS video clips, to provide students with a greater understanding of the Vietnam War. Available for Macintosh and Windows.

## Videos

*Dear America: Letters Home from Vietnam.* New York: Ambrose Video, 1988. (84 minutes)

This original HBO project was an Emmy Award-winning special. It provides the words of real soldiers who served in Vietnam in the form of letters written home. It includes NBC News television coverage of the war and previously unreleased film footage from the Department of Defense. A study guide comes with the video and provides background information.

*The Fall of Saigon.* Bethesda, MD: The Discovery Channel, 1995. (90 minutes)

This video contains rare footage and eyewitness accounts from both sides of the conflict. South Vietnamese citizens loyal to the United States tell their stories of the chaos and duplicity that led to the collapse of Saigon.

# End-of-Unit Celebration

## Vietnam War Research Project

In groups of two or three, have students research the following topics. When completed, hold a presentation day.

Antiwar Demonstrations in the United States During the Vietnam War

President Jimmy Carter

The Causes of the Vietnam War

Comparison of the Treatment of Returning Vietnam Veterans to Returning Veterans from World War II and the Persian Gulf War

The Fall of Saigon

President Lyndon B. Johnson

Ho Chi Minh

President Richard Nixon

Post Traumatic Stress Disorder

The Tet Offensive

The Vietnam Veterans Memorial in Washington, D.C.

# Chapter 6

# Celebrating Our Multicultural Heritage

## Introduction

The United States is becoming increasingly more diverse. Historically, it has been called a "melting pot" for the simple reason that it was founded by and has grown because of an influx of immigrants from other countries.

In our schools, the population of children from various religious and ethnic backgrounds is growing. Thus, it is vital for all students to learn about and understand the background and culture of one another. According to the Bradley Commission of History in the Schools, "Our students need to confront the diverse cultural heritages of the world's many peoples, and they need to know the origins and evolution of the political, religious, and social ideas that have shaped our institutions and others."

Maureen Cech expanded on the need for multicultural education in *Globalchild: Multicultural Resources for Young Children* when she said, "Multiculturalism is a sharing of cultures. It empowers individuals who then share that strength among groups. It expands cultural consciousness into global consciousness. As essential as literacy, multiculturalism is no longer an option in education. It is an integrated part of any well developed program."

Trade books covering a wide variety of cultural backgrounds are included in this chapter for your use in expanding the cultural knowledge, understanding, and acceptance of your students.

## Whole Group Reading

Girion, Barbara. *Indian Summer*. New York: Scholastic, 1990.
While spending summer vacation on an Indian reservation, twelve-year-old Joni has a hard time getting along with Sarah Birdsong and her friends, who seem to feel she is responsible for the prejudice they experience outside the reservation. Girion portrays the struggle of children from two very different cultures to understand and appreciate each other. Grades 4–8.

## Author Information

Barbara Girion was born November 20, 1937 in New York City. She received a bachelor of arts degree from Montclair State College in 1958 and she did graduate work at Kean College and New School for Social Research.

Girion was a junior high school history teacher in Hillside, New Jersey from 1958 to 1962. She has also worked as a substitute special education teacher and a guest lecturer and instructor in creative writing and writing for young people at Hofstra University. She has worked as a writer since 1968.

Several of Girion's books for children have won awards. *A Tangle of Roots* was named one of the Best Books for Young Adults by the American Library Association in 1979. *A Handful of Stars* was also named a Best Book for Young Adults by the American Library Association in 1982.

Of her writing, Girion told an interviewer for *Something About the Author* (volume 78), "Writing is one of the most exciting professions in the world. After the hard work of writing and rewriting comes the fun of seeing a story in print, getting letters from young readers and parents who have enjoyed it, and meeting lots of new and interesting people, some of whom become close friends."

## Activities

1.  On a world map, have students locate:
    Buffalo, NY                          New Jersey
    Mississippi River                    South America

2.  Have students research the six nations of the Iroquois. How are they different and how are they alike? They should locate information on Iroquois laws and culture, then present what they have learned to the rest of the class.

3.  Ask your school art teacher, or parent volunteers, to make cornhusk dolls (no faces) with your class.

4.  Have students write a letter to the Bureau of Indian Affairs in Washington, D.C., requesting information about programs the bureau oversees. Students can then display this information in your classroom.

## Discussion

Give the class the following instruction: As we read this book, we will be discussing the following.

1.  Why did Joni write a letter to Sarah Birdsong?

2.  How does Joni feel about her family's plans for the summer?

3.  What upset Joni at her going-away party?

4.  How does Sarah Birdsong feel about Joni coming to stay with her?

5.  Discuss your reaction to Sarah's letter to Joni.

6.  Why is Sarah's father fighting the government?

7.  What is the Indian legend about how Niagara Falls was formed?

8.  Why do you think Sarah is trying to scare Joni?

9.  Why were Mikey and Sarah surprised when they saw the Birdsongs' house?

10. How is Sarah's house different from Joni's?

11. Does your family have any items that have been handed down from your ancestors that are precious to you, as the Birdsongs do?

12. Why don't the Iroquois people trust the government?

13. Why did Sarah become upset when she saw Joni's mother brushing her hair?

14. What did Sarah tell Joni about the walking stick?

15. How did the Iroquois help George Washington and his men survive the winter?

16. What do you think happened to Joni's doll?

17. According to Maw Maw's story, why are cornhusk dolls made without faces?

18. Discuss Joni's reaction to the trick that Sarah and Sarah's friends played on her at the lake. How would you have felt if you had been Joni?

19. What did the author mean when he wrote, "Ever since Joni had run from the lake, Sarah's stomach had felt like a colony of Mexican jumping beans"?

20. Why are Indians still angry with the white man about things that happened many years ago?

21. Why did Sarah's mother really leave the reservation?

22. What did the Iroquois call North America? Why?

23. How was Sarah treated at the store when she and Joni went to get some things for Maw Maw?

24. What did Joni realize about how Sarah treats her?

25. What were wampum belts used for?

26. Why did Joni take Sarah's necklace?

27. What happened at the store between Sarah and her friends? How did it make Joni feel when she heard them?

28. Why did Maw Maw give Mikey the name "Laughing Boy Who Brings Help and Friendship"?

29. What do you think Joni will do with Sarah's necklace?

30. What are the three sisters? Why do you think Maw Maw told Joni the story of the three sisters?

31. Describe the powwow.

32. What happened between Joni and Sarah during the friendship dance? How did everyone react?

33. In what ways are Joni and her friends like Sarah and her friends?

## Vocabulary

**pediatrician** (p3)
    a doctor who specializes in the care of babies and children

**reservation** (p4)
    a tract of government land reserved for a special purpose, such as an Indian reservation

**stern** (p4)
    harsh in nature or manner; strict; severe

**enthusiastic** (p5)
    expressing eager interest or approval

**rigid** (p7)
    not giving or bending; stiff or firm

**garish** (p8)
    too showy or bright; gaudy

**savage** (p13)
    wild, untamed, and often fierce

**porcelain** (p14)
    a fine, hard, white earthenware used for plates, dishes, cups, and sinks

From *Teaching U.S. History Through Children's Literature.* © 1998 Wanda J. Miller. Teacher Ideas Press. (800) 237-6124.

**confederacy** (p16)
> a union or league of persons or states that have joined together for mutual support or action

**exhibition** (p17)
> an open showing; a display

**wampum** (p26)
> small beads made of polished shells, often worked into belts and bracelets, once used as money or ceremonial pledges by North American Indians

**grimace** (p33)
> a twisting of the face expressing pain, annoyance, disgust, or other feelings

**Peace Corps** (p37)
> a United States government organization that trains American volunteers and sends them to work with and help the people of underdeveloped countries

**hospitality** (p38)
> friendly, welcoming treatment of guests or strangers

**stethoscope** (p44)
> a small, portable instrument by which doctors can hear sounds produced in the chest, especially in the lungs and heart

**suburbs** (p45)
> the area surrounding a large city

**heirloom** (p50)
> an object that has been passed through several generations of a family

**alcove** (p57)
> a small section of a room opening out from the main section

**tomahawk** (p57)
> an axlike weapon used by North American Indians

**ancestor** (p57)
> a person from whom one is descended, generally a person further back than a grandparent; a forebear

**precious** (p57)
> cherished

**family crest** (p58)
> a special symbol that represents a family's name

**prominent** (p60)
> well-known

**privilege** (p64)
> a special benefit, favor, or advantage enjoyed only under special conditions

**paleface** (p70)
> a white person

**traitor** (p79)
> a person who betrays friends, a cause, or an obligation, especially a person who betrays a country

**parcel** (p81)
> a portion of land

**mortified** (p89)
> deprived of self-respect or pride; humiliated

**maiden** (p96)
> an unmarried woman, especially if young

**petrified** (p106)
> extremely frightened

**clan** (p116)
> a group of families claiming descent from a common ancestor

**calico** (p119)
> cotton cloth printed with a figured design

**heritage** (p122)
> traditions, beliefs, or attitudes handed down from the past

**culture** (p122)
> the way of life of a particular people, including its customs, religions, inventions, and tools

**powwow** (p129)
> a conference with or of North American Indians

**commotion** (p133)
> great confusion; excitement; disturbance

**indigestion** (p134)
> the inability to digest food or a difficulty in digesting food

**tension** (p134)
> mental strain; nervous anxiety

**chamomile** (p142)
> a strongly scented plant from whose leaves and daisylike flowers a medicinal tea is brewed

**purify** (p143)
> to make or become pure or clean

**taunted** (p149)
> insulted, provoked, or made fun of with scornful, mocking, or sarcastic remarks

**cunning** (p150)
  clever or tricky

**tetanus** (p153)
  a disease marked by stiffening and spasms of the muscles, especially of the neck and jaw, caused by bacterium that enters the body through a wound

**novocaine** (p153)
  a drug that deadens sensation, used in medicine and dentistry as a local anesthetic

**desperate** (p163)
  considered almost helpless

**harmony** (p164)
  agreement; accord

**mournful** (p170)
  showing or causing grief; sorrowful

**dignified** (p174)
  having dignity; proud; calm and stately

**elders** (p174)
  older people

# Small Group Reading

Ada, Alma Flor. *My Name Is María Isabel*. New York: Atheneum, 1993. Third-grader María Isabel, born in Puerto Rico and now living in the United States, wants badly to fit in at school. A writing assignment, "My Greatest Wish," gives her the opportunity to fit in. Grades 3–5.

## Author Information

Alma Flor Ada was born January 3, 1938, in Camaguey, Cuba. She received her diploma from Universidad Complutense de Madrid in 1959. She received her master's degree (1963) and her Ph.D. (1965) from Pontifica Universidad Catolica del Peru. From 1965 to 1967, Ada did postdoctoral study at Harvard University.

Ada's career has taken her to many colleges and universities as a professor, including the Collegio Alexander von Humbolt in Lima, Peru; the University of San Francisco in California; the University of Texas in El Paso, Texas; and the Universidad Complutense in Madrid, Spain.

Ada has written dozens of books for children, textbooks, and many other educational materials. She has translated many children's books by other authors into Spanish. Many of her children's books have been published in Spanish and English. Several of Ada's books present stories set in Latin America, and describe the feelings of children as they confront cultural misunderstanding and learn to take pride in their heritage.

Ada's work has received several honors. *The Gold Coin* was designated as a Notable Children's Trade Book in the Field of Social Studies by the National Council for the Social Studies and the Children's Book Council.

## Activities

1.  On a world map, have students locate:
    Cuba                                Puerto Rico
    Miami, FL                          Santo Domingo, Dominican Republic

2.  Have students write their own essays titled "My Greatest Wish."

3.  Have students write a short skit for *My Name Is María Isabel* and perform it for the rest of the class. The scene should take place at school when the teacher calls on María Isabel by a different name. At the end, María Isabel should explain to the class why it is important to her to be called by her real name.

4. Ask your school's Spanish teacher or a community member who speaks Spanish to visit your class and present a short Spanish lesson to the small group .

## Discussion

Give the small group the following instruction: As your group reads this book, discuss the following questions.

1. How does María Isabel feel about going to her new school?

2. What happened to María Isabel on the way to the bus?

3. What did María Isabel's teacher say that upset her?

4. Why didn't María Isabel answer her teacher when she was called on?

5. Why did María Isabel's family move?

6. How is María Isabel going to participate in the winter pageant? Why?

7. How do you think María Isabel felt when she saw Clara again?

8. Why does María Isabel feel that she is caught in a sticky spider's web?

9. What is María Isabel's greatest wish?

10. How did María Isabel's essay change things for her at school?

11. Is there anything you have wanted to change at school? Why?

## Vocabulary

**Belita** (p2)
a nickname for Isabel

**cherish** (p10)
to hold dear; to treat tenderly

**chamomile** (p10)
a strongly scented plant from whose leaves and daisylike flowers a medicinal tea is brewed

**patience** (p20)
the condition of being able to wait for someone or something or to endure unpleasant things without complaining

**glared** (p22)
stared in anger or hostility

**pendant** (p25)
anything that hangs from something else, especially an ornament, such as a jewel on a chain

**enchanted** (p28)
charmed; delighted

**soot** (p30)
a black, powdery substance, mostly carbon, that rises in the air from the burning of a material, such as wood, coal, or gas

**grime** (p30)
dirt, especially soot, rubbed into or coating a surface

**subway** (p32)
an electric railroad that is mainly underground

**Chabelita** (p37)
a nickname for Isabel

**Menorah** (p38)
in Judaism, a candelabrum used during religious ceremonies

**pinata** (p39)
a decorated, candy-filled container that is hung from the ceiling at traditional Latin American celebrations where blindfolded children try to break it open with a stick

**eager** (p46)
impatiently anxious

**pageant** (p56)
a public entertainment, often performed outdoors, that is based on historical events

# Small Group Reading

📖 Buss, Fran Leeper, with Daisy Cubias. *Journey of the Sparrows*. New York: Lodestar, 1991.

María and her sister and brother are Salvadoran refugees who are smuggled into the United States in crates. They attempt to build a life in Chicago with the help of a sympathetic family. Grades 6 and up.

## Author Information

Fran Leeper Buss has spent much time traveling throughout the United States, taping life histories of poor and working-class women from different ethnic and racial backgrounds. These oral histories are placed in the Schlesinger Library on the History of American Women at Radcliffe College.

Buss has worked as a campus minister, a women's studies teacher, an outreach worker, and founder and director of a women's crisis and information center. She is currently a research associate at the Southwest Institute for Research at the University of Arizona.

Daisy Cubias is a poet and activist who came to work in the United States as a young woman from El Salvador.

## Activities

1. On a world map, have students locate:

   | | |
   | --- | --- |
   | Brownsville, TX | Lake Michigan |
   | Chicago, IL | Mexico |
   | El Salvador | New Mexico |
   | Guatemala | Rio Grande River |
   | Honduras | |

2. Have students write an essay explaining what they have learned about illegal immigration. It should include reasons that people come to the United States illegally and the dangers these people face. These essays should then be shared with the rest of the class.

3. Have students write journal entries from María's point of view at the following points in the novel: When they traveled across the border in crates, María's first visit to the church looking for food, the birth of Julia's baby, and María's return to Mexico.

## Discussion

Give the small group the following instruction: As your group reads this book, discuss the following.

1. Why do you think María and the others are hiding in crates?

2. Describe the conditions inside the crates.

3. Why is María so afraid of being sent back to El Salvador?

4. What is wrong with Oscar?

5. Why are Marta and her husband separated?

6. What did Beatriz tell Julia about how they would have to live in the United States?

7. What often happens to people who try to cross the border from Mexico to the United States secretly?

8. Who are the coyotes? What do they do?

9. What did Marta mean when she said, "Life here isn't all fresh coffee and sugar"?

10. Why did Papa feel that María could save their family?

11. How does María feel about being in the North?

12. Where did Alicia take María to work? What were the conditions like?

13. What happened to María's father and Ramon?

14. Why didn't María's mother and Teresa come with them to the United States?

15. Why is it important for María to learn English?

16. Discuss your feelings about the way the man with the white hair treated María at work.

17. What did the harmonica man give to María? Why do you think it meant so much to her?

18. Why are María and Julia afraid of the hospital?

19. What happened at the factory on the day María and the other workers were to be paid?

20. What did the Quetzal Lady tell María to do when the church ran out of food?

21. What did María do to earn more money?

22. What did Dona Elena tell María about goodness? Do you agree?

23. Why did María feel joy and sorrow when Julia's baby was born?

24. What news did María and Julia receive from Beatriz in Mexico?

25. What happened to María and Julia's mother? What plans does María have?

26. What did the women at the bus depot tell María?

27. Why do you think Laura and Manuel are willing to take risks to help María?

28. What did María find when she reached Mexico?

29. If you were María, how do you think you would handle the responsibility she has been given?

30. Discuss your feelings about illegal immigration.

## Vocabulary

**midwife** (p8)
a person whose occupation is assisting women in childbirth

**gracias** (p8)
Spanish for "thank you"

**solemn** (p9)
serious

**nightingale** (p10)
a small reddish-brown European bird; the male sings late into the night and is noted for its song

**pobrecito** (p13)
Spanish for "poor boy"

**adobe house** (p14)
a house made of bricks that are dried in the sun instead of in an oven or kiln

**elegance** (p18)
good taste and luxuriousness, such as in clothes, furnishings, or decorations

**exuberant** (p20)
full of high spirits, joy, and energy

**astonishment** (p23)
the condition of being surprised greatly

**muchas** (p24)
Spanish for "very much"

**bienvenidos** (p25)
Spanish for "welcome"

**tortilla** (p25)
> a round, flat Mexican bread made of coarse cornmeal and baked on a sheet of iron or a slab of stone

**ravine** (p37)
> a long, narrow, deep depression in the earth that has steep sides and was usually cut out by a flow of water; a gorge

**textile** (p38)
> a woven fabric

**norteamericanos** (p39)
> Spanish for "North Americans"

**marimba** (p46)
> a kind of xylophone that has resonating tubes beneath tuned wooden bars

**sedate** (p48)
> calm and steady in manner; composed

**scorn** (p61)
> an expression of contempt or disdain

**deported** (p65)
> expelled from a country by legal order; banished

**processions** (p67)
> parades

**fervently** (p80)
> eagerly

**disdainfully** (p81)
> scornfully

**silhouette** (p86)
> the outline of a person or object seen against a light or a light background

**rosary** (p91)
> a string of beads for keeping count of the prayers recited

**compassion** (p94)
> pity for the suffering or distress of another and the desire to help

**serene** (p110)
> peaceful; tranquil; calm

**sanctuary** (p111)
> a holy or sacred place, especially a church or the place in a church where the main altar is located

**gumption** (p118)
> aggressive energy; initiative

**cassock** (p126)
> a close-fitting, floor-length, black robe worn by the clergy of some churches

**mortar** (p126)
> a bowl in which materials are crushed with a pestle

**pestle** (p126)
> a tool with a blunt end used for pounding or crushing substances in a mortar

**sober** (p130)
> serious, calm, thoughtful, and well-balanced

**refresco** (p135)
> Spanish for "refreshment"

**infirmary** (p138)
> a place for treating the sick, such as in a school or factory

**refugee** (p140)
> a person who flees from persecution or danger

**irrigation ditch** (p151)
> a ditch used to furnish land with water

**thicket** (p153)
> a thick, dense growth, such as of trees and bushes

# Small Group Reading

📖 Crew, Linda. *Children of the River*. New York: Delacorte Press, 1989.
Having fled Cambodia four years earlier to escape the Khmer Rouge army, seventeen-year-old Sundara is torn between remaining faithful to her own people and adjusting to life in her Oregon high school as an American. Grades 6 and up.

## Author Information

Linda Crew was born April 8, 1951, in Corvallis, Oregon. Crew attended Lewis and Clark College from 1969 to 1970. She received her bachelor of arts degree from the University of Oregon in 1973.

Among its honors, *Children of the River* was named a Golden Kite Honor Book, 1989, a Michigan Library Association Young Adult Honor Book, and an American Library Association Young Adult Honor Book for Young Adults. It also received the International Reading Association Children's Book Award in the older readers category. Crews's other books include *Someday I'll Laugh About This*, *Nekomah Creek*, and *Ordinary Miracles* (an adult novel).

Crew lives on a farm with her husband and three children. Her family life has provided much material for her writing. In 1980, a family of Cambodian refugees came to work on the Crews' farm at harvest time. The two families became friends, and the Cambodians' stories became the inspiration for *Children of the River*.

## Activities

1.  On a world map, have students locate:

    California              Philippines
    China                   Portland, OR
    Indonesia               Thailand
    Kampuchea, Cambodia     Vietnam
    Malaysia

2.  Have students contact a local travel agent and request travel brochures for Cambodia. They should design a poster using the information they receive to hang in the classroom.

3.  Throughout the reading of *Children of the River*, have students write journal entries from Sundara's point of view, including the journey from Cambodia to the United States, Sundara's feelings about Jonathan as they become closer, and Sundara's fear for the safety of her family back in Cambodia. Have each student in the group choose one of their entries to read aloud to the rest of the class.

4.  Have students contact your county migrant office to find out if migrants come to your area to work, how long they stay, and what type of work they do.

## Discussion

Give the small group the following instruction: As your group reads this book, discuss the following.

1.  Why did Sundara leave her home to go to her relatives' fishing village?

2.  Why does Soka wish to stay in the fishing village? Why must the family leave?

3.  Why is Sundara worried about Soka's baby?

4.  How did Sundara feel when the teacher read her poem aloud?

5.  What news did Soka receive from the United Nations about her sister?

6.  Why does Soka keep news of work to herself?

7.  What is Soka saving money for?

8.  How does Sundara's grandmother feel about working in the fields?

9.  To whom did Sundara talk at the market on Saturday? Why didn't she want her brother to tell Soka about it?

10. How did Jonathan's father inspire Sundara?

11. What did Sundara tell Jonathan about the fighting in Cambodia?

12. What is All Soul Day?

13. What happened after Sundara left Cambodia?

14. What happened to Moni's husband and baby?

15. Why do other people want advice from Soka?

16. How is it easier for the younger children to adjust to life in America than it is for Sundara?

17. What does Sundara miss about Cambodia?

18. What type of problems do the Cambodians encounter in America?

19. Where did Sundara and her family go when they first came to America?

20. According to their custom, who will choose a husband for Sundara? How does Sundara feel about this now?

21. How is school different for Sundara in America than in Cambodia?

22. Why does Pok Simo resent Sundara and her family?

23. What American ideas does Sundara like best?

24. Why does Sundara feel that she doesn't fit in anywhere?

25. What happened between Sundara and Cathy Gates?

26. What surprised Sundara when she went boating with Jonathan and his parents?

27. Why was Sundara frightened when Jonathan came to her house? Was she right to be so upset?

28. What do the letters that Soka receives from Cambodia ask for?

29. What does Sundara plan to do about Jonathan? Do you think it will work?

30. How is the climate different in Oregon than in Kampuchea?

31. What news did Sundara receive about Chamroeun? How did she react?

32. Why hasn't Sundara cried since she left Cambodia?

33. How has Jonathan changed since he met Sundara?

34. Why is Jonathan angry with his parents?

35. Why do you think Naro defended Sundara to Soka?

36. What does Dr. McKinnon want Sundara to teach him? Why?

37. After an outburst from Soka, Sundara thought, "Maybe their mistake was in feeling they had to choose, fearing they couldn't be American without giving up being Khmer. Why couldn't they be both? In the end, after all, what was more American than coming from someplace else, bringing another culture with you?" Do you agree with her conclusion? Why or why not?

38. What happened on Thanksgiving to bring Sundara and Soka closer?

39. What news did Valinn bring to Sundara? How did this news change Sundara's outlook on life and the future?

40. Discuss your feelings after you have finished reading *Children of the River*.

## Vocabulary

**wafted** (p1)
carried or moved gently

**hammock** (p2)
a bed or couch formed by hanging a strong fabric between two supports

**Communist** (p2)
a member of a political party that advocates a political organization in which a single political party controls the state and manages the production and distribution of goods

**teeming** (p2)
overflowing

**refugee** (p2)
a person who flees from persecution or danger

**dominated** (p2)
controlled or ruled over

**terse** (p2)
short and to the point; concise

From *Teaching U.S. History Through Children's Literature.* © 1998 Wanda J. Miller. Teacher Ideas Press. (800) 237-6124.

**commotion** (p2)
  great confusion; excitement; disturbance

**hideous** (p3)
  very ugly; horrible

**sarong** (p3)
  a skirtlike garment of colored silk or cotton, worn by both sexes in Indonesia, Malaysia, and elsewhere

**satchel** (p4)
  a small bag or case

**parasol** (p4)
  a small, light umbrella carried to protect oneself from the sun

**purifying** (p4)
  the act of making clean or pure

**wharf** (p4)
  a structure, usually a platform, built along or out from a shore, alongside which ships or boats may dock to load or unload

**gangplank** (p5)
  a movable bridge that people cross to get on or off a ship

**averted** (p6)
  turned or directed away

**gratitude** (p7)
  thankfulness for a gift or favor; appreciation

**tarp** (p7)
  a piece of canvas or other waterproof material that has been made waterproof, used to cover exposed objects

**thistle** (p9)
  a plant with prickly leaves, having purple or white flowers

**falter** (p12)
  an uncertainty or hesitation in the voice or action

**coax** (p12)
  to ask or persuade

**subdivision** (p12)
  something produced by subdividing, especially a piece of land divided into building lots

**despair** (p13)
  the heavy feeling that comes when all hope is lost or given up

**decipher** (p13)
  to determine the meaning of

**malaria** (p13)
  a disease spread by the bite of an infected anopheles mosquito and marked by recurrent attacks of chills, fever, and sweating

**stupor** (p13)
  a dazed state in which the power to feel, think, or act is lost or greatly lessened

**tentative** (p13)
  hesitant; halfhearted

**vague** (p16)
  indefinite, unclear, imprecise, or indistinct

**ravenous** (p17)
  wildly hungry

**peasant** (p17)
  a country person of humble birth, such as a small farmer

**deferentially** (p20)
  respectfully

**pungent** (p23)
  sharp or piercing to taste or smell

**exile** (p24)
  to send someone away from his or her native land and forbid a return; to banish

**indignant** (p26)
  angry because of something that is not right, just, or fair

**constrain** (p29)
  to hold back; to restrain

**admonition** (p29)
  a mild criticism, warning, or reminder

**conduct** (p33)
  the way a person acts or lives; behavior

**sly** (p33)
  clever in a secret or sneaky way

**falsetto** (p37)
  a way of singing that makes the voice high but thin

**knack** (p38)
  ability or skill; talent

**quivery** (p40)
  trembling or shaking

**demur** (p41)
  to raise an objection

**inflation** (p43)
  a rise in price levels resulting from an increase in the amount of money or credit relative to available goods

**orphan** (p48)
  a child whose parents are dead

**purge** (p55)
  to rid members considered undesirable or disloyal

**aversion** (p57)
  extreme dislike

**weary** (p58)
  discontented or bored

**quay** (p58)
  a wharf or artificial structure where a ship may dock and load or unload

**welfare** (p59)
  organized efforts by a community or group of people to give money and aid to those who are poor and in need

**languishing** (p59)
  becoming weak or feeble

**squalid** (p59)
  dirty and wretched from poverty or neglect

**bewildering** (p59)
  confusing

**sojourn** (p60)
  a stay or visit in a place

**interlude** (p60)
  a short interval of time that interrupts something

**idle** (p60)
  not busy

**throng** (p62)
  a great crowd; a multitude

**dilemma** (p64)
  a position where either of two choices is as bad or unpleasant as the other

**sustain** (p64)
  to keep up the courage or spirits of

**archaic** (p70)
  belonging to an earlier time; ancient

**complacent** (p73)
  satisfied with oneself, one's possessions, or one's accomplishments

**ominous** (p78)
  threatening or foreboding, like a bad omen

**extravagance** (p82)
  wasteful spending of money

**blunt** (p84)
  extremely frank and outspoken

**exotic** (p86)
  strangely different and fascinating

**composure** (p90)
  calmness; self-control

**venerable** (p92)
  worthy of respect, such as because of age or good qualities

**frank** (p93)
  completely honest in saying or showing what one really thinks or feels

**wry** (p94)
  bent, twisted, or turned to one side

**residency** (p95)
  the period during which a physician receives advanced training in a specialty, usually while serving on the staff of a hospital

**lavish** (p96)
  to give freely; to squander

**mooring** (p98)
  a place where something is secured or fastened with cables, ropes, or anchors

**reservoir** (p98)
  a basin, either natural or constructed, for collecting and storing a large supply of water

**vulnerable** (p112)
  capable of being hurt, injured, or wounded

**audible** (p113)
  heard or capable of being heard

**tirade** (p115)
  a long, angry speech

**intrigued** (p116)
  interested or curious

**optimistic** (p124)
  full of hope and cheerfulness

**resolutely** (p133)
  boldly; courageously

**esplanade** (p135)
  an open, level area of grass or pavement used as a promenade or driveway, especially along the shore

**respite** (p136)
  a pause for rest

**bestow** (p136)
  to present as a gift

**genocide** (p138)
  the extermination of an entire people or cultural or political group

**amulet** (p138)
an object worn as a charm to ward off evil or bad luck

**alcove** (p138)
a recess or small section of a room opening out from the main section

**apartheid** (p141)
the governmental policy of racial segregation and social, economic, and educational discrimination in the Republic of South Africa

**bureaucrat** (p148)
a member of a government with many departments made up of appointed officials who follow set rules and regulations

**omen** (p155)
something that is looked on as a prophetic sign of what is going to happen

**premonition** (p170)
a feeling or warning that something is going to happen, usually something bad

**dispel** (p179)
to drive away

**aura** (p179)
a special air or quality that seems to surround or come from a particular source

**solicitude** (p181)
concern, anxiety, or care for someone or something

**monsoon** (p189)
the rainy season in India and adjacent countries, extending from June to September

**karma** (p192)
fate; destiny

**paramedic** (p194)
a person who is trained to assist a doctor or to give first aid or emergency treatment, such as from an ambulance

**conviction** (p197)
a strong, firm belief

**missionary** (p210)
a person sent out to convert people to a certain religion

# Small Group Reading

📖 Mead, Alice. *Crossing the Starlight Bridge*. New York: Bradbury Press, 1994.

Nine-year-old Rayanne's life is turned upside down when her father leaves and she moves off of the Penobscot reservation to live with her grandmother. Grades 4–7.

## Author Information

Alice Mead is an art teacher as well as a writer. She lives in Cumberland, Maine. Mead became interested several years ago in learning about Wabanaki culture, including artwork and legends. She studied with Barry Dana, a Penobscot, and his family in workshops and at their Native Studies encampment. This study led to the writing of *Crossing the Starlight Bridge*.

## Activities

1. On a map of the United States, have students locate:

   Augusta, ME                    Penobscot, ME
   Bangor, ME                     Penobscot River, ME
   Binghamton, ME                 Springbrook, ME
   Kennebec River, ME             Two Rivers Island, ME
   Montana                        Wyoming

2. Ask your school art teacher or a parent volunteer to show your class how to make ash splint baskets.

3. Have students research the Abenaki and Penobscot tribes, then present their information to the rest of the class.

4. Have students write letters from Rayanne to a friend on the Penobscot reservation, telling him or her about her new life with her grandmother and Springbrook Central School.

## Discussion

Give the small group the following instruction: As your group reads this book, discuss the following.

1. Why do you think Rayanne chooses a special crayon every week?

2. Why does Rayanne choose books that have no dads in them?

3. What does Rayanne wish for?

4. Why does Rayanne's father think they should have left the island?

5. What finally made Rayanne's father decide to leave?

6. Why did Rayanne ask the librarian for an atlas?

7. Why did Rayanne's mother sell some of their furniture?

8. Have you ever had to move and go to a different school? How do you think Rayanne feels?

9. Why was Rayanne afraid of going to Springbrook Central School?

10. How do you feel on the first day of school?

11. Discuss the incident between Rayanne and Scott on the playground.

12. What did the logo that Rayanne drew stand for?

13. What does Zak want Rayanne to do? Why?

14. What did Rayanne's grandmother tell her about being surrounded by white culture?

15. Why did Rayanne's father want her to grow up on the island?

16. What plans does Rayanne have for Hop?

17. What did Miss Pinkham ask Rayanne?

18. How did the loon make Rayanne and Julie feel?

19. What news did Rayanne's father bring her? How did she react?

20. How did Rayanne feel about her new home and school at the end of the story?

## Vocabulary

**reservation** (p6)
a tract of government land reserved for a special purpose, such as an Indian reservation

**corridor** (p6)
a long hallway with rooms opening onto it

**mahtekwehswo** (p8)
Abenaki for "rabbit"

**linger** (p9)
to stay on as if unwilling to go; to loiter

**aggravate** (p10)
to make worse, more serious, or more unpleasant

**prairie** (p17)
a large tract or area of more or less level, grassy land having few or no trees

**fragile** (p20)
easily shattered or broken; delicate

**taunts** (p21)
scornful, mocking, or sarcastic remarks

**defiant** (p25)
full of a bold opposition to power or authority; resisting

**inlet** (p27)
a narrow strip of water leading into the land from a larger body of water

**daybed** (p40)
a couch that can be turned into a bed

**ecology** (p41)
the study of the relationships between living things and their surroundings

**ecosystem** (p41)
an ecological community thought of as a functioning unit along with its nonliving environment

**logo** (p41)
a symbol to represent something, such as a group or a business

**starch** (p44)
a preparation of a vegetable substance without taste or smell, used to stiffen clothes

**scorn** (p52)
a feeling of despising someone or something

**granite** (p58)
a hard, igneous rock that will take a high polish and is often used as a building material

**heritage** (p58)
something, such as a tradition, belief, or attitude, handed down from the past

**writhing** (p60)
twisting or distorting the body or part of the body, such as in pain

**torment** (p61)
to make miserable or annoy

**rummy** (p65)
a card game in which points are scored for three or four of a kind or sequences of three or more of the same suit

**pursed** (p65)
drawn into wrinkles; puckered, such as the lips

**escalator** (p67)
a moving stairway for carrying people from one floor to another

**mock** (p71)
not real but made to look so

**fungus** (p75)
a plant with no chlorophyll, flowers, or leaves, such as a mold or mushroom

**drawbridge** (p75)
a bridge that is built so that all or part of it can be raised, lowered, or drawn aside

**harmony** (p77)
agreement; accord

**prominently** (p77)
easily seen; conspicuous

**indignant** (p77)
angry because of something that is not right, just, or fair

**flouncy** (p79)
fancy; decorated with gathered or pleated ruffles for trim

**idly** (p83)
lazily

**medieval** (p87)
of, relating to, or belonging to the Middle Ages

**loon** (p90)
a web-footed diving bird resembling a duck, but with a pointed bill and a strange, laughing cry

**legends** (p97)
stories that have been passed down from earlier times and are often thought by many people to be partly true

**noble** (p112)
impressive and handsome

**wolverine** (p113)
a strong, heavily built, carnivorous animal of North American forests, related to the weasel

## Small Group Reading

📖 Mohr, Nicholasa. *Going Home*. New York: Dial Books for Young Readers, 1986.

Eleven-year-old Felita feels like an outsider when she visits relatives in Puerto Rico for the first time. Ultimately she comes to terms with the heritage she had always taken for granted. Grades 5 and up.

## Author Information

Nicholasa Mohr was born in New York City's El Barrio and now lives in Brooklyn, New York. Mohr was a graphic artist before she began to write full-time. She has written several books, including *In Nueva York, El Bronx Remembered*, and *Felita. Felita* was selected as an ALA Notable Children's Book in the Field of Social Studies.

## Activities

1.  On a world map, have students locate:
    Colombia, South America        San Juan, Puerto Rico
    Philadelphia, PA               Spain

2.  Have students contact an area travel agency and request information and brochures on Puerto Rico. The materials they receive should be incorporated into a poster and hung in the classroom.

3.  Have students write a letter from Felita to Vinny, telling him about her experiences in Puerto Rico. They can then share their letters with the rest of the class.

4.  Felita had to learn more Spanish before going to Puerto Rico. Have students locate an English/Spanish dictionary at your library, choose ten words to learn, and teach them to the rest of the class.

## Discussion

Give the small group the following instruction: As your group reads this book, discuss the following.

1.  What plans did Felita's parents tell her and her brothers about?

2.  Why was Felita especially excited about their plans?

3.  How did Tito react to the news?

4.  Compare and contrast the weather in Puerto Rico with the weather where you live.

5.  How are Tito and Felita treated differently by their mother? Discuss your reaction to this.

6.  Describe the relationship between Felita and her mother.

7.  How do Felita and Gigi feel about having siblings?

8.  What was the deal that Felita and Vinny made?

9.  What worry does Felita have about going to Puerto Rico?

10. Why was Felita's mother impressed by Vinny?

11. What did Tito tell Felita that surprised her?

12. How have Felita's feelings about going to Puerto Rico for the summer changed?

13. Why were some students sad after graduation?

14. How did Felita and her family feel when they reached Puerto Rico?

15. Why was Felita's grandfather upset with her parents? What did Felita's father say to calm him?

16. Why did Felita's parents feel that San Juan had changed?

17. How did Felita feel when they reached Barrio Antulio?

18. What happened at Santa Teresa's that made Felita want to go home?

19. What did Felita tell Provi, Saida, and Judy about New York City?

20. What plans does the church have to raise money?

21. What did Felita learn about the Tainos?

22. Compare and contrast how Anita and her friends treat Felita with how Felita is sometimes treated in New York.

23. What made Felita realize that maybe her mother wasn't so bad after all?

24. Describe what Felita found when she arrived at Santa Teresa's for the final dress rehearsal.

25. Have you ever felt the way Felita did following the play? Discuss your experiences.

26. What will Felita miss when she leaves Puerto Rico?

27. How do you think her visit to Puerto Rico changed Felita?

## Vocabulary

**Abuelo** (p5)
Grandfather

**un macho** (p6)
a young man

**basta** (p6)
enough

**respect** (p6)
to have or show high regard for; esteem; honor

**mango** (p7)
a juicy tropical fruit having a slightly acidic taste

**humidity** (p7)
moisture; dampness, especially of the air

**Abuelita** (p9)
Grandma

**asthma** (p10)
a chronic illness that makes breathing difficult and causes wheezing and sometimes coughing

**tio** (p11)
uncle

**bodega** (p12)
warehouse

**mira** (p13)
look

**senorita** (p20)
miss

**humiliated** (p21)
stripped of pride or self-respect; humbled; embarrassed

**ally** (p21)
a close friend or helper

**bueno** (p29)
good

**merchant seaman** (p30)
a sailor of a ship who is engaged in trade

**toilet water** (p30)
a scented liquid that is used after bathing or shaving

**boulevard** (p32)
a broad city avenue or main road

**chica** (p43)
little girl

**un hombrecito** (p45)
a young man

**smirk** (p53)
a smile that is silly or self-satisfied

**delirious** (p54)
extremely excited

**Anglo** (p57)
a white North American who is not of Hispanic descent

**sí** (p59)
yes

**sarcastic** (p59)
mocking; taunting

**truce** (p60)
a temporary stop in warfare or fighting by agreement of both sides

**foyer** (p61)
an entrance room or hall

**smug** (p65)
very satisfied with oneself to the extent of irritating others

**buenos dias** (p67)
good day

**senor** (p68)
gentleman

**communion** (p71)
a Christian ceremony in which bread and wine are blessed and consumed in memory of the death of Christ

**confirmation** (p71)
a ceremony in which a person is admitted to full membership in a church

**buena suerte** (p78)
good luck

**authentic** (p83)
genuine

**remedy** (p85)
to make right

**gringos** (p85)
slang used in Latin America for foreigners, especially Americans or English persons; usually considered offensive

**cathedral** (p87)
the main church of a diocese of some Christian churches, containing the bishop's throne

**fortress** (p91)
a fort, a series of forts, or a fortified town; a stronghold

**gringito** (p94)
young North American boy

**architect** (p96)
a person who designs and draws up plans for buildings or other structures, then oversees their construction by builders

**holy sacrament** (p111)
any of certain very holy rites in Christian churches, such as baptism and communion

**sulking** (p113)
acting sullen

**sacrilegious** (p113)
having to do with, or characterized by, disrespect

**buena gente** (p115)
good people

**gringita** (p119)
little girl

**siesta** (p124)
in Spain and parts of Latin America, an afternoon nap

**conquistador** (p136)
any of the Spanish conquerors of Mexico and Peru in the sixteenth century

**jíbara** (p144)
a real country girl

**clique** (p145)
a small group whose members stick together and shut out outsiders

**lenient** (p162)
gentle or merciful; not stern or severe; mild

**yucca** (p165)
any of various plants of the southern United States and Mexico having long pointed leaves and clusters of white bell-shaped flowers growing on a tall stalk

**ancestry** (p174)
line of descent; birth

**descendant** (p174)
the child or grandchild of an ancestor; offspring

**indigenous** (p174)
native to the place where found; not brought in from other places or exotic

**liberty** (p175)
freedom from control by others

**rosary beads** (p186)
a string of beads for keeping count of prayers recited

# Small Group Reading

📖 Pitts, Paul. *Racing the Sun*. New York: Avon Books, 1988.
When twelve-year-old Brandon's Navajo grandfather moves into his family's middle-class suburban home, the boy comes to learn and appreciate his heritage. Grades 6–8.

## Activities

1. On a map of the United States, have students locate Flagstaff, Arizona; Montezuma Creek, Utah; and New Mexico.

2. According to Brandon's grandfather, "If you get up early each morning and run to greet the sun, you'll always be healthy and quick." With their parents' permission (due to the time of day), encourage your students to try racing the sun themselves for a week. When the light is just beginning to appear above the horizon, students should run in that direction. They should run until the sun rises above the earth, then run back. Have them write about their experiences in a journal. In what ways were their experiences similar to Brandon's?

3. Have students in this group interview their parents, grandparents, and other relatives about what their lives were like growing up. Did they have any special family traditions? What do they remember about family reunions? Students can then write this information in a booklet titled "The Stories I Will Pass On."

4. At the end of the novel, Brandon's father planned to make a speech about what his father taught him. Have students write a speech together that they believe he would have given. Then have a volunteer give the speech to the rest of the class.

5. If possible, bring in some sagebrush and cedar chips for students to smell.

## Discussion

Give the small group the following instruction: As your group reads this book, discuss the following.

1. Why did the author find it necessary to change the spelling of some Navajo words in this book?

2. What does *UGA* stand for?

3. How does Brandon describe the difference between the American dream and the Navajo dream?

4. Why did Brandon's father leave the Navajo reservation?

5. What did Aunt Helen say in her letter? How did Brandon's parents react?

6. What is Brandon's theory about family organization?

7. How would you feel if you were in Brandon's situation?

8. Why did Brandon say that the relationship between his father and grandfather is like a war?

9. How did Brandon's mother explain the difference between their family's life and the Navajo way of life?

10. Describe Brandon's grandfather's first day with Brandon and his parents.

11. What did Brandon do for his grandfather early in the morning? Why?

12. Why didn't Brandon want to take his grandfather to Food World?

13. What did Brandon's friends say when they saw his grandfather at the mall? How would you have felt if you were Brandon?

14. What did Brandon's grandfather tell him when they were planting squash in the garden?

15. What did Brandon's parents learn about Brandon's grandfather's sickness when they took him to the doctor?

16. What did Brandon's grandfather receive in the mail? How did it make him feel?

17. What does Brandon have planned for his grandfather and himself? Do you think it will work?

From *Teaching U.S. History Through Children's Literature.* © 1998 Wanda J. Miller. Teacher Ideas Press. (800) 237-6124.

18. What did Brandon's grandfather tell Brandon about life when they were at Uncle Stan and Aunt Ethel's house?

19. When Brandon was with his grandfather at his grandfather's house, what important things did his grandfather tell him?

20. After completing the novel, discuss your feelings about Brandon, his father, and his grandfather. How has Brandon changed by learning to love his Navajo heritage?

## Vocabulary

**bilingual** (pvii)
able to speak two languages

**reservation** (pvii)
a tract of government land reserved for a special purpose, such as an Indian reservation

**endearments** (pviii)
expressions of love or affection, such as by words or actions

**pity** (p1)
a feeling of regret or sorrow for the misfortunes or sufferings of others; sympathy

**customary** (p1)
based on custom; usual

**algebra** (p1)
a branch of mathematics that deals with the relations between numbers

**honor** (p2)
fairness, rightness, and honesty

**ecology** (p2)
the study of the relationships between living things and their surroundings

**underachiever** (p2)
a student who performs at a lower level than expected

**resonant** (p2)
deep, rich, and full in tone or sound

**ingenuity** (p3)
skill or cleverness, as shown in inventing or solving things

**reciprocal** (p3)
shared or given by both sides; mutual

**bar mitzvah** (p4)
in the Jewish religion, a ceremony in which a boy who is thirteen is publicly recognized as having reached the age of religious duty and responsibility

**tidbit** (p5)
a choice bit, such as of food or gossip

**intrigue** (p5)
a secret, crafty plot or scheme

**mellow** (p5)
made gentle and sympathetic by age or experience

**berserk** (p6)
in a frenzy of wild rage

**enticing** (p6)
attracting or luring by offering or tempting with something attractive or desirable

**affluent** (p6)
wealthy

**upheaval** (p8)
a violent disturbance or change

**methodical** (p10)
using or showing the use of a strict, orderly system

**spontaneous** (p10)
done naturally from impulse; unplanned

**intuitive** (p10)
knowing or working by an inner feeling, not a conscious reasoning

**manipulate** (p14)
to manage, control, or influence in a shrewd or dishonest way

**hogan** (p15)
a Navajo Indian hut made of sticks and branches covered with earth

**mammoth** (p17)
huge

**prolong** (p18)
to make longer in time or space; to continue; to lengthen

**agony** (p18)
terrible suffering of body or mind; anguish

**miscellaneous** (p20)
composed of many different things or elements

**civilization** (p22)
   the society and culture of a particular people, place, or period

**negotiate** (p22)
   to arrange by bargaining and talking with others

**notion** (p23)
   a general idea or impression

**antisocial** (p25)
   unsociable; aloof

**ingenious** (p30)
   worked out, made, or done in a clever way

**versatile** (p31)
   having many uses

**modesty** (p37)
   the condition or quality of being humble, not boastful

**sagebrush** (p39)
   a bitter small shrub with white or yellow flowers, found on the dry plains of the western United States

**essential** (p43)
   something extremely important or basic

**optimistic** (p51)
   full of hope and cheerfulness

**perspective** (p67)
   a way of seeing and judging things in relation to one another; a point of view; an outlook

**pancreas** (p71)
   a large gland behind the lower part of the stomach that discharges digestive juices into the intestine and insulin into the blood

**exclusive** (p75)
   not shared with any other; belonging only to one

**intermission** (p75)
   a pause between periods of activity

**access** (p77)
   the opportunity to approach, acquire, or enter

**potential** (p81)
   qualities that make the development of a talent, power, or skill possible or likely

**fraternity** (p82)
   a group of people sharing the same interests

**desolate** (p85)
   dreary; barren

**eloquent** (p87)
   effective or skillful in expressing feelings or ideas

**syllabus** (p88)
   a brief outline that explains the main points of a course of study

**primitive** (p90)
   simple or crude, like that of early ages

**solemn** (p94)
   serious, grave, and earnest

**futile** (p105)
   done in vain; useless

**adobe** (p113)
   a brick that is dried in the sun instead of in an oven or kiln

**telepathy** (p117)
   communication from one mind to another, apparently received without use of hearing, sight, or touch

**mongrel** (p120)
   a dog of mixed breed

**skeptical** (p121)
   showing doubt

## Small Group Reading

Yarbrough, Camille. *The Shimmershine Queens*. New York: G. P. Putnam's Sons, 1989.

Yarbrough tells the story of Angie and Michele, best friends growing up in a tough inner-city neighborhood. Ninety-year-old Cousin Seatta comes to visit and teaches Angie and Michele about the shimmershine feeling, the good feeling and pride that people have for their racial heritage and physical features. Grades 5–8.

## Author Information

Camille Yarbrough was born in 1938 in Chicago, Illinois. She studied acting and voice in the United States and in Australia. She attended Roosevelt University.

Yarbrough has worked as a drama teacher and dance instructor, and was employed in the dance company of Katherine Dunham. Along with writing children's books and poems, she is also a songwriter. Yarbrough describes herself as a griot, an "oral historian, preacher, teacher, social catalyst who uses song, rhyme, dance, and mime to illuminate and perpetuate, to revitalize and re-direct the culture which he or she serves."

## Activities

1.  On a world map, have students locate:

    Alabama

    Atlanta, GA

    Ghana, West Africa

    New York City

2.  Have students research the Asante customs of people in the capital city of Ghana, West Africa.

3.  Have students write an essay explaining what in their lives gives them a "shimmershine" feeling.

4.  Have students write a journal entry upon the completion of each chapter of *The Shimmershine Queens*. When they finish the novel, each student in the group can choose an entry that he or she feels is especially important to read aloud to the rest of the class.

## Discussion

Give the small group the following instruction: As your group reads this book, discuss the following.

1.  What causes Angie to have the shimmershine feeling?

2.  What did Cousin Seatta tell Angie about the shimmershine feeling?

3.  What does Angie dream about?

4.  How does Cousin Seatta describe Angie?

5.  What advice does Angie's mother give her about what she should do when people call her names?

6.  According to Cousin Seatta, why are some people mean to those who are different? Discuss your feelings about this.

7.  How does Cousin Seatta feel about education?

8.  What did Mr. Tucker say to Cheryl, Charlene, Pat, Darrell, and Hector about their behavior?

9.  Why do you think Charlene and her friends decided to attack Angie?

10. Why did Angie have to stay home from school?

11. What class are Angie and Michele excited about taking?

12. What happened between Angie and Charlene in Ms. Collier's class?

13. What was the surprise that Ms. Collier brought for Angie and the rest of the class? How did the students react?

14. What did Ms. Collier offer to do to help Angie?

15. How does Michele's Grandmama feel about what Angie and Michele are learning in school?

16. Have you ever felt the way Michele and Angie do about the play? Discuss what you did that gave you this feeling.

17. How do you think Angie felt when she read the introduction of the play for the class?

18. How has working on the play changed the way the students act toward each other?

19. What is worrying Angie so much?

20. Why do you think Angie did what she did at Woolworth's?

21. Discuss the scene at Woolworth's when Ms. Collier and Angie's mother arrived.

22. What does Angie and Michele's rap poem mean?

23. How did reading this novel make you feel?

## Vocabulary

**attitude** (p19)
a way of feeling or regarding; a mental view

**anchor** (p21)
something that gives security or support

**savages** (p25)
people living in a wild or primitive condition

**Ku Klux Klan (KKK)** (p25)
a secret organization, founded in the United States after the Civil War, that advocates white supremacy

**pot-belly stove** (p25)
a stove that has a rounded, bulging part that looks like a large belly

**culture** (p26)
the entire way of life of a particular people, including its customs, religions, ideas, inventions, and tools

**ridicule** (p26)
to make fun of

**maimed** (p28)
crippled

**hoecake** (p35)
a flat bread made of coarse cornmeal

**ignorant** (p51)
having little or no learning or knowledge

**akimbo** (p54)
with hands on the hips and elbows outward

**aggressor** (p60)
a person who attacks first or starts a quarrel

**bewilderment** (p79)
the condition of being puzzled and confused

**Ghanaian stools** (p91)
stools made in Ghana

**calabash bowls** (p91)
bowls made from the hard-shelled, gourdlike fruit of a calabash tree

**proverb** (p95)
an old and often repeated saying of advice or wisdom

**unity** (p95)
the quality of being one or the power of acting as one

**defiance** (p96)
bold opposition to power or authority; refusal to submit or obey

**plantation** (p97)
a farm or estate of many acres having a crop that is planted and tended by laborers who live there

**feigning** (p106)
pretending

**pride** (p106)
someone or something of which one is proud

**admiration** (p115)
a feeling of wonder, approval, and satisfaction for someone or something of quality

**monologue** (p116)
a long speech by one person

**intercom** (p119)
a telephone or radio system for communicating within a limited space

**dispute** (p123)
an argument, debate, or quarrel

**cattycorner** (p128)
diagonally across from

# Bibliography

## Individual Titles

Adoff, Arnold. *All the Colors of the Race*. New York: Beech Tree Books, 1982.

This is a collection of poems written from the point of view of a child who has a black mother and a white father. Grades 2–5.

Adoff, Arnold, ed. *My Black Me: A Beginning Book of Black Poetry*. New York: E. P. Dutton, 1974.

This book contains fifty poems that were first published in 1974. Twenty-six African American poets, from Langston Hughes to Sonia Sanchez, have contributed poems to this book. Grades 3–7.

Ancona, George. *Powwow*. San Diego, CA: Harcourt Jovanovich Brace, 1993.

Men, women, and children of Native American heritage come together to celebrate their shared culture and ancestry at powwows across the country. Grades 3–7.

Ashabranner, Brent. *An Ancient Heritage: The Arab-American Minority*. New York: HarperCollins, 1991.

Through photos and text, Ashabranner traces the history of Arab immigration to the United States and the various experiences of Arab Americans. Grades 5–9.

Ashabranner, Brent, and Melissa Ashabranner. *Into a Strange Land: Unaccompanied Refugee Youth in America*. New York: Dodd, Mead, 1987.

Text and photos reveal the experiences of teenagers newly arrived and alone in the United States. Grades 6–9.

Atkin, S. Beth. *Voices from the Fields: Children of Migrant Farmworkers Tell Their Stories*. Boston: Little, Brown, 1993.

Atkin combines photographs of interviewed children, first-person narratives, and poetry written in English and Spanish to tell the stories of the children's lives. Grades 5 and up.

Bial, Raymond. *Amish Home*. Boston: Houghton Mifflin, 1993.

Photographs and text give readers insight into the way of life of the Amish. Grades 3–7.

Bingham, Caroline, and Karen Foster, eds. *Crafts for Celebration*. Brookfield, CT: Millbrook Press, 1993.

This book introduces festivals in countries around the world by way of the crafts used in different ceremonies. Instructions for several simple craft projects are included. Grades 5 and up.

Brimner, Larry Dane. *A Migrant Family*. Minneapolis, MN: Lerner, 1992.

This book portrays the life of twelve-year-old Juan Medina and his family, migrant workers living in Encinitas, California. Grades 3–7.

Brown, Tricia. *Konnichiwa! I Am a Japanese-American Girl*. New York: Henry Holt, 1995.

Text and photographs of Lauren Kamiya and her family introduce readers to Japanese traditions and Japanese American culture. Grades 2–5.

Bruchac, Joseph. *Flying with the Eagle, Racing the Great Bear: Stories from Native North America*. Mahwah, NJ: Troll Medallion, 1993.

This is a collection of traditional tales that present the heritage of various Native American nations, including the Wampanoag, Cherokee, Osage, Lakota, and Tlingit. Grades 4 and up.

———. *Fox Song*. New York: Philomel, 1993.

A grandmother and grandchild share the experiences of collecting fresh birch bark, tasting sweet maple sap straight from the tree, and discovering a fox's tracks. Grades 1–4.

———. *Native American Animal Stories*. Golden, CO: Fulcrum, 1992.

Bruchac tells stories of animals from many different Native American nations. Grades 4–8.

———. *Native American Stories*. Golden, CO: Fulcrum, 1991.

The stories included are drawn from the native cultures of North America and have the world as a family as a common thread. A map showing the cultural areas and tribal locations of Native American groups is included. Grades 4–8.

Bryan, Ashley. *Sing to the Sun: Poems and Pictures*. New York: HarperCollins, 1992.

This is a collection of original poems that praise the beauty of nature and everyday joys. Illustrations depict characteristics of African American culture combined with flowers, birds, fish, rising suns, and full moons. Grades 1–9.

Bunting, Eve. *A Day's Work*. New York: Clarion Books, 1994.

When Francisco, a young Mexican American boy, tries to help his grandfather find work, he discovers that even though the old man cannot speak English, he has something even more valuable to teach Francisco. Grades 2–4.

——. *Going Home*. New York: HarperCollins, 1996.

Although a Mexican family comes to the United States to work as farm laborers so that their children will have opportunities, the parents still consider Mexico their home. Grades 2–4.

——. *How Many Days to America? A Thanksgiving Story*. New York: Clarion Books, 1988.

Present-day refugees from a Caribbean island embark on a dangerous boat trip to America, where they have a special reason to celebrate Thanksgiving. Grades 2–4.

Burden-Patmon, Denise. *Imani's Gift at Kwanzaa*. New York: Simon & Schuster Books for Young Readers, 1993.

This book is a celebration of African heritage. It is one of a series of tales that complement customs already established in the United States and encourage young people to expand their world to include others of different backgrounds. Grades 2–5.

Caduto, Michael J., and Joseph Bruchac. *Keepers of the Night: Native American Stories and Nocturnal Activities for Children*. Golden, CO: Fulcrum, 1994.

This book contains stories and hands-on activities that help readers understand, live with, and care for nature at night. Topics include astronomy, nighttime weather, and other aspects of the night sky. Grades 4 and up.

Carlson, Lori M., ed. *Cool Salsa: Bilingual Poems on Growing Up Latino in the United States*. New York: Henry Holt, 1994.

This is an anthology of poems in Spanish with English translation. Grades 4 and up.

Cavan, Seamus. *Coming to America: The Irish-American Experience*. Brookfield, CT: Millbrook Press, 1993.

Cavan traces the history of Irish immigration to the United States and discusses why the Irish emigrated, their problems in a new land, and their contributions to American culture. Grades 5–8.

Chaikin, Miriam. *Menorahs, Mezuzas, and Other Jewish Symbols*. New York: Clarion Books, 1990.

The author describes many symbols that have been important to Jews for thousands of years. Grades 3 and up.

Chang, Heidi. *Elaine, Mary Lewis, and the Frogs*. New York: Crown, 1988.

A classroom project involving frogs brings together a Chinese American girl who recently moved to Iowa and a white girl whose family has lived there for generations. Grades 2–4.

Chin, Steven A. *Dragon Parade: A Chinese New Year Story*. Austin, TX: Raintree Steck-Vaughn, 1993.

This book is about how Chinese and Chinese Americans begin the new year—with a celebration and a new start. Grades 2–5.

Chocolate, Deborah M. Newton. *My First Kwanzaa Book*. New York: Cartwheel Books, 1992.

The author introduces Kwanzaa, the holiday in which African Americans celebrate their cultural heritage. Grades 1–3.

Cohen, Barbara. *Make a Wish, Molly*. New York: Doubleday Books for Young Readers, 1994.

Molly, who recently emigrated with her family from Russia to New Jersey, learns about birthday parties and who her real friends are. Grades 2–5.

Crum, Robert. *Eagle Drum: On the Powwow Trail with a Young Grass Dancer*. New York: Four Winds Press, 1994.

In this photo essay, Crum presents nine-year-old Louis Pierre's experiences on the powwow trail in detail and offers insight into the stories, traditions, and customs that have helped the Native American powwow flourish in contemporary times. Grades 3–7.

Garza, Carmen Lomas. *Family Pictures*. San Francisco, CA: Children's Book Press, 1990.

Garza describes, in bilingual text and illustrations, her experiences growing up in a Hispanic community in Texas. Grades 2–5.

Gilson, Jamie. *Hello, My Name Is Scrambled Eggs*. New York: Lothrop, Lee & Shepard, 1985.

Harvey Trumble's parents host a family of Vietnamese refugees. Problems occur when Harvey tries to help the new boy. Grades 5–8.

Giovanni, Nikki. *Spin a Soft Black Song: Poems for Children*. New York: Hill and Wang, 1985.

This is an illustrated book containing thirty-five poems about African American children. Grades 2–6.

Girard, Linda Walvoord. *We Adopted You, Benjamin Koo*. New York: Whitman, 1989.

Nine-year-old Benjamin tells the story of his birth in Korea and his adoption by American parents. Grades 2–4.

Goss, Linda, and Marian E. Barnes, compilers. *Talk That Talk: An Anthology of African-American Storytelling*. New York: Simon & Schuster, 1989.

This is a compilation of tales from African American folklore. Storytellers include Nikki Giovanni and Martin Luther King, Jr. Grades 8 and up.

Graff, Nancy Price. *Where the River Runs: A Portrait of a Refugee Family*. Boston: Little, Brown, 1993.

This is a photo essay about a Cambodian immigrant family of the 1990s that tries to retain its heritage while learning to be American. Grades 5–8.

Greenfield, Eloise. *Nathaniel Talking*. New York: Black Butterfly Children's Books, 1988.

Nathaniel is a nine-year-old African American boy who rhymes and raps about his world, from what it is like to be nine, to his education, and his family life. Grades 1–5.

Hajdusiewicz, Babs Bell. *Mary Carter Smith: African-American Storyteller*. Springfield, NJ: Enslow, 1995.

This is a biography of the African American woman who gained fame as a storyteller and became "America's Mother Griot," or official storyteller of African stories. Grades 4–7.

Halliburton, Warren J. *Coming to America: The West Indian-American Experience*. Brookfield, CT: Millbrook Press, 1994.

Halliburton traces the history of West Indian immigration to the United States, discussing why West Indians emigrated, their problems in a new land, and their contributions to American culture. Grades 5 and up.

Hamanaka, Sheila. *All the Colors of the Earth*. New York: Morrow Junior Books, 1994.

In verse the author points out that despite outward differences, children everywhere are essentially the same. Grades K–3.

———. *Peace Crane*. New York: Morrow Junior Books, 1995.

After learning about the Peace Crane, created by Sadako Sasaki, a survivor of the bombing of Hiroshima, a young African American girl wishes it would carry her away from the violence of her own world. Grades 1–3.

Hamilton, Virginia. *Cousins*. New York: Philomel, 1990.

Concerned that her grandmother may die, Cammy is unprepared for the death of another relative. Grades 4–6.

———. *Her Stories: African American Folktales, Fairy Tales, and True Tales*. New York: Blue Sky Press, 1995.

This book contains nineteen stories of African American women. Grades 4 and up.

Haskins, James. *The New Americans: Cuban Boat People*. Hillside, NJ: Enslow, 1982.

Haskins discusses the conditions in Cuba that have led to mass immigration of Cubans to the United States, the expectations that refugees bring

to their new country, and the realities of their life in the United States. Grades 4–8.

———. *The New Americans: Vietnamese Boat People*. Hillside, NJ: Enslow, 1980.

Haskins describes the mass exodus from Vietnam as a result of the Vietnam War and the lives of the Vietnamese who found refuge in the United States. Grades 4–8.

Haslam, Andrew, and Alexandra Parsons. *North American Indians*. New York: Thomson Learning, 1995.

This book contains much information about the food, family life, artwork, transportation, communication, housing, clothing, and origins of North American Indians. Grades 4–8.

Herold, Maggie Rugg. *A Very Important Day*. New York: Morrow Junior Books, 1995.

Two hundred and nineteen people from thirty-two different countries make their way to New York City in a snowstorm to be sworn in as citizens of the United States. Grades 2–4.

Hewett, Joan. *Hector Lives in the United States Now: The Story of a Mexican-American Child*. New York: J. B. Lippincott, 1990.

This is a black-and-white photo essay in which ten-year-old Hector talks about his experiences as an immigrant. Grades 4–7.

Houston, Gloria. *My Great-Aunt Arizona*. New York: HarperCollins, 1992.

An Appalachian girl, Arizona Houston, grows up to become a teacher who influences generations of children. Grades 1–3.

Hoyt-Goldsmith, Diane. *Celebrating Kwanzaa*. New York: Holiday House, 1993.

Through text and photographs, readers learn how a Chicago family celebrates the African American holiday of Kwanzaa. Grades 1–4.

———. *Cherokee Summer*. New York: Holiday House, 1993.

Ten-year-old Bridget, a Cherokee Indian, shares her personal history and the history of her tribe. Grades 4–7.

Hurwitz, Johanna. *Class President*. New York: Morrow Junior Books, 1990.

A battle begins over a fifth-grade class election between the teacher's pet and the class clown. Julio, of Puerto Rican heritage, has leadership qualities that are encouraged by his Hispanic teacher, and he wins the election. Grades 4–6.

Ingpen, Robert, and Philip Wilkinson. *A Celebration of Customs and Rituals of the World*. New York: Facts on File, 1996.

The authors explore initiation rites, wedding feasts, harvest celebrations, religious rituals, and many other customs used around the world to mark special occasions. Grades 7 and up.

Keegan, Marcia. *Pueblo Boy: Growing Up in Two Worlds*. New York: Cobblehill Books, 1991.
Text and photographs depict the home, school, and cultural life of a young Indian boy growing up on the San Ildefonso Pueblo in New Mexico. Grades 2–5.

Kennedy, Pamela. *A Christmas Celebration: Traditions and Customs from Around the World*. Nashville, TN: Ideals Children's Books, 1992.
Kennedy explains the customs and traditions of Christmas, including those of pre-Christian origin, and discusses how the holiday is celebrated around the world. Grades 7 and up.

Kindersley, Barnabas, and Anabel Kindersley. *Children Just Like Me*. New York: Dorling Kindersley, 1995.
Photographs and text depict the homes, schools, family life, and culture of children around the world. Grades 4–8.

Knight, Margy Burns. *Who Belongs Here? An American Story*. Gardiner, ME: Tilbury House, 1993.
A young Cambodian refugee's experience is interspersed with thoughts about the many immigrants who have come to the United States and the question of who is a real American. Grades 2–5.

Krull, Kathleen. *City Within a City: How Kids Live in New York's Chinatown*. New York: Lodestar, 1994.
Chinatown in New York City is part China and part America. Sze Ki Chau and Chao Liu are growing up in two worlds at once. They speak both Chinese and English. They celebrate Chinese holidays, but they also like going to malls, listening to music, and reading magazines. Grades 4 and up.

———. *The Other Side: How Kids Live in a California Latino Neighborhood*. New York: Lodestar, 1994.
Krull depicts the life of two Mexican American brothers and a girl in San Diego and their enjoyment of a bilingual culture. Grades 4–7.

Kuklin, Susan. *How My Family Lives in America*. New York: Bradbury Press, 1992.
Kuklin describes family cultural traditions through the eyes of Sanu, an African American girl; Eric, a Latino boy; and April, a Chinese American. Grades 3–5.

Lankford, Mary D. *Hopscotch Around the World*. New York: Morrow Junior Books, 1992.

The multicultural aspects of hopscotch are illustrated with seventeen versions of the game. Grades 3-6.

Leathers, Noel L. *The Japanese in America*. Minneapolis, MN: Lerner, 1991.
This book follows the history of Japanese Americans from Commodore Matthew C. Perry's arrival at Edo Bay in 1853 to famous Japanese Americans of the modern age. Grades 4 and up.

Lee, Marie G. *Finding My Voice*. Boston: Houghton Mifflin, 1992.
Korean American Ellen Sung, a high school senior, is trying to decide which college to attend after graduation. She must deal with the prejudice of some of her classmates and pressure from her parents to get good grades. Grades 5 and up.

———. *If It Hadn't Been for Yoon Jun*. Boston: Houghton Mifflin, 1993.
Alice isn't interested in her Korean heritage until her adoptive parents pressure her to be friendly with newly arrived immigrant Yoon Jun. Once they are introduced, Alice finds Korean customs fascinating and meaningful. Grades 4–7.

Lehrer, Brian. *The Korean Americans*. New York: Chelsea House, 1988.
Lehrer discusses the history, culture, and religion of Korean Americans. Grades 7 and up.

Levine, Ellen. *I Hate English!* New York: Scholastic, 1989.
When her family moves to New York from Hong Kong, Mei Mei finds it difficult to adjust to school and learn the unfamiliar sounds of English. Grades 2–5.

Littlechild, George. *This Land Is My Land*. Emeryville, CA: Children's Book Press, 1993.
Littlechild tells about the relationship between Native Americans and their land and his own experiences growing up as a member of the Plains Cree nation. Grades 1–5.

Lord, Betty Bao. *In the Year of the Boar and Jackie Robinson*. New York: Harper & Row, 1984.
This is the story of Chinese immigrant Shirley Temple Wong and her first year of life in America. Grades 5–8.

Lowry, Lois. *The Giver*. Boston: Houghton Mifflin, 1993.
Jonas is given his lifetime assignment at the Ceremony of Twelve, becomes the receiver of memories shared by only one other in his community, and discovers the terrible truth about the society in which he lives. Grades 6 and up.

MacGill-Callahan, Sheila. *And Still the Turtle Watched*. New York: Dial Books for Young Readers, 1991.

A turtle carved in rock on a bluff over a river by Native Americans long ago watches with sadness the changes people bring over the years. Grades 1–3.

Manushkin, Fran. *Latkes and Applesauce*. New York: Scholastic, 1990.

A blizzard leaves a family housebound during Hanukkah. They share the little food they have with some starving animals who later return the favor. Grades K–3.

Martin, Rafe. *The Rough-Face Girl*. New York: G. P. Putnam's Sons, 1992.

In this Algonquin Indian version of the Cinderella story, the Rough-Face Girl and her two beautiful but heartless sisters compete for the affections of the Invisible Being. Grades 2–5.

Mayberry, Jodine. *Recent American Immigrants: Koreans*. New York: Franklin Watts, 1991.

This book portrays the lifestyles of this group of new Americans and shows how they have adjusted to their new home while preserving many of their old customs. Grades 6 and up.

Mazer, Anne, ed. *America Street: A Multicultural Anthology of Stories*. New York: Persea Books, 1993.

This book contains fourteen short stories by such distinguished writers as Gary Soto, Robert Cormier, and Nicholasa Mohr. Grades 5 and up.

McGill, Allyson. *The Swedish Americans*. New York: Chelsea House, 1988.

The author discusses the history, culture, and religion of the Swedes, and why many immigrated to America. Grades 7 and up.

Meltzer, Milton. *The American Promise: Voices of a Changing Nation 1945–Present*. New York: Bantam Books, 1990.

Meltzer provides an overview of the concerns of minority groups, along with information on the Cold War, the Korean War, and the civil rights and women's movements. Grades 7–8.

Montroll, John. *Easy Origami*. New York: Dover, 1992.

Montroll gives easy-to-follow, step-by-step directions to introduce students to the Japanese art of paper folding. Grades 2–7.

Mussari, Mark. *The Danish Americans*. New York: Chelsea House, 1988.

Mussari discusses the culture, history, and reasons why the Danes immigrated to America. Grades 7 and up.

Myers, Walter Dean. *Mop, Moondance, and the Nagasaki Knights*. New York: Delacorte Press, 1992.

After T.J. and his younger brother are adopted, the biggest problems they face are winning an international baseball tournament, held in their New Jersey hometown, and helping a homeless teammate. Grades 4–7.

———. *One More River to Cross: An African American Photograph Album*. New York: Harcourt Brace, 1995.

The stories of twelve African Americans, including Crispus Attucks, Malcolm X, Madame C.J. Walker, and Eddie Robinson, convey the determination and excellence of these courageous men and women. Grades 4–7.

———. *Scorpions*. New York: Harper & Row, 1988.

Jamal reluctantly takes on the leadership of the Harlem gang the Scorpions and finds that his enemies treat him with respect when he acquires a gun—that is, until tragedy occurs. This book was chosen as a Newbery Honor Book. Grades 8 and up.

Namioka, Lensey. *April and the Dragon Lady*. San Diego, CA: Browndeer Press, 1994.

A Chinese teenager struggles to reconcile her traditional Chinese upbringing and her American wish for self-fulfillment. Grades 7 and up.

Neuberger, Anne E. *The Girl-Son*. Minneapolis, MN: Carolrhoda Books, 1995.

This story is based on the life of Induk Pahk, a Korean educator, whose widowed mother disguised her as a boy at the age of eight so she could attend school, which was forbidden to girls in the early twentieth century in Korea. Grades 4–8.

Niiya, Brian, ed. *Japanese American History: An A-to-Z Reference from 1868 to the Present*. New York: Facts on File, 1993.

This encyclopedia includes a chronology of major events and a bibliography of Japanese American materials. Grades 5 and up.

Nikola-Lisa, W. *Bein' with You This Way*. New York: Lee & Low Books, 1994.

A group of children share a sunny day and discover that, despite their differences, they are all really the same. Grades K–3.

Nowakowski, Jacek, ed. *Polish-American Ways*. New York: Harper & Row, 1989.

This book is a good introduction to Polish Americans and their way of life. Grades 3 and up.

Olsen, Victoria. *The Dutch Americans*. New York: Chelsea House, 1989.

The author gives a thorough history of Dutch Americans from Holland's early history to the Dutch in America today. Grades 7 and up.

Oughton, Jerrie. *Music from a Place Called Half Moon*. Boston: Houghton Mifflin, 1995.

This story takes place in Half Moon, North Carolina in 1956. When Edie Jo Houp's father suggests that Vacation Bible School should be open to all children, including Native Americans, the town becomes divided. Grades 7 and up.

Palacios, Argentina. *Standing Tall: The Stories of Ten Hispanic Americans*. New York: Scholastic, 1994.

This book includes the stories of ten American heroes, influential and important Hispanic American men and women from very different backgrounds and times who made history and are making history today. Grades 6 and up.

Patrick, Diane. *Family Celebrations*. New York: Silver Moon Press, 1993.

This book shows readers how different families share special times. Grades 3–5.

Paulsen, Gary. *The Crossing*. New York: Orchard, 1987.

Fourteen-year-old Manny, a street kid fighting for survival in a Mexican border town, develops an unusual friendship with an emotionally disturbed American soldier who decides to help him get across the border. Grades 8 and up.

———. *Sentries*. New York: Viking Penguin, 1986.

The lives of four young people—an Ojibway Indian, an illegal Mexican migrant worker, a rock musician, and a sheep rancher's daughter—are interwoven with the lives of three veterans of past wars. Grades 7 and up.

Payton, Sheila. *Cultures of America: African Americans*. New York: Marshall Cavendish, 1995.

Payton discusses the tremendous obstacles that African Americans have had to overcome to survive, as well as to succeed. She discusses the African American culture and contributions to society. Grades 5 and up.

Pfeffer, Susan Beth. *The Riddle Streak*. New York: Henry Holt, 1993.

Amy decides to try to beat her brother Peter at riddles. This is an honest sibling story about an African American middle-class family. Grades 2–4.

Pfeiffer, Christine. *Poland: Land of Freedom Fighters*. Minneapolis, MN: Dillon Press, 1991.

Pfeiffer provides readers with an introduction to the culture, history, and daily life of people in Poland. A chapter is devoted to Polish Americans and their contributions to the United States. Grades 5 and up.

Pinkney, Andrea Davis. *Seven Candles for Kwanzaa*. New York: Dial Books for Young Readers, 1993.

Pinkney describes the origins and practices of Kwanzaa, the seven-day festival during which people of African descent celebrate their ancestral values. Grades 1–4.

Polacco, Patricia. *Rechenka's Eggs*. New York: Philomel, 1988.

An injured goose rescued by Babushka, having broken the painted eggs intended for the Easter Festival in Moscva, lays thirteen colored eggs to replace them. She then leaves behind one final miracle in egg form before returning to her own kind. Grades 2–4.

———. *The Trees of the Dancing Goats*. New York: Simon & Schuster Books for Young Readers, 1996.

During a scarlet fever epidemic one winter in Michigan, a Jewish family helps make Christmas special for their sick neighbors by making their own Hanukkah miracle. Grades 2–5.

———. *Uncle Vova's Tree*. New York: Philomel, 1989.

Grandparents, aunts, uncles, and children gather at a farmhouse to celebrate Christmas in the Russian tradition. Grades 2–5.

———. Porter, A. P. *Kwanzaa*. Minneapolis, MN: Carolrhoda Books, 1991.

Porter describes the origins and practices of Kwanzaa, an African American holiday created to remind African Americans of their history and cultural origins. Grades 2–5.

Pushker, Gloria Teles. *Toby Belfer Never Had a Christmas Tree*. Gretna, LA: Pelican, 1991.

Toby Belfer gives a party for her friends to explain Hanukkah. Grades 1–4.

Rattigan, Jama Kim. *Dumpling Soup*. Boston: Little, Brown, 1993.

This story takes place on New Year's Eve in Hawaii. Marisa helps make dumplings for her family, which is of Korean, Japanese, Chinese, Hawaiian, and Anglo ancestry. Grades K–4.

Rosenberg, Maxine B. *Making a New Home in America*. New York: Lothrop, Lee & Shepard, 1986.

The author presents five stories of children who have come to the United States as immigrants or resident aliens from Japan, Cuba, India, Guyana, and Vietnam. Grades 5 and up.

San Souci, Robert D. *Cut from the Same Cloth: American Women of Myth, Legend, and Tall Tale*. New York: Philomel, 1993.

This is a collection of twenty stories about legendary American women from various cultural backgrounds taken from folktales, popular stories, and ballads. Grades 4–8.

Sarnoff, Jan, and Reynold Ruffins. *Light the Candles! Beat the Drums! A Book of Holidays*. New York: Charles Scribner's Sons, 1979.

This book describes a variety of holidays that are celebrated in the United States. Grades 5 and up.

Say, Allen. *El Chino*. Boston: Houghton Mifflin, 1990.

This is the true story of a Chinese boy who grew up in the Southwest and who believed his father when he said, "In America, you can be anything you want to be." Grades 3–8.

Schoener, Allon. *The Italian Americans*. New York: Macmillan, 1987.

This book is a comprehensive guide to Italian American culture. Grades 7 and up.

Sharpe, Susan. *Spirit Quest*. New York: Bradbury Press, 1991.

While vacationing on an Indian reservation off the coast of Washington, eleven-year-old Aaron becomes friends with Robert, a young Quileute Indian who is preparing for his spirit quest. Grades 4–8.

Shefelman, Janice. *A Peddler's Dream*. Boston: Houghton Mifflin, 1992.

A Lebanese man comes to seek his fortune in America, where, even though he suffers several setbacks, he finally achieves his dream. Grades 2–5.

Silverthorne, Elizabeth. *Fiesta! Mexico's Great Celebrations*. Brookfield, CT: Millbrook Press, 1992.

Silverthorne describes the cultural and historical background and ways of celebrating many religious and patriotic festivals of Mexico. Instructions for making some of the traditional crafts and foods are included. Grades 4 and up.

Soto, Gary. *Baseball in April and Other Stories*. San Diego, CA: Harcourt Brace Jovanovich, 1990.

Eleven short stories portray the everyday life of Hispanic youth in California. Grades 6–9.

———. *Canto Familiar*. San Diego, CA: Harcourt Brace, 1995.

This book contains twenty-five poems about the pleasures and sadness that Mexican American children experience growing up. Grades 3–7.

———. *The Skirt*. New York: Delacorte Press, 1992.

When Miata leaves the skirt she is to wear in a dance performance on the school bus, she needs all her wits to get it back without her parents finding out that she has lost something again. Grades 4–7.

———. *Too Many Tamales*. New York: G. P. Putnam's Sons, 1993.

Maria tries on her mother's wedding ring while helping to make tamales for a family Christmas party. Hours later, Maria realizes the ring is missing. In a *Horn Book* review, Anita Silvey said, "With a fresh voice and a keen eye for the familiar, Gary Soto presents the Hispanic culture in a way we have rarely encountered in children's books." Grades 2–5.

Spier, Peter. *People*. New York: Doubleday, 1980.

Through text and illustrations, Spier reminds readers that each of us is a unique individual, different from all others, and deserving of respect and tolerance. Grades 2–5.

Stanek, Muriel. *I Speak English for My Mom*. Niles, IL: Whitman, 1989.

Lupe, a young Mexican American, must translate for her mother, who speaks only Spanish. Then Mrs. Gomez decides to learn English to get a better job. Grades 2–4.

Steptoe, John. *Mufaro's Beautiful Daughters: An African Tale*. New York: Lothrop, Lee & Shepard, 1987.

Mufaro's two beautiful daughters, one bad-tempered, one kind and sweet, go before the King, who is choosing a wife. Grades 2–5.

Surat, Michele Maria. *Angel Child, Dragon Child*. Milwaukee, WI: Raintree, 1983.

This is the story of Ut, a Vietnamese child who comes to the United States by herself and who has a difficult time adjusting to her new life. Grades 1–4.

Tate, Eleanora E. *The Secret of Gumbo Grove*. New York: Franklin Watts, 1987.

While helping restore the cemetery of the old Baptist church, eleven-year-old Raisin solves the mystery surrounding the founding of her hometown and gains pride in her family's past. Grades 5–7.

Taylor, Theodore. *Maria: A Christmas Story*. San Diego, CA: Harcourt Brace Jovanovich, 1992.

Eleven-year-old Maria and her family are the first Mexican Americans to enter a float in the annual Christmas parade in San Lazaro, California. Grades 4–8.

Toor, Rachel. *The Polish Americans*. New York: Chelsea House, 1988.

Toor discusses the history, culture, and religion of the Poles, along with factors encouraging their emigration. Grades 7 and up.

Uchida, Yoshiko. *The Invisible Thread*. Englewood Cliffs, NJ: Messner, 1991.

This is a memoir of Uchida's life growing up in California and later being imprisoned in a detention camp during World War II. Grades 4 and up.

———. *The Magic Listening Cap: More Folk Tales from Japan*. Berkeley, CA: Creative Arts, 1987.

A collection of fourteen Japanese folktales. Grades 3–6.

Van Laan, Nancy. *In a Circle Long Ago: A Treasury of Native Lore from North America*. New York: Apple Soup Books, 1995.

Van Laan has chosen twenty-five stories, songs, and poems from more than twenty different tribal traditions to retell. Grades 3 and up.

Vuong, Lynette Dyer. *The Brocaded Slipper and Other Vietnamese Tales*. New York: HarperCollins, 1982.

This is a collection of five Vietnamese fairy tales, including "Little Finger of the Watermelon Patch" and "The Lampstand Princess." Grades 5–8.

Waldstreicher, David. *The Armenian Americans*. New York: Chelsea House, 1989.

The author discusses the history, culture, and religion of the Armenians, factors encouraging their emigration, and their acceptance as an ethnic group in North America. Grades 7 and up.

Walter, Mildred Pitts. *Have a Happy. . . .* New York: Avon Books, 1989.

Chris is sad because his December 25th birthday will be lost in the Christmas rush. He feels better when his family decides to celebrate the seven-day African holiday of Kwanzaa. Grades 3–7.

Watts, J. F. *The Irish Americans*. New York: Chelsea House, 1988.

Watts discusses the history, culture, and reasons the Irish immigrated to America. Grades 7 and up.

Weber, Judith Eichler. *Melting Pots: Family Stories and Recipes*. New York: Silver Moon Press, 1994.

This book looks at the way different cultures celebrate with food. Recipes are included for readers to try. Grades 4–8.

Westridge Young Writers Workshop, ed. *Kids Explore America's African-American Heritage*. Santa Fe, NM: John Muir, 1993.

This book examines the contributions of African American culture in such areas as music, food, literature, and celebrations. Grades 3–8.

———. *Kids Explore America's Hispanic Heritage*. Santa Fe, NM: John Muir, 1992.

This book presents writings by students in grades three to seven on topics of Hispanic culture, including dance, cooking, games, history, art, music, and role models. Grades 3–8.

———. *Kids Explore America's Japanese American Heritage*. Santa Fe, NM: John Muir, 1994.

This book gives a kid's-eye view of Japanese American culture, including their history, language, heroes, and foods. Grades 3–8.

Williams, Sherley Anne. *Working Cotton*. San Diego, CA: Harcourt Brace Jovanovich, 1992.

A young African American girl relates the daily events of her migrant family's life in the cotton fields of central California. Grades 1–4.

Woodson, Jacqueline. *Between Madison & Palmetto*. New York: Delacorte Press, 1993.

This is the third book of a trilogy. When Margaret's best friend, Maizon, returns from boarding school and joins her in the eighth grade, they try to resume their friendship while dealing with personal problems and watching their Brooklyn neighborhood change. Grades 5 and up.

———. *Last Summer with Maizon*. New York: Dell, 1990.

This is the first book of a trilogy. The summer that Maizon and Margaret are eleven, Margaret's father dies. Then Maizon is offered a scholarship to a boarding school where she's afraid she might be the only African American student. Grades 5 and up.

———. *Maizon at Blue Hill*. New York: Delacorte Press, 1992.

After winning a scholarship to an academically challenging boarding school, Maizon finds herself one of only five African American students. Will she ever fit in? This book is a sequel to *Last Summer with Maizon* and the second book in a trilogy. Grades 4–7.

Yarbrough, Camille. *Cornrows*. New York: Coward, McCann & Geoghegan, 1979.

Yarbrough explains how the hairstyle of cornrows, a symbol in Africa since ancient times, can today in the United States symbolize the courage of outstanding African Americans. Grades 2–6.

Yep, Laurence. *Child of the Owl*. New York: Harper & Row, 1977.

When Casey's father goes to the hospital, Casey is sent to live with her grandmother PawPaw in Chinatown, where she learns a lot about herself and her heritage. Grades 6–9.

Yep, Laurence, ed. *American Dragons: Twenty-Five Asian American Voices*. New York: HarperCollins, 1993.

This is a collection of poems, stories, and one short play about fitting in and growing up. Grades 6 and up.

# Theme Resources

## *Commercial Resources*

Albyn, Carole Lisa, and Lois Sinaiko Webb. *The Multicultural Cookbook for Students*. Phoenix, AZ: Oryx Press, 1993.

The authors present a collection of recipes from more than 120 countries and briefly discuss the culture and culinary habits of each country. For use with students in grades 5 and up.

Angell, Carole S. *Celebrations Around the World: A Multicultural Handbook*. Golden, CO: Fulcrum, 1996.

This resource contains information regarding more than twenty celebrations, festivals, or religious holidays observed by countries and cultures around the world. Many activities are included, as well as recipes. For use with students in grades 4 and up.

Caballero-Hodges, Jane, Ph.D. *Children Around the World: The Multicultural Journey*. Atlanta, GA: Humanics Learning, 1994.

This is a revised edition that introduces various cultures and people from around the world with native recipes, music, games, and activities for use with students in grades 4 through 7.

Caduto, Michael J., and Joseph Bruchac. *Keepers of the Earth: Native American Stories and Environmental Activities for Children*. Golden, CO: Fulcrum, 1989.

The authors focus on stories and activities concerning the environment. For use with students in grades 4 and up.

———. *Teacher's Guide to* Keepers of the Earth. Golden, CO: Fulcrum, 1988.

This guide is for use with students in grades 4 and up.

Cech, Maureen. *Globalchild: Multicultural Resources for Young Children*. New York: Addison-Wesley, 1991.

Cech presents a wealth of activities, games, and celebrations for teachers to use with students in grades K through 4 to build understanding of our multicultural world.

Ciment, James. *Scholastic Encyclopedia of the North American Indian*. New York: Scholastic, 1996.

This encyclopedia contains information about 149 North American Indian tribes from the Arctic Circle to Central America and the Caribbean. An excellent book for students in grades 4 through 8 to use for research purposes.

*Cobblestone: The History Magazine for Young People*. Peterborough, NH: Cobblestone.

The subject of the November 1991 issue for students in grades 4 and up is "The Story of American Jews." Articles include "German Jews: Making a Place in America," "Through the Golden Door," and "Yiddish Legacy."

The subject of the December 1992 issue for students in grades 4 and up is "Italian Americans." Articles include "Five Generations of Italian Immigrants" and "The Importance of Heritage: A Chat with Tomie dePaola."

The subject of the May 1995 issue for students in grades 4 and up is "Polish Americans." Articles include "The First Polish Americans," "The Big Wave: Polish Immigration from 1870 to 1914," and "A Children's Tour of the Polish Museum of America."

The focus of the April 1996 issue for students in grades 4 and up is "Japanese Americans." Articles include "Evacuation and Internment During World War II" and "Japanese Americans Today."

The focus of the December 1996 issue for students in grades 4 and up is "Greek Americans." Articles include "Greek Americans" and "Following the Traditions of Family, Faith, and Feasts: An Interview with Paula Magoon."

Cole, Ann, Carolyn Hass, Elizabeth Heller, and Betty Weinberger. *Children Are Children Are Children*. Boston: Little, Brown, 1978.

The authors describe the life and customs of Nigeria, Brazil, Japan, Iran, France, and the Soviet Union, with suggestions for related activities and projects. For use with students in grades 4 through 7.

Edwards, Gerry, Ph.D. *Discovering World Cultures Through Literature*. Glenview, IL: Good Year Books, 1995.

This resource provides activities for trade books in which students will learn about different cultures. For use with students in grades 3 through 6.

Gerke, Pamela. *Multicultural Plays for Children: Volume 1: Grades K–3*. Lyme, NH: Smith and Kraus, 1996.

Scripts for ten plays to be put on by or for primary-grade children appear in this resource.

Gust, John, M.A., and J. Meghan McChesney. *Learning About Cultures: Literature, Celebrations, Games and Art Activities*. Carthage, IL: Teaching & Learning, 1995.

This comprehensive resource includes numerous activities, literature recommendations, and descriptions of celebrations for the following cultures: African American, Arabic, Chinese, Japanese, Jewish, Korean, Mexican, and Native American. For use with students in grades 3 through 6.

Hayden, Carla D., ed. *Venture into Cultures: A Resource Book of Multicultural Materials and Programs*. Chicago: American Library Association, 1992.

This bibliography includes program ideas and resources on seven cultural groups in the United States: African American, Arabic, Asian, Hispanic, Jewish, Native American, and Persian.

Helbig, Alethea K., and Agnes Regan Perkins. *This Land Is Our Land: A Guide to Multicultural Literature for Children and Young Adults*. Westport, CT: Greenwood Press, 1994.

The authors list books of fiction, oral tradition, and poetry by African American, Asian American, Hispanic American, and Native American cultures.

Jasmine, Julia. *Multicultural Holidays: Share Our Celebrations*. Huntington Beach, CA: Teacher Created Materials, 1994.

This book provides a variety of activities and information about holidays celebrated by various religions and cultures. For use with grades 3 through 6.

Kanellos, Nicolás, ed. *The Hispanic Almanac: From Columbus to Corporate America*. Detroit, MI: Visible Ink Press, 1994.

This book examines Hispanic civilization and culture in the United States, including law and politics, population growth, theater, music, and film. Grades 7 and up.

McElmeel, Sharron L. *Bookpeople: A Multicultural Album*. Englewood, CO: Teacher Ideas Press, 1992.

McElmeel presents suggestions for integrating literature and multicultural awareness with students in kindergarten through grade 8. The book features fifteen creators of books for children and young adults.

Milford, Susan. *Hands Around the World: 365 Creative Ways to Build Cultural Awareness and Global Respect*. Charlotte, VT: Williamson, 1992.

Milford presents a variety of games and other activities to foster awareness of various cultures around the world. For use with students in grades 3 through 8.

Rochman, Hazel. *Against Borders: Promoting Books for a Multicultural World*. Chicago: American Library Association/Booklist, 1993.

Rochman explores multicultural literature for children and young adults. Bibliographies group titles by culture for students in grades 2 and up.

*Schooldays: Practical Ideas for Primary Teachers*. Torrance, CA: Frank Schaffer.

The April/May/June 1993 issue of *Schooldays* includes the article "Multicultural Art." This thematic unit features arts from around the world. Students will learn about totem poles, African clothing designs, Chinese painting, Mexican bark painting, Ukrainian Easter eggs, and Japanese paper folding (origami). For use with students in grades 2 through 5.

Scriabine, Christine. *Jackdaw: Modern Immigration: 1930–1965*. Amawalk, NY: Jackdaw, 1997.

This is a portfolio of primary source material including fifteen reproduction historical documents. Among them are a 1994 Application for Naturalization document and "Immigrating USA: Guide for Irish Immigrants," from Catholic Charities of the Archdioceses of New York in 1990. Comprehensive notes on the documents, a reading list, and critical thinking questions are also included. For use with students in grades 5 and up.

Sierra, Judy. *The Oryx Multicultural Folktale Series: Cinderella*. Phoenix, AZ: Oryx Press, 1992.

The author presents versions of the Cinderella story that represent many cultures, geographical areas, and styles. Information about the tales, related activities, and resources are included. For use with students in grades 3 through 7.

Trotter, Tamera, and Joycelyn Allen. *Talking Justice: 602 Ways to Build and Promote Racial Harmony*. Saratoga, CA: R&E, 1993.

Trotter and Allen provide 602 things people can do to promote racial harmony. Grades 4 and up.

Weitzman, David. *My Backyard History Book*. Boston: Little, Brown, 1975.

Activities and projects demonstrate that learning about the past begins at home. For use with students in grades 4 and up.

Wolfman, Ira. *Do People Grow on Family Trees? Genealogy for Kids and Other Beginners*. New York: Workman, 1991.

This introduction to genealogy serves as a wonderful tool to aid in researching a family's history. For use with students in grades 4 and up.

## *Videos*

*Greek Americans*. Bala Cynwyd, PA: Schlessinger Video Productions, 1993. (30 minutes)

This video introduces first-, second-, and third-generation Greek Americans who describe their experiences in the United States.

*Japanese Americans*. Bala Cynwyd, PA: Schlessinger Video Productions, 1993. (30 minutes)

This video explores the cultural heritage of Japanese Americans in the United States through the experiences of three generations of a family.

*Kwanzaa: An African-American Cultural Holiday*. Visual Alchemy, 1993. (30 minutes)

This informative step-by-step video chronicles the origins, terminology, symbols, and practices associated with Kwanzaa.

*United States History Video Collection: Immigration & Cultural Change*. Bala Cynwyd, PA: Schlessinger Video Productions, 1996. (35 minutes)

This video takes a look at old and new immigration, the world of the immigrants, a new working class, the limits of mobility and ethnic diversity, the Chinese Exclusion Act, new forms of leisure and mass entertainment, and the American Dream.

# End-of-Unit Celebration

## Celebrating Our
## Multicultural Heritage Research Project

Individually or in groups of two, have your students research the following cultures. Students should research the customs, crafts, food, and holidays celebrated by Americans from these cultural backgrounds. When these projects are completed, hold a presentation day.

| | |
|---|---|
| African American Culture | Korean American Culture |
| Amish Culture | Latin American Culture |
| Arab American Culture | Mexican American Culture |
| Chinese American Culture | Native American Culture |
| Dutch American Culture | Polish American Culture |
| Irish American Culture | Russian American Culture |
| Italian American Culture | Swedish American Culture |
| Japanese American Culture | Vietnamese American Culture |
| Jewish American Culture | |

Students could also prepare food to bring in from the culture they studied to share with the rest of the class on presentation day. The *Multicultural Cookbook for Students* listed in the bibliography of this chapter is an excellent resource for recipes.

### Recipe

Students who research Dutch American culture could prepare the following recipe at home or at school (with adult supervision) to share with the rest of the class. This is my mother's recipe for Dutch lettuce, which she adapted from my grandmother's recipe. My grandmother, Suzanna Boerman Jansen, immigrated to the United States from Holland on March 31, 1909.

# Dutch Lettuce

### INGREDIENTS

Potatoes

4 to 5 hard-boiled eggs

½ pound chopped cooked bacon

½ head of lettuce, cut up

1½ cups vinegar (at least)

### PROCEDURE

1. Boil desired amount of potatoes (may be mashed if desired).
2. Add 4 to 5 chopped hard-boiled eggs.
3. Add ½ pound of chopped cooked bacon.
4. Cut up half a good-sized head of lettuce and add that plus 1½ cups vinegar (at least) to the bacon grease.
5. Pour vinegar mixture over potatoes, egg, and bacon.
6. Stir in 1 teaspoon salt.

A note from my mother: Delicious according to Dad!

## Introduction

Iraq, under the rule of Saddam Hussein, invaded Kuwait on August 2, 1990. This invasion was immediately condemned by the United Nations Security Council. U.S. President George Bush sent the first United States armed forces to the Persian Gulf under Operation Desert Shield on August 6, 1990.

On November 29, 1990, the Security Council gave Saddam Hussein a deadline for the removal of Iraqi troops from Kuwait. If they didn't retreat by January 15, 1991, "all necessary means" could be used to remove them.

Iraqi troops were still in Kuwait on the day of the deadline, prompting President Bush to order the beginning of an air attack to force their withdrawal on January 16, 1991. Operation Desert Shield had become Operation Desert Storm. An allied ground war followed thirty-nine days later, on February 24, 1991. The American forces were joined by troops from nine other nations. The fighting ended on February 27, 1991, only 100 hours after the ground war began. Many Iraqi troops were unprepared for the ground war, and Iraqi soldiers surrendered by the thousands.

Operation Desert Storm used modern military technology, including Tomahawk cruise missiles preprogrammed with their targets' coordinates, F-117A Stealth fighters that dropped "smart bombs," which could fix on and destroy very specific targets, and Patriot antimissile systems.

A rough estimate of Iraqi casualties during the war was 100,000, with 60,000 to 75,000 Iraqi soldiers taken as prisoners. The total number of combat deaths for the United States was 124, with an additional forty-five listed as missing in action.

Because the Gulf War was the most recent war fought that involved the United States, there are few trade books written for children and young adults on the topic at this time. Those that are listed here were chosen to give students an understanding of the Persian Gulf War and the U.S. involvement in it.

To begin your discussion of the Persian Gulf War, play a recording of "God Bless the USA," written and performed by Lee Greenwood at the time of the Persian Gulf War. Follow this with a discussion of the meaning of the lyrics.

# Whole Group Reading

📖 Deegan, Paul J. *Operation Desert Storm*. Edina, MN: Abdo & Daughters, 1990.

Deegan describes the military campaigns of Operation Desert Storm, in which more than 500,000 American troops and troops from nine other nations joined forces to liberate Kuwait from Saddam Hussein and his Iraqi troops. Grades 4–8.

## Author Information

Paul Joseph Deegan was born March 19, 1937, in Mankato, Minnesota. He received a bachelor of arts degree in 1959 from the University of Minnesota. Deegan's career has included working as a reporter and editor with newspapers in Austin, Texas; Mankato, Minnesota; and St. Paul, Minnesota. He was an editorial director for Creative Education and for Children's Book Company from 1969 to 1980. Deegan has since owned and managed Deegan Associates and Total Concept Software.

Deegan began writing while still in grade school. While in high school and college, he worked on school newspapers. He majored in editorial journalism at the University of Minnesota.

Deegan has written dozens of books for young people, including several biographies and a sports instructional series. He has also edited or designed 100 juvenile books by Creative Education, Amécus Street, and Children's Book Company.

## Activities

1.  On a world map, have students locate:

    | | |
    |---|---|
    | Baghdad, Iraq | Kuwait |
    | Basra, Iraq | Persian Gulf |
    | Euphrates River, Iraq | Riyadh, Saudi Arabia |
    | Germany | Commonwealth of Independent States |
    | Haifa, Israel | (formerly the Soviet Union) |
    | Iran | Tel Aviv, Israel |
    | Japan | Turkey |
    | Jordan | Washington, DC |
    | Jubail, Saudi Arabia | |

2.  Have students research the following people and the roles they played in the Persian Gulf War:

    | | |
    |---|---|
    | President George Bush | General Colin Powell |
    | Saddam Hussein | General Norman Schwarzkopf |

3.  Have students in the group use additional sources to find out more about the devastation caused by the Persian Gulf War on the Gulf itself. They can then use the information they find to give an oral report to the class.

4.  Have students compare and contrast the air war during the Persian Gulf War versus that in World War II. They could then incorporate their statements into a poster to display in your classroom.

# Discussion

Give the class the following instruction: As we read this book, we will be discussing the following questions.

1. Why were American troops sent to Saudi Arabia?

2. What was Operation Desert Shield?

3. When did Operation Desert Shield become Operation Desert Storm?

4. What were some of the modern weapons used during Operation Desert Storm?

5. What was the general feeling among the American people toward U.S. involvement in the Gulf?

6. Why were the Israelis angry with the United States on the second day of the war?

7. What did President Bush send to Israel? What promise did he make to the Israelis?

8. What weapon proved to be the most helpful to the United States? Why?

9. What comparison can be made about air warfare between the Persian Gulf War and World War II?

10. What was the United States focus in the air war? Why?

11. What problems did the destruction of public utility systems create?

12. How many American soldiers died in the air war?

13. What was the economic cost of the war to the United States?

14. Why did Congress want to request financial aid in the war from Japan and Germany?

15. What effect did the Persian Gulf War have on the Gulf itself?

16. Why did Defense Secretary Dick Cheney and General Colin Powell believe a ground war was necessary?

17. Why did the possibility of a ground war worry Americans?

18. When did the allied ground assault begin? What other nations joined the United States in this attack?

19. At the beginning of the ground attack, what surprised the United States and the coalition forces?

20. How long did Operation Desert Storm last?

21. Who directed the war from Riyadh, Saudi Arabia?

22. How did the American people view the United States forces who fought in the Gulf?

23. How many Iraqi troops were killed in the war?

24. What was the total number of combat deaths of United States soldiers in the Persian Gulf War?

25. What did Iraqi forces do before retreating from Kuwait?

26. What did reporters find in Kuwait after the war ended?

27. How were the Kuwaitis treated by Iraqi soldiers?

28. What was Resolution 687? What did this resolution demand?

# Vocabulary

**coalition** (p6)
a temporary alliance of leaders, parties, or nations

**diplomat** (p6)
a person engaged in the handling of relations, friendly or unfriendly, short of war, between nations

**liberation** (p7)
the act of setting free

**missile** (p9)
an object, especially a weapon, intended to be thrown or shot, such as a bullet, arrow, stone, or guided missile

**radar** (p9)
a device for locating objects and determining their size and speed by sending out radio waves and observing how and from where they are reflected by the objects

**sorties** (p10)
air missions

**reserve unit** (p11)
troops who live as civilians and train at certain times to be ready to enter the regular armed forces in an emergency

**congregation** (p11)
a group of people, especially those who meet together for worship

**ally** (p14)
a person or country joined with another for a particular purpose

**proximity** (p14)
nearness; closeness

**intercept** (p14)
to meet and block the passage of

**aerial** (p16)
of or in the air

**civilian** (p16)
a person who is not in active military service

**casualties** (p16)
soldiers who are killed during a battle

**network** (p18)
any system having parts that cross or are connected somewhat like the cords of a net

**contagious** (p18)
easily spread from person to person

**modest** (p18)
not excessive or extreme; moderate

**collateral** (p18)
aside from the main subject; secondary

**mobile** (p21)
easily transported or movable

**ventured** (p21)
exposed to chance or risk; placed in danger

**opponent** (p21)
a person or group of people who compete or fight against another, such as in sports, war, or a debate

**neutral** (p21)
not interfering or taking sides, such as in a dispute, contest, or war

**purification** (p23)
the process of making clean and pure

**ecosystem** (p24)
an ecological community along with its non-living environment thought of as a functioning unit

**abandon** (p25)
to leave; to desert; to forsake

**assure** (p26)
to make certain; to guarantee

**diversion** (p26)
the act of diverting or turning aside

**negotiate** (p29)
to bargain and talk with others in hope of reaching an agreement

**commentator** (p29)
a person who reports, analyzes, and explains the news on radio or television

**bunker** (p29)
a hollow place in the earth

**resistance** (p30)
the act of working against

**conscript** (p30)
a person who is drafted into the armed forces and is forced into service

**rout** (p34)
a disastrous defeat

**annihilation** (p34)
complete destruction

**initial** (p34)
of or coming at the beginning; earliest; first

**patriotism** (p36)
love for one's country and loyal devotion to it

**lauded** (p38)
>   highly praised

**flank** (p38)
>   to be located at the side or sides of

**idealist** (p38)
>   a person who has high ideals of conduct and tries to live according to them

**liberty** (p38)
>   freedom from any arbitrary control by others

**twilight** (p40)
>   the light in the sky just after sunset or just before sunrise

**executed** (p40)
>   put to death

**brutality** (p40)
>   cruel and savage acts

**factor** (p40)
>   one of the elements or causes that help to produce a result

**collaborate** (p40)
>   to work against a country by helping the enemy

**liable** (p46)
>   legally responsible

**valor** (p47)
>   great courage or bravery, especially in war

# Small Group Reading

Deegan, Paul J. *Operation Desert Shield*. Edina, MN: Abdo & Daughters, 1990.

Deegan relates the events of Operation Desert Shield and the buildup of the United Nations coalition forces in the Persian Gulf prior to the Gulf War. Grades 4–8.

## Author Information

Paul Joseph Deegan was born March 19, 1937, in Mankato, Minnesota. He received a bachelor of arts degree in 1959 from the University of Minnesota. Deegan's career has included working as a reporter and editor with newspapers in Austin, Texas; Mankato, Minnesota; and St. Paul, Minnesota. He was an editorial director for Creative Education and for Children's Book Company from 1969 to 1980. Deegan has since owned and managed Deegan Associates and Total Concept Software.

Deegan began writing while still in grade school. While in high school and college, he worked on school newspapers. He majored in editorial journalism at the University of Minnesota.

Deegan has written dozens of books for young people, including several biographies and a sports instructional series. He has also edited or designed 100 juvenile books by Creative Education, Amécus Street, and Children's Book Company.

## Activities

1. On a world map, have students locate:

| | | |
|---|---|---|
| Afghanistan | Czechoslovakia | Hungary |
| Argentina | Denmark | Iceland |
| Australia | Egypt | Italy |
| Austria | Finland | Japan |
| Bahrain | France | Kuwait |
| Bangladesh | Geneva, Switzerland | Libya |
| Belgium | Germany | Luxembourg |
| Bulgaria | Great Britain | Malaysia |
| Cairo, Egypt | Haifa, Israel | Mecca, Saudi Arabia |
| Canada | Honduras | Median, Saudi Arabia |

| | | |
|---|---|---|
| Morocco | Portugal | Sweden |
| Netherlands | Quatar | Syria |
| New Zealand | Red Sea | Taiwan |
| Niger | Riyadh, Saudi Arabia | Turkey |
| Norway | Senegal | Tehran, Iran |
| Oman | Sierra Leone | Tel Aviv, Israel |
| Philippines | South Korea | United Arab Emirates |
| Poland | Spain | |

2.  Have students research the following people and their involvement in the Persian Gulf War:

    Secretary of Defense Dick Cheney
    General Colin Powell
    General Norman Schwarzkopf

3.  Have students write reactions to the treatment of the people of Kuwait by Iraqi soldiers, then read their reactions aloud to the rest of the class.

4.  Have students interview family members or teachers to find out what they remember about Operation Desert Shield.

## Discussion

Give the small group the following instruction: As your group reads this book, discuss the following.

1.  Why did Saddam Hussein order Iraqi troops to invade Kuwait?

2.  In response to this invasion, what did U.S. President George Bush do?

3.  What was Operation Desert Shield?

4.  Why were United States military troops based in Saudi Arabia?

5.  Why did President Bush fear that the Iraqis might also invade Saudi Arabia?

6.  Why was King Fahd of Saudi Arabia hesitant to accept United States protection?

7.  What was the deadline set by the United Nations Security Council for Iraq to withdraw from Kuwait? What would happen if Iraqi troops failed to withdraw by the deadline?

8.  How did the Soviet Union react to the Iraqi invasion of Kuwait?

9.  How many nations joined the coalition?

10. Who was the United States field commander in the region for Operation Desert Shield?

11. What jobs did women perform during Operation Desert Shield?

12. Why was Saudi Arabia shocked to see women soldiers?

13. Describe the Gulf region.

14. What did soldiers eat in the Gulf? What were the living conditions like?

15. As time went by, what became an enemy in Operation Desert Shield?

16. Why was Iraq considered a tough opponent? How did the United States and the Western world react to threats from Saddam Hussein?

17. Why didn't the United States want Israel to attack Iraq?

18. How does a Patriot missile work?

19. Why was the use of gas masks necessary?

20. During the invasion, how did Iraqi soldiers treat the people of Kuwait?

21. How did Saddam Hussein use hostages as pawns?

22. How did President Bush compare Saddam Hussein with Adolf Hitler?

23. What did President Bush do as a final attempt to avoid a war before the United Nations deadline for Iraqi withdrawal from Kuwait?

24. When did Operation Desert Shield become Operation Desert Storm?

## Vocabulary

**infantry** (p4)
soldiers, or a branch of the army, trained and equipped to fight on foot

**emir** (p4)
a Muslim prince or chief, especially in the Middle East

**refuge** (p4)
shelter or protection from danger or distress

**ban** (p5)
a law or order forbidding something

**liberating** (p7)
freeing; releasing

**paratroopers** (p7)
soldiers trained to parachute into battle from an airplane

**rein** (p8)
any means of controlling or restraining

**wary** (p8)
watchful and suspicious; very careful; cautious

**ally** (p9)
a person or country joined with another for a particular purpose

**annex** (p9)
to add as an additional part

**deter** (p11)
to prevent from doing something through fear or doubt; to discourage

**lambast** (p11)
to lash with harsh words; to scold severely

**lackeys** (p11)
male servants in uniform

**condemn** (p12)
to speak against as being wrong

**null** (p12)
without legal force or effect

**void** (p12)
without legal force or effect; invalid

**resolution** (p12)
a formal expression of the feelings or will of an assembly

**coalition** (p14)
a temporary alliance of leaders, parties, or nations

**regime** (p16)
a government in power

**archenemy** (p16)
a chief or major enemy

**foe** (p16)
an enemy

**sanctions** (p17)
the steps or measures taken, usually by several nations, to force another nation to obey international law

**culture** (p18)
the entire way of life of a particular people, including its customs, religions, ideas, inventions, and tools

**stability** (p18)
continued existence; permanence

**astounded** (p22)
stunned with amazement

**terrain** (p22)
an area of land, especially as considered with respect to its use for military operations or some other purpose

**humidity** (p23)
moisture; dampness, especially of the air

**enterprising** (p23)
full of energy, daring, and willingness to embark on new undertakings

**oasis** (p24)
an area in a desert made fertile by a water supply

**staunch** (p25)
firm and dependable

**socialize** (p26)
   to take part in social activities

**opponent** (p28)
   a person or group of people who compete or fight against another, such as in sports, war, or a debate

**missile** (p28)
   an object, especially a weapon, intended to be thrown or shot, such as a bullet, arrow, stone, or guided missile

**terrorist** (p28)
   a person who uses violence and threats to frighten a people or a government into submission

**idle** (p28)
   of no worth or importance; useless; meaningless

**shrapnel** (p33)
   fragments scattered when a shell explodes

**hostage** (p34)
   a person given up to or held by an enemy until certain promises or conditions are fulfilled

**safe haven** (p34)
   a safe place; a refuge; a shelter

**pawn** (p34)
   a person used to gain another's ends

**campaign** (p36)
   a series of connected military operations made to gain some special objective

**appeasing** (p36)
   calming or soothing, especially by giving in to demands

**stakes** (p36)
   something bet or risked

**fruitless** (p37)
   useless or unsuccessful

**authorization** (p38)
   legal right granted by someone who has authority

**debate** (p38)
   to discuss or argue for or against, especially in a formal way, between people taking opposite sides of a question

**commentator** (p39)
   a person who reports, analyzes, and explains the news on radio or television

# Small Group Reading

📖 Deegan, Paul J. *Saddam Hussein*. Edina, MN: Abdo & Daughters, 1990.
This is a biography of Saddam Hussein, the President of Iraq, who sent Iraqi troops to invade and take control of Kuwait on August 2, 1990. Grades 4–8.

## Author Information

Paul Joseph Deegan was born March 19, 1937 in Mankato, Minnesota. He received a bachelor of arts degree in 1959 from the University of Minnesota. Deegan's career has included working as a reporter and editor with newspapers in Austin, Texas; Mankato, Minnesota; and St. Paul, Minnesota. He was an editorial director for Creative Education and for Children's Book Company from 1969 to 1980. Deegan has since owned and managed Deegan Associates and Total Concept Software.

Deegan began writing while still in grade school. While in high school and college, he worked on school newspapers. He majored in editorial journalism at the University of Minnesota.

Deegan has written dozens of books for young people, including several biographies and a sports instructional series. He has also edited or designed 100 juvenile books by Creative Education, Amécus Street, and Children's Book Company.

# Activities

1. On a world map, have students locate:

   Auja, Iraq
   Baghdad, Iraq
   Cairo, Egypt
   France
   Great Britain
   Iran
   Saudi Arabia

   Commonwealth of Independent States
      (formerly the Soviet Union)
   Suez Canal
   Syria
   Tel Aviv, Israel
   Turkey
   Washington, DC

2. Have students create a poster depicting Iraq following the Persian Gulf War. It should include information regarding the public health crisis. Display the poster in your classroom.

3. Have students write a personal reaction to the U.S. involvement in the Persian Gulf War. They should include their opinion and substantiate it with reasons.

4. Have students in this group write a short biography of Saddam Hussein and his rise to power in Iraq, then present the biography to the rest of the class.

# Discussion

Give the small group the following instruction: As your group reads this book, discuss the following.

1. How has Saddam Hussein been described?

2. With whom did President George Bush compare Saddam Hussein?

3. What was Hussein's early life like?

4. Why was Hussein unable to enter the Baghdad Military Academy?

5. Discuss the history of the political control of Iraq.

6. What did the Baath Party that Hussein joined favor?

7. What did Hussein plan while he was in prison? Was it successful?

8. How did Hussein achieve his goal of becoming president of Iraq?

9. When friends objected to Saddam's takeover of Iraq, what did Saddam do?

10. Why do many people in Iraq have pictures of Saddam in their living rooms?

11. Why does Saddam take his own food and a food taster with him when he leaves Iraq?

12. What were the economic costs of the war between Iraq and Iran? How many lives were lost?

13. Describe Saddam's hideout in Baghdad.

14. What does the word *Saddam* mean?

15. What is the general consensus regarding the reason Saddam invaded Kuwait? When did the invasion take place?

16. Why did Saddam believe that the United States would not interfere with the invasion of Kuwait?

17. What do some people believe about why Saddam refused to surrender early in the Gulf War?

18. What is the estimate of Iraqi troops killed before the cease-fire on February 27, 1991?

19. What caused a public health crisis in Iraq?

20. Why did the United States launch a ground war against Iraq on February 23, 1991?

21. Why did so many Iraqis surrender after the ground war began?

22. How long did the ground attack last?

23. What terms did Iraq agree to following the cease-fire?

24. Why did many Iraqi citizens believe President Bush wanted to destroy Iraq?

25. What problems did Saddam face in Iraq after the war ended?

26. What did Saddam do in his attempt to keep the military loyal to him?

27. By late March 1991, why did the United States worry about what might happen if Saddam Hussein fell from power?

28. What was Operation Provide Comfort?

## Vocabulary

**dominate** (p5)
to control or rule over

**amoral** (p5)
lacking standards of right and wrong; neither moral nor immoral

**pity** (p5)
a feeling of keen regret or sorrow for the misfortunes or sufferings of others; sympathy

**fate** (p5)
what happens to a person; fortune; lot

**inspire** (p5)
to arouse (a feeling or idea) in someone

**hostility** (p5)
an unfriendly feeling; dislike or hate

**peasant** (p6)
a country person of noble birth, such as a small farmer

**turbulent** (p8)
restless; disorderly; rebellious

**conspiracy** (p8)
a secret plan of two or more persons to commit an evil or unlawful act; a plot

**norm** (p8)
a pattern, standard, or model considered typical or average

**ethnic** (p8)
of, having to do with, or belonging to a specific group of human beings whose members share the same culture, language, or customs

**nationalism** (p8)
a desire or movement for independence as a nation

**revolt** (p8)
an uprising against authority; a rebellion or mutiny

**mandate** (p8)
a formal, usually written, command from someone in authority

**radical** (p9)
favoring or having to do with rapid or widespread changes or reforms, especially in politics or government

**socialism** (p9)
the ideas that the means of production and distribution, such as factories, railroads, and power plants, should be owned by the government or associations of workers and operated without private profit

**assassinated** (p9)
murdered by a secret or surprise attack

**interrogator** (p10)
a person who asks questions; an examiner

**regime** (p10)
a government in power

**coup** (p11)
a sudden and brilliant maneuver; a clever or lucky move

**sympathetic** (p12)
agreeable to one's tastes, opinions, or feelings

**suppress** (p12)
to put down or end by force; to crush

**opposition** (p12)
an obstacle or hindrance

**ruthless** (p12)
without pity, mercy, or compassion; cruel

**propaganda** (p12)
a group of facts or ideas used to persuade a group of people to adopt or support certain ideas, attitudes, or actions

**autocratic** (p12)
having absolute power

**vast** (p13)
of very large size; enormous; huge

**dictator** (p13)
a person who rules a country with absolute power

**glorified** (p14)
honored or exalted; worshipped

**skirmish** (p16)
a brief fight between small groups of troops

**export** (p16)
to send to other countries

**uprising** (p17)
a revolt; a rebellion

**multitude** (p18)
a great number of persons or things; a crowd; a throng

**schematic** (p19)
a scheme or rough design

**province** (p20)
a main division of a country, similar to a state in the United States, having its own local government, such as any of the provinces of Canada

**adversary** (p20)
an opponent, such as in a contest; an enemy

**looted** (p21)
robbed

**aggressive** (p22)
quick to attack or start a fight

**conduct** (p22)
the way a person acts or lives; behavior

**analyst** (p22)
a person who examines critically or closely

**sanctions** (p22)
the steps or measures taken, usually by several nations, to force another nation to obey international law

**ambition** (p22)
an eager desire to succeed or to achieve something, such as wealth or power

**conviction** (p22)
a strong, firm belief

**ambassador** (p22)
an official of the highest rank, sent as a government representative to another country

**cunning** (p24)
clever or tricky

**extremist** (p24)
a person who holds extreme opinions, favors extreme measures, or goes to extremes in actions or behavior

**coalition** (p26)
a temporary alliance of leaders, parties, or nations

**materialist** (p26)
a person with too much regard for the material or physical side of life, rather than for the mind or spirit

**secular** (p26)
of or for the world rather than the church; not sacred or concerned with religion

**imperialist** (p26)
a person who believes in the policy of increasing the power or domination of a nation, such as by conquering other nations and exerting influence in political and economic areas

**sabotage** (p27)
the destruction of a country's property, resources, or productive capacity by enemy agents in wartime

**humiliate** (p29)
to strip of pride or self-respect; to humble; to embarrass

**flamboyant** (p31)
too gaudy or showy

**prevail** (p31)
to gain control

**comply** (p33)
to act in agreement

**renounce** (p33)
to give up, especially by formal statement

**annexation** (p33)
the control of

**reparations** (p33)
money or goods exacted from losing nations to pay the winners for wartime damage

**justify** (p34)
to provide good reason for

**unrest** (p34)
angry discontent or turmoil sometimes not far from rebellion

**dissenters** (p34)
people who hold or express different beliefs

**turmoil** (p36)
a condition of great confusion or agitation; a disturbance; a tumult

**discontent** (p36)
an unhappy, dissatisfied feeling

**futile** (p36)
done in vain; useless

**stifle** (p36)
to keep back; to suppress

**pardon** (p38)
the decision of the legal order that frees a
person from punishment

**oust** (p38)
to force out or remove

**refugee** (p40)
a person who flees from persecution or
danger

# Small Group Reading

Kerr, M. E. *Linger*. New York: HarperCollins, 1993.
When his older brother suddenly joins the army and is sent to the Persian Gulf, sixteen-year-old Gary begins to take a new look at the restaurant that has been the focal point of his family and their small Pennsylvania town. Grades 8 and up.

*A word of caution*: This novel contains some strong language. I would suggest that it be read aloud to this group by the teacher, an aide, or a parent volunteer. Chapter 12, pages 67–68; Chapter 14, page 75; Chapter 24, pages 124–129; and Chapter 27, pages 138–148 should be skipped.

## Author Information

M. E. Kerr was born Marijane Meaker on May 27, 1927, in Auburn, New York. Meaker has worked as a freelance writer since 1949.

Meaker's books have won several awards. *Gentlehands* was selected as one of the *New York Times* Outstanding Books of the Year in 1978. *If I Love You, Am I Trapped Forever?* was chosen as a Book World's Children's Spring Book Festival Honor Book and as a Child Study Association of America's Children's Book of the Year in 1973. Other books written by Meaker include *Dinky Hocker Shoots Smack!*, *Night Kites*, and *The Son of Someone Famous*.

Marijane Meaker has written under several pseudonyms, including Ann Aldrich, M. E. Kerr, M. J. Meaker, and Vin Packer. When she couldn't get an agent to handle her work, she became her own agent and had stationery printed up with her name and "Literary Agent" on it. She then sent out her own stories under pseudonyms. Her first story, "Devotedly, Patrick Henry Casebolt," was published in September 1951 under the pseudonym Laura Winston by *Ladies' Home Journal*. Her first book for young adults as M. E. Kerr in 1972, *Dinky Hocker Shoots Smack!*, was an instant success and is still going strong. It was chosen as an ALA Notable Book by the American Library Association.

## Activities

1. On a world map, have students locate:

| | |
|---|---|
| Baghdad, Iraq | Ecuador |
| Bangladesh | Egypt |
| Berryville, PA | El Salvador |
| Boston, MA | Indianapolis, IN |
| Colombia | Israel |
| Denver, CO | Key West, FL |
| Dominican Republic | Kuwait |

| | |
|---|---|
| Mexico | Philadelphia, PA |
| Montpelier, VT | San Diego, CA |
| New Jersey | Saudi Arabia |
| New York City | Vermont |

2. Have students research General Norman Schwarzkopf and Saddam Hussein.

3. Have students in this group write an essay about their feelings about the Vietnam War protests and their effect on the returning soldiers. Students can then read their essays aloud to the rest of the class.

4. Have students write a personal reaction to Mr. Dunlinger's treatment of Movie Star. How did it make them feel? What would they have said to Mr. Dunlinger if they were Bobby?

# Discussion

Give the small group the following instruction: As your group reads this book, discuss the following.

1. To whom did Bobby write from the Gulf? Why did this surprise his brother Gary?

2. What is Linger?

3. How did Sergeant Andala treat the new recruits?

4. Why did Bobby join the army?

5. What is Movie Star worried about?

6. Why does Mr. Raleigh, the English teacher, speak out against the United States defending the Persian Gulf?

7. What does Mr. Raleigh think the Persian Gulf crisis is about?

8. What did the button say that Lynn gave to Gary? Why were some words and word parts capitalized?

9. Why do they have chickens where Bobby is stationed?

10. What is life like for Bobby in the Persian Gulf?

11. What did Uncle Chad tell Bobby to do to get rid of Dunlinger's competition? Do you think he did it?

12. What did Sugar tell Bobby and the others about the people of Kuwait?

13. What did Senator Edward Kennedy of Massachusetts say in a speech to Congress about the possible number of casualties?

14. Why does Mr. Raleigh want Gary to read a book about Vietnam?

15. What did Gary's mother say to the Vietnam veteran who was protesting U.S. involvement in the Gulf?

16. What did Mr. Dunlinger have against the Mexicans?

17. What did Mr. Raleigh think would be different about television coverage of the Gulf War? Why?

18. How did Gary learn that war had started in the Gulf?

19. What souvenirs do the soldiers trade for with Iraqi deserters?

20. What happened to Carlos Elizondo?

21. Why do many of the regular customers at Linger want Jules Raleigh to leave?

22. What did Lynn ask Gary to do for her?

23. Describe the first sign of war for Bobby.

24. What happened to Bobby, Movie Star, and Sugar after the cease-fire?

25. What did Gina Sanchez tell Bobby about Movie Star in her letter?

26. What did Bobby tell Mr. Sweet about how their tank was hit?

27. Mr. Raleigh told Bobby in a letter, "Experience is a hard teacher, because you get the test first and the lesson afterward." What did he mean? Do you agree?

28. What was the surprise for Bobby in Mr. Dunlinger's office?

29. How did Bobby react to Mr. Dunlinger in his office?

30. What happened to Linger after the Fourth of July?

## Vocabulary

**alumnus** (p2)
a male graduate or former student of a school or college

**sarcasm** (p2)
a cutting, unpleasant remark that mocks or makes fun of something or someone

**destiny** (p2)
the outcome or fate that is bound to come

**unique** (p4)
being the only one of its type; without an equal

**cupola** (p4)
a circular, dome-shaped roof

**tacky** (p7)
lacking style or taste; dowdy

**recruit** (p9)
a newly enlisted member of the armed forces

**mines** (p14)
hidden explosives set to go off when an enemy (such as a ship, tank, or soldier) comes near them

**ethnic** (p18)
of, having to do with, or belonging to a specific group of human beings, whose members share the same culture, language, or customs

**slur** (p18)
an insulting remark or insinuation

**bigotry** (p19)
an attitude, belief, or action characteristic of a person who has narrow-minded and intolerant attitudes, especially with regard to religion, politics, or race

**optimism** (p20)
the tendency to see things on their bright side

**authentic** (p22)
genuine

**chicano** (p23)
Mexican American

**galley** (p25)
kitchen

**provocative** (p25)
tending to arouse someone, such as by making one puzzled, angry, interested, or amused

**cope** (p25)
to deal with successfully; to handle

**novelty** (p27)
the quality of being new and unusual

**courtesy** (p31)
politeness and consideration for others

**corporate** (p31)
of or related to a corporation

**saber** (p36)
a heavy cavalry sword with a curved blade

**disclosure** (p40)
the act of making known

**vital** (p41)
having great or essential importance

**incubator** (p41)
a container for keeping a prematurely born baby warm

**activist** (p41)
a person who participates in public action in support of a cause

**nomadics** (p44)
people who move from place to place in search of food or pasture

**petrochemical** (p45)
any chemical derived from petroleum or natural gas

**ambition** (p48)
an eager desire to succeed or to achieve something, such as wealth or power

**runt** (p49)
an unusually small animal, person, or plant

**chide** (p49)
to scold

**indifferent** (p54)
    uncaring; unconcerned

**reservist** (p55)
    a member of the military reserves who lives as a civilian and trains at certain times to be ready to enter the regular armed forces in an emergency

**sardonic** (p56)
    bitterly scornful; mocking

**noble** (p56)
    having a high rank or title; aristocratic

**emir** (p57)
    a Muslim prince or chief, especially in the Middle East

**disrespect** (p57)
    a lack of proper respect or courtesy

**casualty** (p60)
    a soldier who is killed, wounded, or missing during a battle

**unsubstantiated** (p64)
    not established as true by evidence; not proven

**maudlin** (p64)
    tearfully emotional or too sentimental

**manipulative** (p64)
    managing, controlling, or influencing in a shrewd or dishonest way

**bayonet** (p64)
    a daggerlike weapon that may be attached to the muzzle of a rifle

**histrionics** (p64)
    exaggerated display of emotion to gain the attention or sympathy of others

**liberate** (p64)
    to set free; to release

**prep school** (p67)
    a private school that prepares students for college admission (preparatory)

**correspondent** (p70)
    a reporter who regularly sends news back to a newspaper or magazine, often from a distant place

**patriotic** (p71)
    having or showing love, loyalty, and devotion toward one's country

**custom** (p72)
    something that has become an accepted practice by many people

**gravitated** (p76)
    moved as though pulled by a powerful force; to be attracted

**sanctions** (p77)
    the steps or measures taken, usually by several nations, to force another nation to obey international law

**placard** (p77)
    a poster publicly displayed

**sentiment** (p77)
    an attitude, opinion, or feeling

**amateur** (p77)
    a person who practices any art, study, or sport for enjoyment but not for money

**welfare** (p81)
    organized efforts by a community or group of people to give money and aid to those who are poor and in need

**pride** (p82)
    someone or something of which one is proud

**contrary** (p82)
    stubbornly determined to oppose or contradict

**encroaching** (p83)
    intruding on the rights or property of another

**intruding** (p83)
    coming without being invited or wanted

**territory** (p83)
    the geographical area ruled by a nation, state, or country

**beholden** (p83)
    under obligation; indebted

**ransacked** (p85)
    searched through every part of

**rendition** (p87)
    a performance of a musical composition or a part in a play

**aspire** (p90)
    to have great hope or ambition for something; to seek

**complimentary** (p91)
    given free

**festooned** (p91)
    decorated with material hung in a curve

**turret** (p92)
    a rotating armed tower, large enough to contain powerful guns, forming a part of a warship, tank, or airplane

**sorties** (p93)
  military missions against an enemy

**scuds** (p93)
  missiles used by Iraqi troops

**Patriot missiles** (p93)
  antimissile missiles, programmed to
  intercept and destroy incoming enemy
  missiles

**ravenous** (p97)
  wildly hungry

**regulations** (p97)
  rules of conduct

**loot** (p97)
  to rob

**superstition** (p97)
  the unreasonable fear or belief that many
  helpful and harmful supernatural forces exist
  and that certain actions will anger or pacify
  them

**brow** (p100)
  the front, upper part of the head; the
  forehead

**coincidence** (p101)
  a seemingly remarkable chance occurrence
  or appearance of two things at the same
  place or time

**itinerant** (p101)
  a person who travels from place to place,
  especially one who moves from job to job

**scapegoat** (p101)
  a person, group, or animal made to bear the
  blame for the sins or errors of others

**hyperbole** (p103)
  an obvious exaggerated statement made for
  dramatic effect

**bunker** (p113)
  a hollow or a mound of earth

**grenade** (p113)
  a small bomb thrown by hand or fired from a
  rifle

**hammock** (p114)
  a bed or couch formed by hanging a strong
  fabric between two supports

**idle** (p114)
  to operate without transmitting power

**medevac** (p114)
  medical evacuation

**debate** (p116)
  the act of discussing or arguing for or
  against, especially in a formal way between
  persons taking opposite sides of a question

**liberal** (p117)
  a person who is not narrow-minded or
  prejudiced; tolerant; broad-minded

**capital punishment** (p121)
  a penalty of death for a crime

**limbo** (p134)
  a place or condition for unwanted or
  forgotten people or things

**recoup** (p137)
  to recover; to get well

**compassionate** (p150)
  feeling compassion or pity; sympathetic;
  merciful

**ominous** (p153)
  threatening or foreboding, like a bad omen

**era** (p154)
  a period of time

**gloat** (p161)
  to think about with an intense, often
  malicious or evil delight

**irony** (p165)
  a fact, result, or happening that seems the
  opposite of what one would naturally expect

**breach** (p174)
  a hole; a gap

**infantry** (p175)
  soldiers, or a branch of the army, trained and
  equipped to fight on foot

**ultimately** (p176)
  in the end; at last; finally

**Purple Heart** (p176)
  a decoration given to members of the United
  States armed services who have been
  wounded in action against an enemy

**carillon** (p192)
  a set of bells on which a melody can be
  played, often by hammers operated from a
  keyboard

**cadence** (p193)
  a rhythmic flow of words

**throng** (p193)
  a great crowd; a multitude

**remotes** (p194)
  television broadcasts from a distance

**epaulet** (p199)
an ornament worn on each shoulder of a naval or military officer's uniform

**mustered out** (p200)
discharged from military service

**sympathetic** (p202)
feeling, expressing, or coming from sympathy or compassion

**humiliate** (p203)
to strip of pride or self-respect; to humble; to embarrass

**blackball** (p207)
to keep away from

**patronize** (p207)
to support or encourage as a patron

**recession** (p208)
a slight drop in business activity; a slight depression

**principle** (p208)
good moral standards; honesty; fairness

# Small Group Reading

📖 Westall, Robert. *Gulf*. New York: Scholastic, 1992.

Tom Higgins, a British schoolboy, narrates his younger brother's struggle with an apparent mental illness, or "mystery of nature," which drives the boy to assume the role of an Iraqi soldier during the Persian Gulf War. Grades 8 and up.

## Author Information

Robert Westall was born October 7, 1929, in Tynemouth, England. He died April 15, 1993, in Cheshire, England.

Westall received a bachelor of arts degree in 1953 from the University of Durham. He also attended the University of London. He was an art teacher and head of the art department at Sir John Deane's College in Northwich, England from 1960 to 1985. Westall also worked as an antiques dealer from 1957 to 1987. Westall began his full-time writing career in 1987. His books have won several awards, including the Carnegie Medal from the Library Association of Great Britain in 1976 for *Machine-Gunners* and in 1982 for *The Scarecrows*. *Machine-Gunners* was later used as the basis for a television series.

## Activities

1. On a world map, have students locate:

   Atlantic Ocean
   Baghdad, Iraq
   Bangladesh
   Cambodia
   El Salvador
   Ethiopia
   France
   India
   Iraq
   Japan
   Korea
   Kuwait
   Lebanon
   London, England
   Niagara Falls, NY
   Nicaragua
   Nigeria
   Pakistan
   Riyadh, Iraq
   Spain
   Sudan
   Tikrit, Iraq
   Vietnam

2. Have students research Saddam Hussein and General Norman Schwarzkopf.

3. Have students write an essay about Figgis's experiences with Latif in the Persian Gulf War. They should include their own feelings about the war's effect on the lives of soldiers and their families. Students can then share these essays with the rest of the class.

4. Have students write short journal entries for each chapter of *Gulf* from Tom's point of view.

## Discussion

Give the small group the following instruction: As your group reads this book, discuss the following.

1. Why do you think Tom invented an imaginary invisible friend when he was a child?

2. How did Tom feel when his brother, Andy, was born?

3. Describe what Andy was like as a young child. Was there anything unusual about him?

4. Have you ever felt as strongly about something as Andy felt about the squirrel?

5. Who is Bossa? How did Bossa affect Andy (Figgis)?

6. How would you feel if you had a brother like Figgis?

7. Why did Figgis have his hair cut the way he did?

8. What do you think Figgis was dreaming about in chapter 6?

9. How do you think Tom felt after he played rugby with his father?

10. How do Tom and Figgis's parents feel about a possible war in the Gulf?

11. Why does Tom envy Figgis?

12. How are Figgis's dreams affecting Tom's schoolwork?

13. What event took place on Figgis's first night in the hospital?

14. Where was Figgis taken after leaving the hospital?

15. What did Dr. Rashid suggest that might help Figgis's family to understand him?

16. Discuss Figgis's behavior now. What do you think is happening?

17. How does Figgis's father feel about Figgis?

18. Why does Tom feel that he is responsible for Figgis's behavior?

19. Why did Dr. Rashid visit Tom at his school?

20. What is the "mystery of nature" that Dr. Rashid told Tom that Figgis suffers from?

21. Discuss your feelings about children under the age of fifteen fighting in a war.

22. According to Dr. Rashid, why do the Iraqis hate Americans?

23. What do you think will happen to Figgis as the war progresses?

24. Why does Tom watch television nonstop?

25. Why did the hospital supply Figgis with mattresses, pillows, and broken chairs? What does Figgis do with them?

26. What did Figgis tell Tom about his experiences with Latif? How does it make you feel about war?

27. Why do you think Dr. Rashid said that it was not Figgis who was mad, but the rest of the world? Do you agree or disagree? Why?

28. What makes Tom think that the Figgis part of Andy died with Latif and Akbar?

29. Why did Tom feel that Figgis was their family's conscience?

# Vocabulary

**smashing** (p1)
strikingly good or effective; wonderful

**hearth** (p2)
the floor of a fireplace or furnace

**rugby** (p2)
a type of football

**hoops** (p3)
a striped rugby shirt

**bated breath** (p3)
barely breathing because of excitement or fear

**councillor** (p4)
a member of a council of people called together to discuss something or make decisions

**linger** (p4)
to stay on as if unwilling to go; to loiter

**nappy** (p5)
diaper

**indignant** (p5)
anger aroused by something that is not right, just, or fair

**envious** (p5)
full of jealousy

**geology** (p7)
the study of the origin, history, and structure of the earth, especially as recorded in rocks

**solemnly** (p8)
seriously

**crafty** (p8)
clever at deceiving others; sly

**bloke** (p9)
a British slang word meaning "fellow" or "guy"

**telepathy** (p10)
communication from one mind to another, received without use of hearing, sight, or touch

**slipshod** (p10)
careless

**misery** (p13)
a condition of great suffering

**callous** (p14)
unfeeling; hard-hearted

**inquisitive** (p16)
full of questions; eager for knowledge; curious

**kayak** (p18)
an Eskimo canoe made of a light frame fully enclosed by skins, with an opening for the user

**avalanche** (p18)
the falling of a large mass of snow, ice, or rock down a slope

**cunning** (p19)
clever or tricky

**laden** (p19)
weighed down; loaded; burdened

**marina** (p20)
a place where small boats and yachts can dock and get supplies

**famine** (p20)
a widespread lack of food that causes many to starve

**psychic** (p20)
sensitive to things that are supernatural

**gaunt** (p20)
very thin and bony, such as from illness or hunger

**dignified** (p21)
having dignity; proud

**sunstroke** (p21)
a sudden illness caused by staying too long in the sun

**excavator** (p22)
a person or machine that makes holes by digging

**bankrupt** (p22)
unable to pay debts

**charity** (p23)
the giving of help, usually money, to the poor and unfortunate

**peseta** (p23)
a Spanish unit of money comparable to the United States cent

**anesthetized** (p26)
caused to be made unconscious or having senses deadened by means of an anesthetic

**paddock** (p28)
a pasture or lot near a stable for exercising horses

**silhouette** (p29)
the outline of a person or object against a light or a light background

**fanatical** (p29)
unreasonably enthusiastic

**mauve** (p30)
a purplish rose color

**lorry** (p30)
truck

**petrol** (p31)
fuel; gas

**contemporaries** (p35)
people living at the same time as others

**communal** (p36)
public

**arrogant** (p36)
too proud and disdainful of others

**nostalgic** (p38)
having, showing, or coming from something that took place in the past

**vigor** (p39)
active strength or force of mind or body; healthy energy

**suffice** (p39)
to be sufficient; enough

**vague** (p45)
indefinite, unclear, imprecise, or indistinct

**frigate** (p48)
a modern ship used on escort and patrol missions

**atomic bomb** (p49)
a powerful bomb using the energy suddenly released when the nuclei of uranium and plutonium split

**crimson** (p49)
a deep red color

**puce** (p51)
a dark brownish purple color

**epileptic** (p55)
a person who suffers from a disorder of the nervous system, attacks of which sometimes cause loss of consciousness and convulsion

**concussion** (p56)
a violent shock to the brain caused by a fall, blow, or blast

**amnesia** (p56)
a partial or complete loss of memory caused by injury, sickness, or severe shock

**maneuvers** (p59)
planned movements or actions, such as of troops or warships

**cold war** (p60)
an international conflict expressed in diplomatic and economic rivalry rather than war

**shell shock** (p62)
a nervous condition resulting from long exposure to the strain of modern warfare

**psychiatrist** (p62)
a doctor who treats people who are mentally ill

**amiable** (p63)
pleasing in disposition; agreeable; friendly

**sorties** (p63)
military missions against an enemy

**tornadoes** (p63)
British fighter planes

**liberal** (p64)
not narrow-minded or prejudiced; tolerant; broad-minded

**inaudible** (p68)
incapable of being heard

**unperturbed** (p69)
not alarmed or agitated

**schizophrenia** (p70)
a severe mental disorder in which a person confuses what is real and what is imaginary, with disturbances in behavior, thought, and emotion

**biro** (p72)
ballpoint pen

**ostentatious** (p74)
showing off too much or an uncalled-for display of something to attract attention or admiration

**racist** (p74)
a person who favors a particular race

**brigade** (p75)
a unit of troops smaller than a division

**pendulum** (p78)
a weight hung from a support and allowed to swing back and forth, often used to regulate clocks because the time required for one complete swing is constant

**jargon** (p80)
special words or terms used by the members of a particular profession or class

**friendly fire** (p80)
the accidental firing of weapons at one's own people

**gaiters** (p82)
coverings, such as of cloth or leather, for the lower leg or ankle

**potty** (p95)
crazy

From *Teaching U.S. History Through Children's Literature.* © 1998 Wanda J. Miller. Teacher Ideas Press. (800) 237-6124.

# Bibliography

## Individual Titles

Allen, Thomas B., F. Clifton Berry, and Norman Polmar. *War in the Gulf: From the Invasion of Kuwait to the Day of Victory and Beyond.* Atlanta, GA: Turner, 1991.

This book provides a thorough account of the Persian Gulf War by CNN. Grades 8 and up.

Boyne, Walter J. *Gulf War: A Comprehensive Guide to People, Places and Weapons.* Lincolnwood, IL: Publications International, 1991.

As the title suggests, this is a thorough accounting of the Gulf War, complete with many color photographs. Grades 7 and up.

Bratman, Fred. *War in the Persian Gulf.* Brookfield, CT: Millbrook Press, 1991.

Bratman's coverage includes the Iraqi invasion of Kuwait; the historical background of Iraq, Kuwait, and the Persian Gulf region; biographical information on Saddam Hussein; United Nations and United States actions; and the Persian Gulf War. Grades 6–9.

Cornum, Rhonda, as told to Peter Copeland. *She Went to War: The Rhonda Cornum Story.* Novato, CA: Presidio Press, 1992.

This is the story of Rhonda Cornum—Army officer, helicopter pilot, physician, and mother. Cornum was aboard a U.S. Army helicopter on a search and rescue mission when the helicopter was shot down. Five on board were killed instantly. Cornum was one of three who survived and was captured by the enemy. Grades 8 and up.

Deegan, Paul J. *Persian Gulf Nations.* Edina, MN: Abdo & Daughters, 1990.

Through text and photographs, Deegan profiles the nations of the Persian Gulf, including Iran, Iraq, Jordan, Kuwait, Saudi Arabia, and Turkey. Grades 4–7.

Foster, Leila Merrell. *The Story of the Persian Gulf War.* Chicago: Childrens Press, 1991.

Foster examines the causes and events of the Persian Gulf War following Iraq's invasion of Kuwait in 1990. Numerous photographs are included. Grades 4–7.

Friedrich, Otto, and the editors of *Time* magazine. *Desert Storm: The War in the Persian Gulf.* New York: Time Warner, 1991.

This book is considered to be the first book to cover every aspect of the Persian Gulf War. Fifteen *Time* magazine writers put this book together from reports of some two dozen of its best correspondents. Included are more than 100 photographs and fourteen pages of maps and charts. Grades 7 and up.

King, Dr. John. *The Gulf War.* New York: Dillon Press, 1991.

King examines the causes, events, and aftermath of the Persian Gulf War. Grades 4 and up.

Mazarr, Michael J., Don M. Snider, and James A. Blackwell, Jr. *Desert Storm: The Gulf War and What We Learned.* Boulder, CO: Westview Press, 1993.

This book gives a thorough history of the Persian Gulf War. It is an excellent research tool for older students. Grades 8 and up.

Rabinowitz, Richard. *What Is War? What Is Peace? 50 Questions and Answers for Kids.* New York: Avon Books, 1991.

This book answers many of the questions that students have about war. It includes a glossary and an appendix that tells what students themselves can do in the quest for world peace. Grades 4–7.

Salzman, Marian, and Ann O'Reilly. *War and Peace in the Persian Gulf: What Teenagers Want to Know.* Princeton, NJ: Peterson's Guides, 1991.

The authors discuss the Persian Gulf War, including U.S. involvement, media coverage, military campaigns, the people, culture, and traditions of the Middle East, and sources of further information. Grades 7 and up.

Steins, Richard. *The Mideast After the Gulf War.* Brookfield, CT: Millbrook Press, 1992.

Stein provides information and background on the Mideast after the 1991 Persian Gulf War, including refugee problems, environmental damage, and an unsettled political situation. Grades 6 and up.

# Theme Resources

## Computer Resource

*Desert Storm: The War in the Persian Gulf.* Burbank, CA: Warner New Media, 1991. (CD-ROM)
This CD-ROM includes correspondents' reports, eyewitness accounts, photographs, audio recordings, maps, charts, research, and documents gathered by the editorial staff of *Time* magazine.

## Videos

*The Black Americans of Achievement Video Collection: Colin Powell.* Bala Cynwyd, PA: Schlessinger Video Productions, 1992. (30 minutes)
This is a video biography of General Colin Powell, Chairman of the Joint Chiefs of Staff during the Persian Gulf War.

*A Line in the Sand.* Orland Park, IL: MPI Home Video, 1990. (50 minutes)
This is an MPI Home Video presentation of an ABC News special on the Persian Gulf Crisis, hosted by Peter Jennings.

*Military Aircraft: Desert Storm, War in the Air.* Seattle, WA: Pool & Crew. (75 minutes)
This video shows viewers the modern military technology used during the Persian Gulf War. It focuses on aircraft and pilots and contains no scenes of human suffering.

*Operation Desert Storm: The Victory.* Cable News Network, 1991. (101 minutes)
This is an award-winning CNN documentary that presents the military strategy, quick-fire combat, and valor displayed in the Persian Gulf.

*Schwarzkopf: How the War Was Won.* Orland Park, IL: MPI Home Video, 1991. (70 minutes)
This video contains the military briefing in which General Norman Schwarzkopf explains the military tactics that led to the end of the Persian Gulf War. Narrated by ABC News anchor Peter Jennings.

# End-of-Unit Celebration

## Persian Gulf War Research Project

In groups of two or three, have students research the following topics. When completed, hold a presentation day.

President George Bush

Secretary of Defense Dick Cheney

The Economic Cost of the Persian Gulf War to the United States

Saddam Hussein

The Invasion of Kuwait by Iraqi Troops

Media Coverage of the Persian Gulf War

The Mideast After the Persian Gulf War

Modern Military Technology Used by the United States in the Persian Gulf War

Operation Desert Shield

General Colin Powell

General Norman

## Persian Gulf War Vocabulary Activity

In addition to the research project, you might wish to celebrate the end of the unit by having students work in teams to complete the vocabulary activity presented in figure 7.1 (p. 210). This could be competitive or noncompetitive, with appropriate prizes awarded to all.

210 7—The Persian Gulf War

**Directions:** Place the letter of the correct definition in the blank next to the vocabulary word.

1.  coalition _____

2.  dictator _____

3.  sanctions _____

4.  imperialist _____

5.  regime _____

6.  patriotism _____

7.  liberation _____

8.  Patriot missiles _____

9.  sorties _____

10. scuds _____

11. paratroopers _____

12. propaganda _____

13. friendly fire _____

**a.** love for one's country and loyal devotion to it

**b.** the accidental firing of weapons at one's own people

**c.** air missions

**d.** the act of setting free

**e.** a person who rules a country with absolute power

**f.** missiles used by Iraqi troops

**g.** a temporary alliance of leaders, parties, or nations

**h.** a person or country joined with another for a particular purpose

**i.** a group of facts or ideas used to persuade a group of people to adopt or support certain ideas, attitudes, or actions

**j.** the steps or measures taken, usually by several nations, to force another nation to obey international law

**k.** a government in power

**l.** antimissile missiles, programmed to intercept and destroy incoming enemy missiles

**m.** a person who believes in the policy of increasing the power or domination of a nation, such as by conquering other nations and exerting influence in political and economic areas

**Fig. 7.1.** Persian Gulf War vocabulary activity.

# Chapter 8

# Supplemental U.S. History Resources

## Theme Resources

Caney, Steven. *Kids' America*. New York: Workman, 1978.

This book includes aspects of American life from the colonial period to the present. Caney gives suggestions for craft projects, genealogy searches, and games. For students in grades 3–8.

Goldstein, Toby. *Waking from the Dream: America in the Sixties*. New York: Messner, 1988.

This book covers the Vietnam War, the civil rights movement, international politics, and the race to space. Grades 8 and up.

*National Geographic Picture Atlas of Our World*. Washington, DC: National Geographic Society, 1993.

This resource contains 120 maps and offers students in grades 4 and up an inviting look at more than 170 countries.

Rubel, David. *Scholastic Timelines: The United States in the 20th Century*. New York: Scholastic Reference, 1995.

This resource contains more than 300 photographs and illustrations, along with information on politics, everyday life, arts and entertainment, and science and technology of the twentieth century. For use with students in grades 4 and up.

Tunnell, Michael O., and Richard Ammon, eds. *The Story of Ourselves: Teaching History Through Children's Literature*. Portsmouth, NH: Heinemann, 1993.

This is a book of essays on American history by authors such as Milton Meltzer and Russell Freedman. An annotated bibliography of American historical literature is included for use with students in grades K–9.

Van Meter, Vandelia. *American History for Children and Young Adults: An Annotated Bibliographic Index*. Englewood, CO: Libraries Unlimited, 1990.

This is an annotated bibliography of trade books covering American history for children and young adults.

Weizmann, Daniel. *Take a Stand! Everything You Never Wanted to Know About Government*. Los Angeles: Price Stern Sloan, 1996.

Weizmann describes how the United States government works and how to get involved in politics, including school elections, letter-writing campaigns, and mock political debates. For use with students in grades 4–8.

## Computer Resources

*Chronicle of the 20th Century*. New York: Dorling Kindersley, 1996. (CD-ROM)

This CD-ROM is an interactive guide to the people, places, and events of the twentieth century. It includes a 3-D "Newsroom," a "News in Brief" section containing an entry for each day of the century, and a "Chronicle Finder," which makes it possible for students to search by word, date, or media. A built-in Internet link provides access to "Chronicle Online," a Web site magazine.

Landmark Documents in American History. New York: Facts on File, 1995. (CD-ROM)

This CD-ROM contains more than 1,000 primary source documents, including legislation, famous speeches, Supreme Court decisions, treaties, and presidential inaugural addresses. Introductions explain the significance of each document. Photographs, illustrations, video, and sound clips are also included. Available for DOS/Windows.

# Literature Response Guide
### Written by Leslie Wood

The use of literature response journals is an excellent way to guide students' reading of individual trade books. Literature response journals can be used for independent reading at home or at school.

Each student will need a notebook of some type for responding to his or her reading. The following is a guide to help lead students in responding to literature. Each student should have a copy of this guide stapled to the inside of his or her notebook. Although you may have more specific events you would like students to respond to in certain books, this general guide is very helpful. I have seen it used with upper elementary students and the results have been wonderful! In a short span of three months, growth in their responses was remarkable. Students put a lot more thought into their reading and their written responses.

---

## LITERATURE RESPONSE GUIDE

1. **Pointing Response**
   What did you like about what you read? (I liked. . . .)
   What does the author make you see or feel? (The author made me see or feel. . . .)
   Use quotes from the book to point out things you liked.

2. **Questioning Response**
   What questions do you have about the reading? (I wonder. . . .)
   What would you like to find out more about? (I would like to find out more about. . . .)

3. **Memory Response**
   What do things or events in the book make you think of? Explain. (The events in this
      book make me think of. . . .)
   Does the reading remind you of something you read in another book? Explain. (This
      book made me think of. . . .)
   Does a character remind you of a person you know in your life or a character you met
      in another story? (_____ reminds me of _____ because. . . .)

4. **Prediction Response**
   What do you think will happen next and why? (I think. . . .)

5. **Information Response**
   What did you learn from the book? ( I learned. . . .)
   What do you want to learn more about? (I want to learn more about. . . .)

6. **Vocabulary Response**
   Make a note of any vocabulary words you don't know, look up the words, and write
      down the definitions.

7. **Feeling Response**
   How are you feeling about events or characters? Have your feelings changed while
      reading? How and why have they changed? (This book makes me feel _____
      because. . . .)

8. **Summary Response**
   Write a three- or four-sentence summary of the chapter or what you have read so far.
      Remember to only include the most important events of the chapter.

---

**Fig. 8.1.** Literature response guide.

Student Name _____

Topic _____

## OUTLINE

I.  **Introduction of Topic**:

II.  **Notes** (Important facts from library sources); use notebook paper for additional space:

III.  **Conclusion**:

IV.  **Bibliography** (Be sure to write down all necessary information for each source used. This includes: Author, title, publisher, copyright date. Also, if you are using a magazine article, include the name of the article and page numbers.):

**Fig. 8.2.** Research guide.

## GRADING SHEET

Student Name _____

Topic _____

Graded by Social Studies Teacher: _____

    Grade for historical facts present in the paper: _____

    Comments:

Graded by English Teacher: _____

    Grade for written presentation: _____

    Comments:

Overall Project Grade: _____

**Fig. 8.3.** Social studies/ language arts integrated project.

# Index

# About the Author

Wanda Miller received her bachelor's degree in psychology and her master's degree in reading from Nazareth College of Rochester in Pittsford, New York. Besides being certified to teach reading, she also holds New York State certification in elementary education and special education.

Wanda has worked as a freelance writer and editor for Perma-Bound, and has had eight teacher guides published. She also wrote a short story titled "Mom, I'm a Reader!" which was published in the Our Own Stories section of the October 1996 issue of *The Reading Teacher*, a journal of the International Reading Association.

Wanda teaches remedial reading in grades three through five in Williamson Elementary and Middle Schools in Williamson, New York. She served on the Board of Directors for the Rochester Area Reading Council from 1994 to 1997.

Wanda lives in Marion, New York with her husband, Randy, and their two children, Randy and Kari.